John McDowell on Worldly Subjectivity

Also available from Bloomsbury

Advances in Experimental Philosophy of Mind, edited by Justin Sytsma
Certainty in Action, by Danièle Moyal-Sharrock
Free Will and Epistemology, by Robert Lockie
Kant's Transition Project and Late Philosophy, by Oliver Thorndike
The Philosophy of Being in the Analytic, Continental, and Thomistic Traditions,
by Joseph p. Li Vecchi, Frank Scalambrino and David K. Kovacs

John McDowell on Worldly Subjectivity

Oxford Kantianism Meets Phenomenology and Cognitive Sciences

Tony Cheng

BLOOMSBURY ACADEMIC
LONDON • NEW YORK • OXFORD • NEW DELHI • SYDNEY

BLOOMSBURY ACADEMIC
Bloomsbury Publishing Plc
50 Bedford Square, London, WC1B 3DP, UK
1385 Broadway, New York, NY 10018, USA
29 Earlsfort Terrace, Dublin 2, Ireland

BLOOMSBURY, BLOOMSBURY ACADEMIC and the Diana logo are trademarks of
Bloomsbury Publishing Plc

First published in Great Britain 2021
This paperback edition published in 2022

Copyright © Tony Cheng, 2021

Tony Cheng has asserted his right under the Copyright, Designs and Patents Act, 1988, to be identified as Author of this work.

For legal purposes the Acknowledgements on p. vii constitute an extension of this copyright page.

Cover photograph by Rose Lenehan

All rights reserved. No part of this publication may be reproduced or transmitted in any form or by any means, electronic or mechanical, including photocopying, recording, or any information storage or retrieval system, without prior permission in writing from the publishers.

Bloomsbury Publishing Plc does not have any control over, or responsibility for, any third-party websites referred to or in this book. All internet addresses given in this book were correct at the time of going to press. The author and publisher regret any inconvenience caused if addresses have changed or sites have ceased to exist, but can accept no responsibility for any such changes.

A catalogue record for this book is available from the British Library.

Library of Congress Cataloging-in-Publication Data
Names: Cheng, Tony, author.
Title: John McDowell on worldly subjectivity: Oxford Kantianism meets phenomenology and cognitive sciences / Tony Cheng.
Description: London; New York: Bloomsbury Academic, 2021. | Includes bibliographical references and index. |
Identifiers: LCCN 2020054784 (print) | LCCN 2020054785 (ebook) | ISBN 9781350126718 (hardback) | ISBN 9781350126725 (ebook) | ISBN 9781350126732 (epub)
Subjects: LCSH: McDowell, John, 1942-
Classification: LCC B1647.M144 C49 2021 (print) | LCC B1647.M144 (ebook) | DDC 192—dc23
LC record available at https://lccn.loc.gov/2020054784
LC ebook record available at https://lccn.loc.gov/2020054785

ISBN: HB: 978-1-3501-2671-8
PB: 978-1-3502-3687-5
ePDF: 978-1-3501-2672-5
eBook: 978-1-3501-2673-2

Typeset by RefineCatch Limited, Bungay, Suffolk

To find out more about our authors and books visit www.bloomsbury.com and sign up for our newsletters.

For John McDowell

Contents

Preface	viii
Prologue: Oxford Kantianism and Pittsburgh Hegelianism	1
1 The Many Faces of Human Subject	7
2 *Cogito* and *Homo sapiens*	17
3 Perceiver and Knower	29
4 Thinker and Speaker	53
5 Agent and Person	75
6 *Apperceiver* and *Homo sentiens*	101
7 Rational Animal and Conceptual Being	127
Epilogue: Self-Determining Subjectivity	153
Notes	171
Bibliography	191
Index of Names	211
Subject Index	213

Preface

I should have liked to produce a good book. This has not come about, but the time is past in which I could improve it.
Ludwig Wittgenstein, *Philosophical Investigations*

Presumably, Wittgenstein could carry on revising the book, but he decided not to do so. I feel his pain. This essay has been evolving since 2008 or so, out of my thesis *World and Subject: Themes from McDowell* supervised by Chung-I Lin. It could have appeared much sooner, but can also wait until much later. I have decided to finalize it at this point; let me explain.

It could have appeared much sooner, since during the process of thesis writing I had always conceived this project as a book. This is not universally true of theses and dissertations in philosophy these days, as the 'paper/article' model adopted by prominent institutions such as NYU has gained its popularity, amongst other reasons. More specifically, this essay was conceived as a book that goes beyond an introduction of John McDowell's philosophy: after all, it is a thesis, which has to be original in some significant ways. Therefore, this essay has been written as a critical engagement with a specific theme in McDowell's philosophy – full-fledged subjectivity situated in the world. Notice that the notion of 'world' here is appropriated from Hans-Georg Gadamer's distinction between environment and world, so this notion cannot be equated with 'physical world' we often see in contemporary Anglo-Saxon philosophy. I will explain this in the essay itself.

It did not appear much sooner, mainly because after finishing the thesis, I felt that I had been working within a certain comfort zone for too long, and it would be intellectually healthier if I work on issues and approaches quite different from what I was already quite used to. By 'comfort zone' I mean traditional issues concerning intentionality and epistemology, written by philosophers such as W. V. O. Quine, Wilfrid Sellars, Michael Dummett, Donald Davidson, Jerry Fodor, Robert Brandom and Christopher Peacocke, amongst many others. To be sure, their thoughts are so rich and profound that it is totally sensible to stay in that ballpark throughout my lifetime. But at that point I just felt that there are also so many insights elsewhere, and I was determined to depart from this comfort zone and explore other issues, including the hard problem of consciousness, the relation between consciousness and attention, the sense of touch and Molyneux's Question, and varieties of self-consciousness, and so on. I have learned so much during this intellectual journey, and I never regret with my decision to leave my comfort zone for such a long time. However, I did have this essay in mind the whole time, and have planned to come back to it at some point.

But it can also wait until much later, not only because McDowell's philosophy is still evolving, but also because he has covered so much ground that presumably no single commentator could reasonably claim that she or he has expertise in most aspects of the McDowellian framework. One key reason why I still decided to finalize this essay at this point is that McDowell's framework has been quite stable since a decade or so ago, and it is not a stretch to attempt to take stock for now. He still publishes abundantly after 2008, and I have been keeping an eye on the development, which can be seen here and there in this essay, but I have mostly focussed on three decades of McDowell's writings, roughly from 1980 to 2010. Many of his new pieces are ongoing exchanges with others, including Susanna Siegel, Bill Brewer, Anil Gupta and Declan Smithies. I am following this and other new threads closely and plan to write on these matters in the coming years.

Some readers might wonder, why don't I keep waiting, try to accommodate these new elements, and perhaps publish this essay years later? The short answer is, of course I can, but philosophy is an ongoing dialogue, and in a sense any piece will never be ready. It can always wait. I may go on elaborating my decision process, but that would not be of interest for my readers. I shall therefore only single out one thing: 2020 has been a bumpy year for the globe – COVID-19 and unstable geopolitics have created a sense of urgency in me. This is in a sense irrational, especially because now I am back to my home Taiwan and it has been coping with the situations well, but as Hume pointed out, reason is the slave of the passions. In this specific case I let myself succumb to this sense of urgency. I take this as an *interim* conclusion of my engagement with McDowell's thinking; there will be more to come in the future.

I have registered my gratitude to those who have helped me with the thesis in its preface, and I shall not repeat them here. In addition to those, I would like to thank Paul Snowdon, Quassim Cassam and Dan Zahavi, for showing me how this project can be extended in various directions. Along the way many other people have taught me important things, and I have expressed my gratitude to them on other more relevant occasions, such as in my later dissertation *Sense,*

Space, and Self, written when I was at UCL and supervised primarily by Rory Madden and Lucy O'Brien.

I have dedicated the 2008 thesis to my parents, 張艾蓉 and 鄭松茂. I shall dedicate this book to John McDowell himself: thanks for being so inspiring since half a century ago, and for being a personal friend, if I may say so, since 2006.

I thank Shao-An Hsu for spotting the typos in the hardback edition.

Prologue

Oxford Kantianism and Pittsburgh Hegelianism

Background

1. Labels in philosophy can be misleading: they can oversimplify subtleties and gloss over differences, for example. They can sometimes be useful, though: they can help us situate certain views or approaches into wider contexts efficiently, for example. In this introductory chapter, I shall venture to invoke two labels to capture some strands in John McDowell's philosophy. This would be, just to warn my readers, against McDowell's own preference.[1] That being said, McDowell does say something about Strawson's Kant and Sellars's Hegel, as quoted below, so it is natural for commentators to speculate and extrapolate the spirits behind these remarks:

> *I am not sure that Strawson's Kant is really Kant, but I am convinced that Strawson's Kant comes close to achieving what Kant wanted to achieve.*
>
> John McDowell, *Mind and World*

> *[W]hat I have been representing as Sellars's blind spot, his inability to contemplate the possibility that intentionality might be relational, is part of a package with his conviction that to give philosophical reflection about intentionality a Hegelian shape is to abandon objectivity rather than to vindicate it.*
>
> John McDowell, *Having the World in View*

2. 'Oxford Kantianism' does not seem to have anything like an explicit definition on paper. It is, however, clear that this tradition was initiated by P. F. Strawson, notably his *The Bounds of Sense* (1966). Basically, Strawson attempts to preserve Kant's insights as much as possible, while discarding his notorious transcendental idealism. This was coeval with another Oxford Philosopher Jonathan Bennett's interpretations of Kant's *First Critique* (1966, 1974), but this does not mean that Bennett should be classified in this camp. One defining feature of Oxford Kantianism seems to be the combination of interpretations of Kant and contemporary philosophy of mind, language, epistemology and metaphysics. The recent Gomes–Stephenson edited volume on Kant and the philosophy of mind (2017) is a prime example. However, it is certainly not a sufficient condition: Gary Hatfield (1991, 2009), Andrew Brook (1994), and Robert Hanna (2001, 2006) are obviously not Oxford Kantian. Strawson's Kant has a similar status as Kripke's Wittgenstein (1982): perhaps they are not qualified as scholarly interpretations from the viewpoint of Kant and Wittgenstein experts, but these (mis)interpretations are creative and illuminating. McDowell was educated at Oxford from 1963 to 1969, and taught there from 1966 to 1986. He was, needless to say, heavily influenced by Strawson, especially his Kantianism.[2]

Strawson has some prominent followers in this regard – Gareth Evans, John McDowell, Naomi Eilan, John Campbell, Quassim Cassam, José Luis Bermúdez and Anil Gomes – all follow Strawson's Kant in one way or another. One sub-division we can make here is between those who combine this line of thought with considerations from empirical sciences, and those who refuse to, or at least do not do so. The former, which I shall call 'left-wing Oxford Kantians', includes Evans, Eilan, Campbell, Bermúdez and myself, if I can add myself to the list. The latter, which I shall call 'right-wing Oxford Kantians', includes McDowell, Cassam and Gomes. Kant himself would presumably approve the right-wing approach, given his distinction between transcendental and empirical psychology. But the main point here is not to decide who's Kant is real Kant. What I wish to highlight for my readers is this: while I have been studying McDowell's philosophy for years and am sympathetic with his general outlook, I regard myself as 'left wing' and therefore cannot be entirely faithful to McDowell's framework. This should be taken, hopefully, as a positive feature of this book: it is not written by someone who is *so* sympathetic to McDowell's thinking that little critical distance can be retained. In fact, I will explore some challenges from empirical sciences and envisage how McDowell would and should respond to them.

3. How about Pittsburgh Hegelianism? Again it is difficult to find an explicit definition, though it is easy to identify who initiated the tradition. In this case it was Wilfrid Sellars who established this philosophical approach. McDowell moved from Oxford to Pittsburgh in 1986 and briefly overlapped with Sellars. Sellars is an atypical analytic philosopher in that he paid enormous attention to some prominent continental figures, such as Kant, Hegel and Husserl. McDowell's engagements with Hegel's thinking are relatively recent: in addition to the 'unboundedness of the conceptual' in *Mind and World* (1996a), we can find his explicit discussions of Hegel in McDowell (2003a/2008a, 2003b, 2009a, 2009b, 2010a/2008a, 2018a, 2018b). His colleague Robert Brandom, who is also classified in this approach, has been engaging with Hegel's thinking and has finally published his interpretation of Hegel's *Phenomenology of Spirit* in 2019. Pittsburgh Hegelianism, although relatively younger than Oxford Kantianism, has attracted much more attention in the recent literature. Here is a very informative though perhaps partial description from Chauncey Maher:

> Although Sellars, Brandom, and McDowell do not agree on everything, they share some distinctive ideas. In brief, they reject the idea that thinking about things can be assimilated to being merely affected by things; thinking requires a capacity to reason, to know what does and does not follow from a thought; likewise, they reject the idea that acting intentionally can be assimilated to an ability to affect things; acting intentionally also requires a capacity to reason; that capacity, in turn, requires sensitivity to *norms* or *evaluative* standards of proper reasoning.
>
> 2012, p. 1

Note that Maher's book is called *The Pittsburgh School of Philosophy*; 'Hegelianism' is not prominent in this work. For explicit labelling in this regard, see Redding (2007, 2011) and deVries (2017); for scepticism, see Rockmore (2012). In light of the current lack of interest of Oxford Kantianism, the present essay will focus on it and put Pittsburgh Hegelianism in the background.[3]

4. Oxford Kantianism, unpopular in the current climate anyway, is not without its prominent opponents. Indeed, this label is often in the mouths of those who are against it. Oxford Kantianism, as Andrew Brook defines it, is 'the Kantian tradition that grew out of P. F. Strawson's work at Oxford in the 1960s':

> Oxford Kantianism insists upon a deep divide between philosophy and empirical psychology ... This insistence is peculiar. Philosophers make claims about the mind, specifically, about how the mind must be ... Surely it cannot be a matter of indifference whether the mind actually is as they claim to be. Nor is it always clear what is being contrasted to empirical psychology.
>
> 2001, p. 190

There are two claims here; one is that Oxford Kantianism sharply divides *a priori* philosophy and empirical psychology, and the other is that this division is problematic. Concerning the first point, what Brook has in mind is what I call 'right-wing Oxford Kantianism'; if we adopt Brook's rather narrow definition, then Evans, Eilan, Campbell and Bermúdez cannot be said to be in this tradition, and this is a rather odd outcome, though we can agree with Brook that the 'right wing' might be closer to Strawson himself. Concerning the second point, as a left-winger my own approach is closer to Brook's.

David Papineau (2003) has offered a slightly different criticism of Campbell, specifically targeting his *Reference and Consciousness* (2002). Here is Papineau:

> This modern neo-Kantianism has been enormously influential within Oxford, and is establishing notable outposts elsewhere in the English-speaking world ... Throughout most of the twentieth century, academic philosophy organized itself around the great fault-line dividing the "Continental" and "analytic" schools ... Oxford neo-Kantianism has added a new ingredient to the philosophical mix ... [A] new and potentially more fruitful division is emerging within English-speaking philosophy. In place of the old analytic-Continental split, we now have the opposition between the naturalists and the neo-Kantians. The naturalists look to science to provide the starting point for philosophy. The neo-Kantians start with consciousness instead.
>
> 2003, p. 12

Papineau goes on to criticize neo-Kantianism for ignoring the sciences. The spirit is basically the same as Brook's criticism above. I do not agree with Papineau's criticism here, as Campbell obviously takes the relevant sciences seriously not only in *Reference and Consciousness* but also in other works. And for what it's worth, that book was published under the 'Oxford Cognitive Science Series'. Note that there are two similar points to be separated here; one is that this Kantianism is non-naturalism, and the other is that this Kantianism starts with consciousness. These are different points as one can hold the second point without embracing the first point. I myself happen to occupy this position, though the naturalism I hold is no physicalism, and this leads to the distinctive approach of the present project.

Foreground

1. The subtitle of this book is 'Oxford Kantianism Meets Phenomenology and Cognitive Sciences'. This might generate slight vertigo for some readers, as it

involves too many diverse ideologies. Indeed, when McDowell himself encounters challenges from phenomenology and cognitive sciences, he is mostly reactive and does not go into the opponents' territories and offer positive thoughts (1994/1998a, 2007c/2008b, 2007d/2008b). In this essay I will take a different approach: in describing and elaborating McDowell's thinking, I will spontaneously draw connections to phenomenology and cognitive sciences. Here are some examples:

(1) 'Passive synthesis' in Husserl.
(2) Notions of human body in Husserl and Merleau-Ponty.
(3) Experiential imprecision and overflow in vision science.
(4) Conceptions of concepts in cognitive and developmental psychology.

These will not come up as separate chapters, as I do not wish to generate the impressions that these are separate or additional issues. Instead, I would like to treat them as integral to understanding McDowell's thinking.

2. To put these thread more in my own terms, I dub the current approach 'Naturalised Strawsonianism' (Cheng, 2018). 'Strawsonianism' is invoked to capture Strawson's project of understanding Kant and making his thinking relevant to contemporary analytic philosophy. 'Naturalised' is invoked to make sure that although Oxford Kantianism can be anti-naturalistic, it does not have to be. Indeed, even for McDowell himself, he holds (rightly, I shall argue) that his position is a version of naturalism. I go further in insisting on the relevance of some empirical findings, and this will become clear in due course.

This Naturalised Strawsonianism can have a phenomenological reading, and that is what I explicitly intend. Recall Papineau's remark that neo-Kantians start with consciousness instead. This is reminiscent of Husserl's phenomenological project, that one should start with consciousness and *bracket* everything else (Husserl, 1913/1982). Now with a more relaxed mindset, one could even say that Strawson's descriptive metaphysics (1959) is a *phenomenological* project, if that tradition were to be understood 'as the purely descriptive study of structural features of the varieties of experience' (Smith, 2016, p. 7). This is so because while Strawson sets out engaging *descriptive* metaphysics, his project is actually *transcendental* in essence, i.e. finding the 'make-possible' condition for certain capacity. How to make these two elements cohere is a difficult and subtle matter; one way to proceed is to regard the project as *describing the necessary conditions of the possibility of the target of investigation*. This potential tension can also be seen in Husserl, especially when we consider his adoption of Brentano's 'descriptive psychology' (1889/1973): how can a descriptive psychology be part of a transcendental project?[4]

What is offered above is highly schematic, as I do not wish to burden the reader with a lengthy discussion at this early point. I shall turn to substantive discussions of McDowell's thinking now, and the above backgrounds will emerge whenever relevant. One caveat before moving on: this essay is a critical appraisal of McDowell's various views. It is *not* an introductory book, as de Gaynesford (2004a) and Thornton (2019) are. It is also not a thoroughgoing critique, as Gaskin (2006) is. It is something in between. In the next chapter, I will first set up the stage in my own way without following McDowell's writings closely. There are two potential merits in doing so: first, we can thereby see more clearly the relevance of McDowell's thinking to contemporary analytic philosophy, and second, we can have a certain critical distance that enables us to evaluate McDowell's thinking in a more impartial way.

1

The Many Faces of Human Subject

Know thyself.
   Plato, *The First Alcibiades*, quotes Socrates and The Delphian Inscription

The I, the I is what is deeply mysterious.
                              Ludwig Wittgenstein, *Notebooks*

World

1. As Wittgenstein remarked, the I or the first person is indeed deeply mysterious. The present essay is an attempt to understand human subjectivity (i.e. a special property of the first person) and its place in the world through explicating John McDowell's philosophy. This attempt includes the question part and the thinker part, and I shall explain them in turn. The way I put the question makes it sound like the leading question in the contemporary philosophy of mind, that is, 'what is the mind's place in nature?' This question is theory-laden, for often the notion of 'nature' involved is 'physical nature', the domain of physical laws. This implication is neutral between reductive and non-reductive physicalism: even those who regard 'supervenience' as the key notion of their non-reductive theories use 'nature' as an abbreviation for 'physical nature'.[1] Indeed, 'naturalism' and 'physicalism' are often, if not always, interchangeable terms. 'Materialism' is also their kin, but it has become less popular since a few decades ago, mainly because it has a connotation of an outdated conception of matter. I intend to avoid the implication of physical nature in the formulation of the leading question. The notion of 'world' is also theory-laden, to be sure, but it will become clear that the implication I choose to avoid is a much more relevant one.[2]

2. Through a quick browse of the table of contents, or indeed a glimpse of the title of this first chapter, readers might feel that what will be focussed upon is the subjective, as opposed to the objective side. Let me anticipate part of the dénouement: *the world and minded human subjects are constitutively interdependent*. This statement is extremely vague or even empty before further elaborations, but I shall leave it for the later chapters and concentrate here on how it justifies my writing strategy. It is true that an emphasis has been put on the subjective, but notice that the subjectivity in question is *worldly* subjectivity, which implies that the objective side actually plays an equally important role here. To be slightly more specific, the hypothesis put forward is that both the world and minded human subjects are strong *emergent* phenomena, and their emergences are interdependent. This hypothesis will not receive full support in this essay, however. The major case to be made here is a more humble one, namely: the ideas that both the world and minded human subjects are strong emergent phenomena and that their emergences are interdependent are *not* as disturbing as it might seem, and their plausibility can be seen by understanding McDowell's thinking and insights.

Recall the familiar leading question in philosophy of mind, about the mind and its place in nature. As I said, the notion of nature here is heavily theory-laden, and even if I try to avoid this by substituting it with 'world', it is still quite possible for the implication and some related thoughts to slip in. Besides, the notion of 'world' also has different implications for different philosophers. The best way to cure this, I believe, is to start the discussion with some clarifications of this objective side.

But there is a theoretical obstacle here: if 'world' and 'subject' are interdependent in some significant sense, how can we say anything substantial about one of them without also saying something substantial about the other? We might be able to dodge this if we remind ourselves of a certain kind of *neutrality*: do not take the absolute independence of the world for granted; it should be regarded as one of the central issues in the present essay, and it is controversial. Almost everyone agrees that we need to retain some important kind of independence for the world, but whether it is independence *simpliciter* is an issue to be discussed. To see what is at stake, consider the traditional way of conceiving the problem of perceptual directness: do we (at least sometimes) enjoy direct contacts with the world through perceptions? The territory is often divided by direct realism, indirect realism and idealism. First one decides her metaphysical position: if for her the world is mind-dependent, she is an idealist; if she thinks the world is mind-independent, then she needs to choose from direct and indirect realism. In *The Problem of Perception*, A. D. Smith writes:

> [T]he topic of this work is the philosophical position known as "Direct Realism" – a position that *combines* this issue of directness with a Realism about the physical world. Such Realism holds that the physical world has an existence that is not in any way dependent upon its being "cognized"... [And it] is opposed to Idealism: the view that whatever seems to be physical is either reducible to, or at least supervenient upon, cognitive states of consciousness.
>
> Smith, 2002, pp. 1–2; my emphasis

Here Smith implies that the metaphysical part of one's position can be determined independently of, and therefore prior to, the epistemic part. Most past and present philosophers of perception would agree with this move. This is exactly the thought I wish to resist, however. But as indicated above, to argue against this one needs to say more about *both* the subjective and the objective sides, and of course one cannot do this all at once here. What we can do here is just to ask ourselves to stay neutral about whether we can reasonably conceive the situation in *this* factorizing way; in other words, let's not take this 'divide-and-conquer' way of thinking for granted, *pace* Smith and many others. Whether this way of thinking is justified is an important issue to be evaluated, not a self-evident starting point. This is, unfortunately, not recognized by most philosophers in the analytic tradition, probably because of the persisting negative attitude towards the notorious 'idealism', German, British or otherwise.[3]

To divide the question into the metaphysical and the epistemic parts reflects, at least partially, the ideal of division of labour. This methodology as such is innocent, but it does not follow that it would not cause any problem in certain contexts. In our case, the thing to be remembered is that epistemology is a *relation to the world*: notions such as 'knowing' and 'seeing' are factive ones. So if we want to understand how, for example, perceptual directness is possible, we need to be careful about both poles of this epistemic relation, that is, the world and the epistemic subject. Perhaps it will turn out that Smith and many others get things right, but that needs arguments. To assume otherwise is to beg the question against some other positions.

The point of division of labour is well taken, for if all philosophers start their reflections from refuting global scepticism, or vindicating free will, the intellectual progresses of the whole community will be stagnant. So I believe Smith, and indeed all of us, are justified in restricting ourselves to some extent. What I would like to stress is that he restricts too much in the above setting. To rule out idealism temporarily is fine, but to characterize the world as he does is excessive. What he should have done is to insist that what he is going to do in the book is to neglect the view that refuses to acknowledge the independence of the world *in a certain sense*. To do this, there is still room for contemplating upon *the senses* in which the world is independent. I cannot here argue that Smith's way of dividing the territory is indeed problematic, but I invite my readers to take an adventure with me, and indeed, with McDowell, to see if we are in fact too naïve about what the world is like.

The situation here is an example of methodology infecting ontology. Another relevant example goes in the opposite direction. Smith and many others assume the absolute independence of the world; the opposite example refuses to acknowledge the independence of the world altogether, at least for certain purposes. The notable representative of this, not surprisingly, is René Descartes.[4] To be sure, Descartes' contempt against the world is only methodological, indicated by the label the '*Method* of Doubt,' but this method assumes that the constitution of the mind is totally independent of the world. Although with different directions, this strategy and Smith's one are in effect of the same spirit. The philosophers in question are well aware that they should not assume metaphysical theses before they start their argumentations, and that is why they painstakingly emphasize the *methodological* nature of their presuppositions. However, this line of reasoning assumes that methodological considerations are entirely irrelevant to ontological propositions, and this is what I wish to resist. If one thinks he needs to have a full understanding of human being before he goes on to understand gender, he assumes a false ontology of human being in his methodology. Almost no one would commit this kind of mistake here, for in this case the falsity is obvious. In our case, by contrast, the truth or falsity of the metaphysics is far from obvious, so many people have wrongly thought that their methodologies are metaphysically innocent. Again, I invite my readers to *bracket* the sense in which the world is independent, so that we can see whether we are really right about the world in our daily lives and philosophical inquiries. The Cartesian Method of Doubt will be a central target throughout the essay, but we should also bear Smith's case in mind in our investigations.

Subject

1. To repeat, the leading question in this essay concerns human subject or subjectivity and its place in the world. A human subject is a *Homo sapiens* with a *Cogito*; that is, a human animal with mentality and selfhood. So to understand human subject is to understand mentally equipped human animal. Mentality has different aspects, and to understand mentality is to understand the nature of those aspects. A human subject exhibits their mentality when it perceives, knows, thinks, speaks, acts and feels; in this essay I venture to understand these varieties of mentality by explicating McDowell's thinking. Again, let me focus on questions and phenomena before saying more about the philosopher. Eric Olson (2007) proposes various relevant questions that 'are typically not about "the self" at all' (p. 274). His examples include personal identity, first-person reference, the unity of consciousness, moral agency, reflexive thought and self-knowledge. This is of course, as he himself acknowledges, not an exhaustive list. The underlying thought is that there is no single, well-defined problem of the self. I concur with this thought. The so-called 'problem of the self' is not identical to the mind-body problem, though the two are definitely related. It looks like the problem of personal identity, but they are still different. The problem of consciousness is obviously relevant, but again they are not one and the same. So perhaps we should accept that there is no problem of the self as such; instead, there are problems concerning the *functioning* self: the self functions as a perceiver, knower, thinker, speaker, agent, person and (self-) conscious subject, amongst others. In the following chapters I investigate these aspects respectively.

Now, I begin this section by talking about 'mentality', but soon the key concept became 'self' or 'subject'. Have we changed the subject matter? Yes and no. Yes, because as a matter of fact, the questions concerning the self, notably personal identity and free agency, are only a portion of philosophy of mind. No, because I do not think issues concerning mentality and those concerning the self should be studied separately. Like the problem of the self, the problem of mentality can also be divided into various different sub-questions, such as perception, knowledge, thought, language, action, (self-) consciousness, amongst others. Now it would be highly unnatural to think that we can, say, investigate perceiv*ing* without also investigating perceiv*er*. To think we can seems to imply a three-fold picture: world, mind and self, which might be problematic.[5] Philosophers of mind often talk about propositional attitudes, constituted by mental states (attitudes) and mental contents (propositions), but we need to remember that every propositional attitude goes with a self, functions as a perceiver, knower or others. It does not make good sense to confine the problems concerning the self in a corner of philosophy of mind. To be sure, there can be certain branches concentrating on those problems in particular, but it does not follow that in most regions of philosophy of mind we can just forget about the self. Again, division of labour seems to be the troublemaker here, though the method as such is innocent.

The two points I just argued can be put in this way: there is no sharp line between the problems about mentality and those about the self or subject, *and* the problems of the self or subject should be approached by understanding the nature of perceiver, knower, thinker, speaker, agent, person and (self-) conscious being, amongst others. This expels a possible wrong impression that in focusing on *subject* we have confined ourselves in a small region of philosophy of mind. By investigating various aspects of the self or subject, we should have a more comprehensive understanding of human mentality.

A remaining question to be answered is this. So far I use the notions of 'self' and 'subject' interchangeably; does this mean that there is no distinction between them? Grammatically speaking, 'self' is a *reflexive* pronoun. This implies that questions under this title may be primarily about *higher-order* mentality.[6] It should be clear that I am not only discussing that kind of mentality, however. That is why I use 'subject' exclusively in the later discussions. I also use 'self' in this section because in bringing out my points I invoked Olson's discussions, and what he uses is the notion of 'self', though he does not intend to confine himself with higher-order mentality. His usage is understandable, for his opponents often conduct their discussions with 'self', rather than 'subject'. In any case, I believe only the notion of 'subject' is broad enough to accommodate the aspects I would like to investigate in the present essay. Therefore throughout the discussions I will talk about human *subject*, as a perceiver when it perceives, a knower when it knows, and so on and so forth. And relatedly, human subjects exhibit *worldly subjectivity*.

2. It is time to turn to McDowell's thinking itself. I shall start with some very general descriptions. In addition to contemporary influences from Strawson, Evans, Sellars and Brandom, McDowell also invokes resources from important thinkers in the history of Western philosophy. As we shall see in later chapters, he adopts Aristotelian notion of 'second nature', Kantian conception of the 'discursivity of experience', Hegelian absolute idealism, Wittgensteinian notion of 'form of life', and Gadamerian distinction between 'world' and 'environment', and so on. In response to critics from other backgrounds, he also discusses Heidegger and Merleau-Ponty. And I have not mentioned a large amount of contemporary philosophers. This makes it extraordinarily difficult to approach McDowell's thinking. The nature of McDowell's philosophy poses a serious challenge to anyone who is willing to conduct a large-scale exposition of his thinking: given that he touches on so many divergent issues in various branches of philosophy *and* so many unfathomable thoughts of various important philosophers in a highly systematic way, either the question-oriented way or the figure-centred way of exposition will very likely be unsatisfying. If one chooses the former, it will be very hard for one to give due weights to the convoluted relations between issues and those big names; if one adopts the latter, one will probably neglect detailed objections and replies in specific issues. Either way, the exposition is open to objections about its writing strategy. Although these two styles do not strictly exclude each other, still it is quite challenging for commentators to reach equilibrium.

Anthologies aside, there are at least three introductory books exclusively on McDowell's philosophy. The first is *John McDowell* (2019; first edition in 2004) by Tim Thornton. This one is very question-oriented, taking care of different areas of McDowell's thinking in a detailed fashion. *John McDowell* (2004a) by Maximilian de Gaynesford was also question-oriented, but the author concentrates more on McDowell's own thinking. The third one, *On Thinking and the World: John McDowell's Mind and World* (2005) by Sandra M. Dingli, emphasizes the relations between McDowell and other important thinkers, like Kant, Heidegger and Davidson. All of them try to strike a balance between the question-oriented approach and the figure-centred one. The distinctiveness of my interpretation here is that I focus on the very idea of *subjectivity*, which is relatively absent in the extant interpretations; also, this interpretation is the only one that seeks to cover possible points of contact from *both* phenomenology and cognitive sciences.

So obviously I need to make a choice. In the present essay I tend to structure the argumentations with the figure-centred approach. The principal reason is that McDowell's philosophy, as an interconnected system, needs to be understood in this way. I believe we should understand how he integrates miscellaneous elements from divergent areas and thinkers into a unified whole before going deeper in specific questions. Besides, at different stages of the essay, I will evaluate debates between McDowell and other important contemporary philosophers, in order to bring out McDowell's place in contemporary philosophy. 'Figure' here includes McDowell and his important contemporaries. I choose this approach because I hope to offer a more comprehensive exposition of McDowell's thinking, *and* further I want to place McDowell's thinking as a whole on the map of contemporary philosophy, and this requires me to focus mainly on other 'big names'.

3. Let me connect these abstract considerations about the essay structure to the actual contents. The main theme, to repeat, is to understand human subject and its place in the world. There are two strands in this project: first, how does a *Homo sapiens*, an animal, can nevertheless be a *Cogito*, i.e. having the capacities to be responsive to reasons *as such*, and to think about oneself? Second, how can this minded human animal be a perceiver, knower, thinker, speaker, agent, person and (self-) conscious being in the world? The former question pinpoints the tension between our animal, biological nature and spiritual capacities, and the latter concerns how our biologically-rooted spiritual capacities enable us to navigate in the world through varieties of our mentality. In this essay I start with the tension but concentrate on the applications. In Chapter 2 I introduce the tension and discuss how McDowell manages to dissolve it and thereby find a place in the world for minded human subject. From chapters 3 to 7, I discuss how McDowell's resolution to the putative tension applies to various mentalities, including perceiver and knower, thinker and speaker, agent and person, conscious and self-conscious subject, etc.; I discuss how McDowell avoids Brandom's charge of residual individualism, how he criticizes Kripke's Cartesian way of construing the sceptical paradox, how he objects to Dummett's 'full-blooded conception of theory of meaning', how he finds Davidson's and Brandom's 'I-thou' conception of the publicity of intentionality unsatisfying, how he replies to Dreyfus's accusation of 'the Myth of the Mental', how he discerns a Cartesian line of thought in Parfit's view of personal identity, and how he thinks Kant unwittingly lapses into the 'narrow assumption', and so on. In the Epilogue, I will discuss the root of those varieties of mentality, that is, our *self-determining subjectivity*. As we shall see, McDowell thinks human subject is special in the sense that it lives in the 'logical space of reasons', and this space is exhausted by conceptual connectedness, and finally, this space of rational-conceptual connectedness is identical with *the realm of freedom*. So arguably the heart of McDowell's thinking is his elaboration of this self-determining subjectivity. As the concluding chapter, it can hardly provide a full-fledged construction of that important notion, but I shall try to gesture at possible directions for us to think about. This is not supposed to comprehensively cover McDowell's engagements with all the famous philosophers he himself mentions: Hegel, Wittgenstein, Sellars, Strawson and Evans will appear in due course, though I avoid singling them out in the flow of the prose.

A few words about McDowell's 'quietism'. This Wittgensteinian component of his thinking is often understood as a refusal of offering positive or systematic accounts. So conceived, my present project is at odds with this attitude. However, quietism need not be understood that way only. It is a reminder about our ways of seeing issues; it says that before engaging in substantial discussions, one should slow down and see whether there is any compulsory reason for us to accept the challenge in question. 'Quietism' itself is a big issue, especially when one takes it to be a discussion about Wittgenstein scholarship. However, in this essay I adopt a rather weak understanding of it, as just briefly characterized above. Therefore, I will not go into this in the rest of the essay. At times, however, it will come up explicitly, and we might find it useful for understanding why McDowell stops somewhere before saying something more positive for the issues in question.[7]

2

Cogito and *Homo sapiens*

Just as nature developed itself as a whole from the original act of self-consciousness, a second nature will emerge ... from free self-determination.
F. W. J. Schelling, *The System of Transcendental Philosophy*

[M]an (the worker) feels that he is acting freely only in his animal functions – eating, drinking, and procreating, or at most in his dwelling and adornment – while in his human functions, he is nothing more than animal.
Karl Marx, *Economic and Philosophical Manuscripts of 1844*

Nature

1. We are human beings. This plain fact indicates, at least implicitly, that we are at the same time rational and natural. This may seduce us 'to see ourselves as peculiarly bifurcated, with a foothold in the animal kingdom and a mysterious separate involvement in an extra-natural world of rational connections' (1996a, p. 78), John McDowell observes. We do not need reductive physicalism to ensure that we are *Homo sapiens,* and we do not need substance dualism to maintain that each of us is, or has, a *Cogito.* The trouble is that it is hard to see how we can be both natural and rational: if we conceive 'nature' as the domain exhausted by scientific investigations narrowly construed, it seems obvious that there is no room for the notion of 'reason'. But we cannot have a satisfying self-image without accommodating the element that makes us properly human.[1]

2. Wilfrid Sellars once remarked: '[i]n characterizing an episode or a state as that of *knowing,* we are not giving an empirical description of that episode or state; we are placing it in the logical space of reasons, of justifying and being able to justify what one says' (1956, pp. 298–9). Relations in the *space of reasons* are rational, normative ones; they can be evaluated as correct or incorrect. McDowell contrasts the space of reasons with the *realm of law*, which is demarcated by natural sciences (1996a, p. xv).² The Sellars-McDowell line of thought is that the two spaces are *sui generis* (i.e. different in kind; 1996a, p. xix). That is to say, if one attempts to reconstruct the intelligibility of the space of reasons from the resources of the realm of law, one '[falls] into a naturalistic fallacy' (ibid., p. xiv). Furthermore, the *sui generis* nature should not be secured by 'picturing the space of reasons as an autonomous structure – autonomous in that it is constituted independently of anything specifically human (the idea of the human is the idea of what pertains to a certain species of animals) ...' (ibid., p. 77). This pair of thoughts serves to respect our commonsense that we are rational animals, without committing ourselves to a presumably mystical 'supernaturalism' – a thought that renounces our status as *natural* beings (ibid., p. 78). But things are not so simple. If the space of reasons is of its own kind, evading the net of *natural* sciences, how can we understand it without the notion of 'supernatural'? And if we are to avoid unpalatable supernaturalism, how can we preserve the idea that human beings are properly *human* precisely because we live in the space of reasons?

The predicament is well characterized by a Sellarsian metaphor 'the clash of the images', discussed by James O'Shea for example (2007, p. 10).³ The two images – the manifest image and the scientific image – clash because of the *sui generis* thesis, and supernaturalism seems to be the inescapable result of the clash. The Sellarsian task, which is taken up by McDowell as well as other Sellarsians, is to 'fuse the images', put by Jay Rosenberg (2007), O'Shea's teacher.

But not everyone is Sellarsian. There are two main strands in response to the dilemma presented above. One is to '[deny] that the spontaneity of the understanding is *sui generis* in the way suggested by the link to the idea of freedom' (1996a, p. 67). This is called 'bald naturalism'. It is 'bald' because it erases what is distinctively human. McDowell has no intention to argue that bald naturalism is false; he only suggests that the view is 'a less satisfying way to [solve the philosophical puzzlement in question] than [his] alternative' (ibid., p. xxi), which will emerge later. The other way is to regard 'the structure of the space of reasons' as 'simply extra-natural ... as if we had a foothold outside the animal kingdom, in a splendidly non-human realm of identity' (ibid., p. 88) This is called 'rampant platonism'. It is 'rampant' because it overemphasizes what is distinctively human. Here again, McDowell does not, and cannot knock it down. After all, though the view is indeed mysterious, it does not follow that it cannot be true in a mysterious way. What McDowell (and indeed everyone who opposes to it) can do is to elaborate one or another more satisfying way to understand human being.[4]

Nurture

1. The view McDowell recommends 'is a naturalism of *second nature*', and it 'can equally see it as a *naturalized platonism*' (1996a, p. 91, my emphasis). In order to understand this, first we need to learn more about the notion of 'second nature'.

Recall that when the notion of the realm of law is introduced, it is supposed to be contrasted with the space of reasons. The realm of law is coextensive with, and indeed defined by, the domain of natural sciences, especially those that are governed by strict laws. A natural, and indeed seemingly unavoidable thought followed from this is that nature is *exhausted by* the realm of law. This line of thought is neutral with regard to the disagreement between bald naturalism and rampant platonism, for what they disagree is whether the space of reasons is *sui generis*; their common ground is the equation between nature and the realm of law. McDowell manages to steer a middle course between the two by introducing the notion of 'second nature': the realm of nature includes *both* the realm of law and the space of reasons, so the thesis that the space of reasons is *sui generis* is compatible with the insistence that human beings are fully *natural* beings.

To identify nature with the realm of law is distinctively modern; the development of this thought has often been called 'disenchantment' (ibid., p. 70).[5] In order to motivate his broader understanding of nature, McDowell goes back to the era before enlightenment, in particular ancient Greek. Here is what he says,

> Virtue of character properly so called [by Aristotle] includes a specifically shaped state of the practical intellect: "practical wisdom," in the standard English translation. This is a responsiveness to some of the demands of reason ... The picture is that ethics involves requirements of reason that *are there* whether we know it or not, and our eyes are opened to them by the acquisition of "practical wisdom".
>
> ibid., p. 79, my emphasis

In *Nicomachean Ethics*, Aristotle's word for 'practical wisdom' is '*phronesis*'. I emphasize 'are there' in this passage to indicate the *objective* character of ethical demands conceived by McDowell. Now he intends this 'to serve as a model for the understanding, the faculty that enables us to recognize and create the kind of intelligibility that is a matter of placement in the space of reasons' (ibid., p. 79). A further and crucial question is how this line of thought can help us out of the stalemate between bald naturalism and rampant platonism. As indicated above, the gambit is to develop a satisfying notion of second nature. So what we need are reasons for thinking that Aristotelian practical wisdom deserves to be called second 'nature'.[6]

McDowell suggests that '[we] are alerted to these demands by acquiring appropriate conceptual capacities. When a decent *upbringing* initiates us into the relevant way of thinking, our eyes are opened to the very existence of this tract of the space of reasons' (ibid., p. 82, my emphasis). In saying this, what McDowell has in mind 'is what figures in German philosophy as *Bildung*' (ibid., p. 84). Now this can be recognized as genuine *nature* because '[our] *Bildung* actualizes some of *the potentialities we are born with*' (ibid., p. 88, my emphasis): what we are born with is our animal first nature, which is *not different in kind* from those which are possessed by other animals. What is distinctively human is that our animal first nature includes miscellaneous complex potentialities suitable for fostering the space of reasons. We have extraordinary complicated brains and sense organs, and these powerful resources help us, say, begin to parse strings of sounds emitted from other's mouths. McDowell, an empiricist to be sure, does not need to reject Chomskian innate faculties or similar mechanisms in this respect. Our second nature is what makes us special, but our remarkable first nature is also crucial for our rational animal lives. We can see that the Aristotelian distinction between potentiality and actuality is at work here: our *potentialities* relevant to the initiation into the space of reasons are our animal first nature, but when proper upbringing kicks in, those potentialities are *actualized* (or realized) as the capacities to be responsive to reasons *as such*, i.e. recognize reasons as reasons. In this way, we gain a satisfying self-image 'without offering to reinstate the idea that the movement of the planets, or the fall of a sparrow, is rightly approached in the sort of way we approach a text or an utterance or some other kind of action' (ibid., p. 72).[7]

What McDowell rejects is 'an intelligible distortion undergone by the Aristotelian idea that normal human beings are *rational animals*' (ibid., p. 108, my emphasis). The root of this distortion is to conceive 'an animal endowed with reason [as] *metaphysically split*' (ibid., p. 108, my emphasis): we are *natural* because we are confined in the realm of law, but we are also *supernatural* because we are responsive to reasons as such. This distortion can be set straight by recognizing that for Aristotle, responsiveness to reasons as such is our second *nature*, which is realized by our first nature potentialities under suitable upbringing. We should recognize that 'rationality is *integrally part* of [human beings'] animal nature' (ibid., p. 109, my emphasis). Our animal nature includes first and second natures, and this does justice to both the thought that our rational capacities are natural, and the thought that we share something with other animals. In accommodating the latter, we do not need to reject the idea that rationality is *intrinsic* to our animal nature. In the context of the conceptuality of experiences, McDowell says that 'it is not compulsory to attempt to accommodate the combination of something in common and a striking difference in [a] *factorizing* way: to suppose our perceptual lives include a core that we can also recognize in the perceptual life of a mere animal, and *an extra ingredient in addition*' (ibid., p. 64, my emphasis).[8] Although the contexts are different, the general lesson should apply here too.

2. As we have seen, second nature is supposed to '[give] human reason enough of a foothold in the realm of law to satisfy any proper respect for modern natural science' (ibid., p. 84). I shall discuss two objections that run at the opposite directions. The first maintains that in order to secure the foothold in the realm of law, second nature must be located in *both* the space of reasons and the realm of law, but this nonetheless leads to incoherence. The second maintains that the foothold in the realm of law cannot be secured anyway; that is, the insistence on second 'nature' leads to supernaturalism come what may.

The first line of objection is taken by Paul Bartha and Steven Savitt (henceforth B&S, 1998). They assert that McDowell's position is 'simply untenable' (ibid., p. 254). The general principle underlying their argument is that 'there is no way to account for an interactive relationship between [two wholly separate worlds] without undercutting the point of maintaining their separateness' (ibid., p. 257). The main trouble of Cartesian dualism nicely illustrates this: if *res cogitan* and *res extensia* are different in kind, the putative interactions between them become unintelligible. And if one insists that there must be a bridge, this supposed bridge must thereby belong to both realms at the same time, but this violates the premise that the two realms are different in kind.[9]

They first notice, rightly, that second nature belongs to the space of reasons, for it is supposed to account for spontaneity. But they argue that it belongs to the realm of law also, for it 'must involve interaction with the natural environment' (B&S, 1998, p. 258). If so, the *sui generis* character of the space of reasons collapses, given the lesson drawn from Cartesian dualism and, according to B&S, Passmore.

No one, McDowell included, can sensibly deny that 'human perception (and therefore human reason) is also conditioned by the physical processes that govern the interaction between our sensory apparatus and our environment – processes that belong to the realm of law' (ibid., p. 258). But the inference from this to the conclusion that second nature is also an inhabitant of the realm of law is a *non sequitur*. The sense of 'conditioning' here should be 'an *enabling* question', as opposed to 'a constitutive one' (McDowell, 1994/1998a, p. 352, my emphasis). The distinction between the space of reasons and the realm of law, by contrast, is obviously a *constitutive* matter. One can claim that perception and reason nevertheless belong to the realm of law, but that needs arguments, and the above *non sequitur* can do nothing about it. And that is not McDowell's position anyway.[10]

B&S think that McDowell commits that second nature belongs to both the space of reasons and the realm of law, but this is a straightforward misinterpretation. This misunderstanding is understandable, however, given that it seems to be a natural interpretation of the thought that reasons can be causes: if second nature is ultimately *natural*, it must be in the *causal* network, which means it must be in the realm of law as well. The falsity of this inference should now be clear: as discussed in one of the chapter notes earlier, McDowell warns us that the opposite of the space of reasons should not be the space of *causes*, for if it is so, it follows that there is no causal relation in the space of reasons, and therefore reasons cannot be causes. B&S are nevertheless indifferent about this reminder, regarding the realm of law as the space of causes (and thereby unwittingly committing that reasons cannot be causes), and thinking that if McDowell is willing to do justice to the fact that reasons can be causes, he has to admit that second nature belongs to both the space of reasons and the realm of law, and the *sui generis* claim collapses. Their objection is based on a misunderstanding of the distinction between the space of reasons and the realm of law, as we have seen. McDowell would say that if we see the crucial contrast as between the space of *reasons* and the space of *causes*, it is 'too late' to insist that spontaneity belongs to both. And additionally, that position leads to incoherence, as B&S's rehearsal of the Cartesian trouble shows.

The opposite objection is proposed by Crispin Wright (2002). Wright thinks that McDowell has not done enough work to exclude rampant platonism. He identifies and criticizes three criteria allegedly proposed by McDowell:

(i) that the correctness of ethical judgement is constrained by 'contingencies of our life';

(ii) that it needs only an ordinary, unmysterious ethical education to initiate people into 'the rational demands of ethics';
(iii) that correct ethical judgement is 'essentially within reach' of our ethical thinking. (ibid., p. 153).

As I see it, only (ii) deserves our attention here, for (i) and (iii) are more like descriptions of McDowell's picture. I shall therefore focus on (ii). The point I am going to argue, however, applies to (i) and (iii) as well, for the point is that McDowell never attempts to provide *any criterion* (in a certain sense) to distinguish naturalized platonism from its rampant relatives.

In discussing (ii), Wright asks:

> Why should Rampant Platonists find any difficulty in the idea that it takes only an ordinary training to trigger the exercise of the social non-natural epistemic capacities in which they believe? What exactly is the problem in that *combination*?
> 2002, p. 154, my emphasis

Here Wright is pointing out the *compatibility* of *Bildung* and rampant platonism; he thinks, rightly in my view, that McDowell's invocation of *Bildung* and related considerations does not exclude rampant platonism. But why is this compatibility a problem for McDowell?

We need to bear in mind that McDowell never attempts to knock rampant platonism and bald naturalism down. In the case of rampant platonism, as I said in the previous section, though 'the view is indeed mysterious, it does not follow that it cannot be true in a mysterious way'. Rampant platonism, by its nature, is irrefutable given the *sui generis* thesis; it asserts that the space of reasons is autonomous *simpliciter*, which means it is *wholly* (*holily*?) independent of other kinds of intelligibility. Therefore the only way to repel rampant platonism is to refute the *sui generis* thesis, that is, to embrace bald naturalism. So the charge from Wright is unfair: rampant platonism is a thesis that can only be repelled by bald naturalism, but McDowell is clearly not a bald naturalist. It is understandable, nevertheless, why Wright has this demanding task in mind: he himself is a dedicated bald naturalist.[11] But we need to remember that not everyone shares that metaphysical position.

McDowell is well aware that given his anti-bald naturalism, he cannot *refute* rampant platonism. What he can sensibly do is to *urge* us to accept a much more moderate position, naturalized platonism, by elaborating a sensible notion of 'second nature'. Of course a rampant platonist can always say that given the *sui generis* thesis, he can accommodate whatever we say. But why should this matter?

Consider the case of radical scepticism. Nowadays most people recognize that such a radical thesis is not refutable, so what we non-sceptics can do is to argue, in one way or another, that we have no good reason to believe in radical scepticism, or we have good reasons to believe otherwise. The situation is quite similar when it comes to rampant platonism. Although bald naturalism is indeed incompatible with that version of platonism, the latter can always insists that the physicalist reduction in question is not successful, for there is no common ground for evaluating the success of reduction. So what we can hopefully have is something like McDowell's picture: provided a reasonable story about how human beings can become responsive to reasons as such – in his case, through *Bildung*, custom and language – we have good reasons to believe in a naturalized platonism. Why need more?

3. Now, given McDowell's demanding conception of human being, the question about the status of mere animals becomes urgent. This can be fully answered only after we say more about McDowell's views of experience, conceptual capacities, rationality and self-consciousness, but I can here sketch a general picture with Hans-Georg Gadamer's distinction between 'world' and 'environment' (1960/2004, p. 483). Gadamer writes:

> [Although] the concept of environment was first used for the purely human world ... this concept can be used to comprehend all the conditions on which a living creature depends. But it is thus clear that man, unlike all other living creatures, has a "world," for other creatures do not in the same sense have a relationship to the world, but are, as it were, embedded in their environment.
>
> ibid., p. 441

He further relates this openness to the world to human's possession of languages:

> Language is not just one of man's possessions in the world; rather, on it depends [on] the fact that man has a *world* at all. The world as world exists for man as for on other creature that is in the world. But this world is verbal in nature ... that language is originarily human means at the same time that man's being in the world is primordially linguistic.
>
> ibid., p. 440

And the crucial difference between human beings' openness to the world and mere animals' embedment in the environment is the very idea of 'freedom':

> Moreover, unlike all other living creatures, man's relationship to the world is characterized by *freedom from environment*. This freedom implies the linguistic constitution of the world. Both belong together.
>
> ibid., p. 441

Here is not the place to elaborate Gadamer's distinction; I introduce it at this point only because it helps us understand McDowell's general picture of mere animals.[12] McDowell says that for his purposes, the point of the distinction 'is that it shows in some detail how we can acknowledge what is common between human beings and brutes, while preserving the difference that the Kantian thesis forces on us' (1996a, p. 115). What is in common between us and them is that both, as living creatures, embed in and cope with our immediate environments; as animals, all of us are structured by our 'immediate biological imperatives' (ibid., p. 115). '[A] merely animal life', however, 'is shaped by goals whose control of the animal's behavior at a given moment is an immediate outcome of biological forces. A mere animal does not weigh reasons and decide what to do' (ibid., p. 115). In the case of human being, by contrast, we can say that '[to] acquire the spontaneity of the understanding is to become able, as Gadamer puts it, to "rise above the pressure of what impinges on us from the world" (*Truth and Method*, p. 444) – that succession of problems and opportunities constituted as such by biological imperatives – into a "free, distanced orientation" (p. 445)' (ibid., p. 115–16). In a word, human beings enjoy 'full-fledged subjectivity', as opposed to mere animals' 'proto-subjectivity' (ibid., p. 116–17).

Thus, we can avoid a 'peculiarly bifurcated' ontology, exemplified by two strands of the Cartesian thoughts.[13] On the one hand, the Cartesians maintain a position more radical than bald naturalism in their treatment of mere animals, regarding them as zombic automata. On the other hand, they insist on a position more radical than rampant platonism in the case of human being, seeing them as having immaterial mental substances. This strange two-fold view is more radical than bald naturalism, for in holding this naturalism one does not need to regard mere animals as zombies: the zombie thesis is far stronger than the idea that mere animals are locked in the realm of law. And this view is more radical than rampant platonism, for in urging this platonism one does not thereby commit to the idea that human beings have, or are immaterial souls: the soul thesis is far stronger than the idea that human beings can reach a mysterious, non-animal space of reasons. Against both of these, McDowell urges that 'exercises of spontaneity belong to *our* way of actualizing ourselves as animal' (ibid., p. 78, my emphasis).

There might be some worries about McDowell's two presuppositions. One is that human beings really enjoy freedom of the will; the other is that mere animals are non-rational. McDowell himself seems to be confident with both of them, but I think it is reasonable to formulate the essence of his thinking by conditionals: *given that* we humans do enjoy freedom of will, and *given that* mere animals are indeed non-rational, or at least do not possess rationality in the sense that they can respond to reasons *as such*,[14] then the view McDowell recommends is much more satisfying than both bald naturalism and rampant platonism, since his picture reconciles two important facts about us: we are denizens of the animal kingdom, and we are rational beings.[15]

4. I begin my exposition of McDowell's philosophy with the issues concerning human beings' place in nature. I adopt this approach because I regard the following remarks of McDowell as quintessential:

> In order to introduce the attractions of a relaxed naturalism, I have exploited philosophical difficulties about perceptual experience. But this focus was not essential; the difficulties exemplify a type ... Now the difficulty concerns not the *passivity* of experience as such, but its *naturalness*. The problem is that operations of sensibility are actualizations of a potentiality that is part of our nature. When we take sensing to be a way of being acted on by the world, we are thinking of it as a natural phenomenon, and then we have trouble seeing how a *sui generis* spontaneity could be anything but externally related to it. But passivity is *not part of the very idea* of what it is for a natural potentiality to be actualized. So we should be able to construct a train of thought about actualization of active natural powers, duplicating the difficulties I have exploited in the case of passive natural powers.
>
> 1996a, p. 89; my emphasis

This vital passage appears in his Lecture V, and therefore is, unfortunately, often overlooked by philosophers in the analytic tradition. Even his colleague Robert Brandom complains that '[t]he social nature of spontaneity and the space of reasons is acknowledged, but only *belatedly*, in the discussion of the need for knowers and agents to be properly brought up in order to be sensitive to various sorts of norms' (1996, p. 256; my emphasis). He sees this as a ground for arguing that McDowell's overall picture is a 'residual *individualism*' (ibid., p. 258). This line of criticism assumes that McDowell's writing strategy reveals his view about the conceptual order, which means he does *not* assign the conceptual priority to the social elements. But the fact is quite to the contrary. McDowell is the philosopher who insists on *the* conceptual priority for the social. He even finds fault in the picture depicted by Donald Davidson, who painstakingly stresses the essential importance of the social elements:

> In recent work, Davidson has undertaken to build the concept of objectivity out of a "triangulation" between these self-standing subjects, pairwise engaged in

mutual interpretation. This comes into conflict with the Kantian thesis of interdependence that I consider in Lecture V, §5, and reconsider in Lecture VI, §4. By my lights, if subjects are already in place, it is *too late* to set about catering for the constitution of the concept of objectivity.

1996a, p. 186; my emphasis. Also see his 2003c/2008b

It seems to me that McDowell does not present Davidson's position accurately, for Davidson does not try to derive objectivity from 'self-standing subjects'. Rather, he makes clear that his aim is to show that knowing our own minds, knowing others' minds, and knowing the external world 'form a tripod; if any leg were lost, no part would stand' (1991/2001c, p. 220). My purpose here is not to take part in the debate; what I would like to stress is that McDowell often finds other philosophers' do not give due weight to the *priority* of the social, so it is uncharitable to think that he himself does not acknowledge that priority. It is possible to argue that McDowell's 'too late' argument applies to himself after all, but anyway we should recognize that in McDowell's picture, the social elements plays constitutive roles in social *initiation* into the space of reasons; conceptually speaking, his invocation of '*Bildung*' and 'second nature' does not come into the picture 'only belatedly', as Brandom and many others mistakenly suppose.

In this chapter, I introduced the tension between reason and nature, and discussed how McDowell manages to ease the tension without cancelling the *sui generis* character of the space of reasons. To be sure, I do not offer a wholesale defence of second nature and other related notions. My main theme in this essay, as I said in Chapter 1, is the *applications* of second nature – how a creature with second nature can be a perceiver, knower, thinker, speaker, agent, person and (self-) conscious subject – as opposed to second nature *per se*. There is a lot more to be said about this Aristotelian notion, but I would like to leave it to some future occasions. To have a full story for that, explications of notions such as supervenience, emergence, constitution, realization and so on, are essential.

3

Perceiver and Knower

That the objective world would exist *even if there existed no knowing being at all, naturally seems at the first onset to be sure and certain, because it can be thought in the abstract . . . But if we try to* realize *this abstract thought . . . and if accordingly we attempt to* imagine an objective world without a knowing subject, *then we become aware that what we are imagining at that moment is in truth the opposite of what we intended . . . that is to say, precisely that which we had sought to exclude.*

Arthur Schopenhauer, The World as Will and Representation, Vol. II.

This phenomenologically necessary concept of receptivity is in no way exclusively opposed to that of the activity of the ego, *under which all acts proceeding in a specific way from the ego-pole are to be included. On the contrary, receptivity must be regarded as the lowest level of activity.*

Edmund Husserl, Experience and Judgment

Primeness

1. In the previous chapter, we concentrated on how McDowell responds to this difficult question: how can we be *both* rational and natural? His proposal is a *naturalism of second nature*, or *naturalized platonism*. The take-home message is that we can legitimately regard the space of reasons as part of nature. Now, an ensuing question concerns how the operations of the space of reasons enable our minds to directly contact with the world. This big question can be divided into some more specific ones. The present chapter takes up the following one: how does our second nature enable us to have *perceptual*, or more general, *epistemic* contact with the world?

Let me introduce two notions before starting the exposition. They are 'broadness' and 'primeness'. A mental state is broad if and only if its individuation condition involves external factors; a mental state is prime if and only if it cannot be analysed by more primitive states.[1] I shall begin with broadness. Its opposite notion is 'narrowness', which says that the individuation condition of a mental state only involve internal factors; here 'internal' can be glossed by 'in the skull' or at least 'in the body'. To insist on the narrowness of mental states is to commit one to 'internalism' about the mental.[2] By contrast, to think that mental states are generally broad is to hold 'externalism'. Now, there are generally two versions of externalism, weak and strong. Weak externalism holds that the mental state in question can be de-composed into internal and external factors; that is, the identity of the internal/external factors can be independently specified. By contrast, strong externalism maintains that the internal and external factors are *interdependent* in a strong sense; theoretically or conceptually we can talk about internal or external factors, but empirically there is no such distinction. This strong externalism commits to broadness *as well as primeness*: the latter entails the former, but not vice versa. So we can understand weak externalism as subscribing broadness without primeness; the independently specified internal factor is often called 'narrow content'. The motivations for committing narrow content include considerations about self-knowledge and mental causation, amongst others, but for my purposes we do not need to go through the details here.[3]

So much has been said for the terminological matter. As we shall see, McDowell commits to both primeness and broadness; that is, he is a strong externalist. The main theme of the present chapter is primeness; I will leave broadness for Chapter 5. In this section I shall first identify the relevant target and the basic shape of McDowell's criticisms, and more about his positive thinking will be discussed in the next section.

2. McDowell introduces his target in the context of Bertrand Russell's Theory of Descriptions (McDowell, 1986a/1998b). He discerns a Cartesian strand in Russell's overall thinking and characterizes it as follows:

> In a fully Cartesian picture, the inner life takes place in an autonomous realm, transparent to the introspective awareness of its subject; the access of subjectivity to the rest of the world becomes correspondingly problematic, in a way that has familiar manifestations in the mainstream of post-Cartesian epistemology ... [this inner space is] a locus of configurations that are self-standing, not beholden to external conditions ...[4]
>
> ibid., pp. 126–7; also see 1984a/1998b, 1991b/1998b

Here McDowell does not refer to Descartes' texts, but we can reasonably conjecture that what he has in mind here is the 'Method of Doubt': in order to ensure the certainty or purity of our analyses, we should first only consider factors *internal to the subject* (McDowell, 1997c/1998a). The gist of McDowell's negative point here is that there is a harmful metaphysical assumption lurking in this seemingly innocent methodological consideration. The assumption is that there is an autonomous inner space metaphysically speaking. This metaphysics implies a disastrous epistemic loss of the world. McDowell first mentions Barry Stroud's argument against this epistemic disaster (1984, ch.1):

> Barry Stroud, for instance, plausibly traces the Cartesian threat of losing the world to this principle: one can acquire worldly knowledge by using one's senses only if one can know, at the time of the supposed acquisition of knowledge, that one is not dreaming. This sets a requirement that Stroud argues cannot be met; no proposed test or procedure for establishing that one is not dreaming would do the trick, since by a parallel principle one would need to know that one was not dreaming that one was applying the test or procedure and obtaining a satisfactory result. So Stroud suggests that if we accept the requirement we cannot escape losing the world.
>
> McDowell, 1986a/1998b, p. 238

What Stroud identifies is the so-called 'KK principle' in traditional internalist epistemology: in order to know something, I need to know that I know that thing, which implies that I need to know that I am not dreaming. If one subscribes to the Method of Doubt and the Dreaming argument, one thereby commits to a certain variety of the KK principle. But it should be clear that the principle invites a vicious infinite regress, as described in the quotation. Now McDowell thinks that this diagnosis is plausible but not the end of the story.[5] As we shall see, though lots of contemporary philosophers reject, at least implicitly, the KK principle, many of them still accept the inner space model. One of McDowell's main tasks is to show that this model is responsible for our philosophical anxiety concerning perception, knowledge, thought, language, action, personal identity and self-consciousness.

McDowell then proposes two sources for the distinctiveness of the inner space model. The first is that the inner space theorist 'extends the range of truth and knowability to the appearances on the basis of which we naively think we know about the ordinary world'. The motivation of this is that '[this] permits a novel response to arguments that conclude that we know nothing from the fact that we are fallible about the external world' (ibid., p. 238). Recall that the inner space theorist's scepticism is only methodological; his ultimate concern is to bring knowledge back to us. Therefore he adopts the above manoeuvre so that 'we can retreat to the newly recognized inner reality, and refute the claim that we know nothing ...' (ibid., p. 239).

But this cannot be the whole story. The above move allows the truth predicates to apply to our subjective states, but this looks like a piece of commonsense; we do this all the time when we say something like 'it appears to me that such and such is the case'. Of course we can apply the truth predicates to this kind of talk: it is true whenever the subject reports sincerely. So there must be something more contentious that explains the distinctiveness of the inner space model.

The explanation is 'a picture of subjectivity as a region of reality whose layout is transparent – accessible through and through – to the capacity for knowledge that is newly recognized when appearances are brought within the range of truth and knowability' (ibid., p. 240). The infallibility here implies 'not world-involving'. Combined with what has been said above, the inner space model amounts to this: items in the inner space are autonomous, self-standing, which is to say that their relations to the external world are extrinsic. It follows that a given subject has immediate and unproblematic grasps of his mental items. Even in the case of deceptive experiences, the subject can readily grasp his own 'seeming' states.[6]

But isn't this just an outmoded straw man? McDowell does not cite specific passages from Descartes, and nowadays many philosophers admit that there are limits of self-knowledge. Who on earth will fall into the category characterized in this way?

As I said above, McDowell aims to show that this model functions in many domains. Concerning the issues of perception and knowledge, the model appears in the guise of the so-called 'highest common factor theory' (1982b/1998b, p. 386). According to this line of thought, veridical and deceptive experiences are fundamentally of the same kind; because items in the inner space have only extrinsic relations to the external world, we can have complete grasp of them regardless the experience is veridical or not. As for knowledge, true empirical beliefs and deceptive ones (consider the evil demon or the brain-in-a-vat case) are fundamentally of the same kind; for similar reasons in the case of perception, the inner items have the justificatory power they do regardless the empirical belief is true or not.

This line of thought can be elaborated further. Let's start with perception. Normally we can gain correct information through perception, but things do not always go well. In illusions and hallucinations, it seems that we still perceive *something*: some non-existent properties or objects. Now a natural question concerns what instantiates the non-existent properties or objects perceived in deceptive cases. Here there are many complications: some philosophers think that what instantiates those perceived properties or objects are non-intentional *sense-data* (Robinson, 1994); some argue that we perceive uninstantiated sensory profiles in hallucinations (Johnston, 2004); some deny this and think that those properties or objects are *represented* by our experiences (Tye, 2002). There are many entangling puzzles here, and the relevant literature goes very wild.[7] For our purposes here, we only need to note that both the sense-datum theory and representationalism (or intentionalism), no matter how the details go in different versions, regard veridical experiences and deceptive ones as *fundamentally of the same kind*.[8] The argument most frequently cited for this view is the one from *phenomenal indistinguishability*: since subjectively indistinguishable illusions/hallucinations are possible, and 'experience' is essentially a subjective notion, there is a common factor shared by illusions, hallucinations and veridical experiences (Robinson, 1994). A veridical experience is constituted by this inner common factor *plus* external conditions; metaphysically speaking, the inner component is individuated without any reference to external situations, for it is something shared by veridical experiences and deceptive ones. We can call this the 'conjunctive' view of perception.[9]

Simon Blackburn is one of those who find the above argument compelling. He writes that in the thought experiment involving phenomenal indistinguishability,

> [E]verything is the same from the subject's point of view. This is a legitimate thought-experiment. Hence there is a legitimate category of things that are the same in these cases; notably experience and awareness.
>
> 1983, p. 324

Although other philosophers in this camp may have different formulations, the general shape of the argumentation is the same. I will come back to this later.

Here goes the epistemological version. Traditionally, the notion of 'knowledge' is analysed into 'belief', 'truth' and 'justification'. Edmund Gettier's short classic (1963) crashed our faith in this simple analysis, but most of us believe that either we can supplement the original analysis with a fourth condition, or we can revise the 'justification' element in one way or another, to accommodate those putative counterexamples. On a widespread understanding, the 'truth' element is undoubtedly external, and both the 'belief' and the 'justification' elements are internal. After the rise of externalism in both philosophy of mind and epistemology, the claim about belief and justification has long been shaky. In the case of justification, however, the internalist intuition stands firm. Consider the brain-in-a-vat case (BIV for short). If I were a brain envatted in a scientist's lab, presumably I would have perceptual phenomenology indistinguishable from the phenomenology owned by normal subjects. Now I form a belief that I am in a noisy café, based on my auditory phenomenology. Obviously this belief does not constitute knowledge, for actually I (if any) am in a scientist's lab. But it seems unfair to say that I am *not* justified in believing that I am in a noisy café because I am not in a position to know that I am in a bad case. Recall the KK principle. It requires a meta-knowledge for every bit of knowledge, which is unreasonably strong. Now even for those who subscribe to this principle, to demand that I have knowledge about my overall situation before I can have *justification* about the café belief is far too strong. Why think that I, as a brain in a vat, am not justified in believing that I am in a noisy café, given that I do have the relevant phenomenology caused by the electronic device? If this line of thought is accepted, the justification element is internal after all, for a brain in a vat or a subject deceived by the evil demon can have justification about empirical beliefs. This is also a 'conjunctive' view, for knowledge is (at least) composed by an internal justification element *and* an external truth element.[10]

The conjunctive view about perception and knowledge is in effect the inner space model: on this view, there is a common factor shared by subjects in the good case and in the bad case.[11] This implies that the common factor is 'self-standing, not beholden to external conditions', for if it were not, it cannot present in the bad case, where external condition is absent. With this picture at hand, nonetheless, we juxtapose our direct contact with the world: if the inner element is present anyway, regardless our real situations, doesn't it constitute a veil that blocks our access to the world?

In the case of perception, McDowell responds to this predicament this way:

> Of facts to the effect that things seems thus and so to one, we might say, some are cases of things being thus and so within the reach of one's subjective access to the external world, whereas others are mere appearances. In a given case the answer to the question 'Which?' would state a further fact about the disposition of things in the inner realm . . . since this further fact is not independent of the outer realm, we are compelled to picture the inner and outer realms as interpenetrating, not separated from one another by the characteristically Cartesian divide.
>
> 1986a/1998b, p. 241

In the picture McDowell recommends, the 'conjunction' presents in the inner space picture is replaced by a 'disjunction'. There is no highest inner common factor shared by veridical experiences and deceptive ones, so there is no inner factor to be *conjunctive* with external conditions. In the good case, by contrast, perceptual experiences involve external situations essentially, which means that the relation between perception and deception is *disjunctive*: either a perceptible aspect of the world, or a mere appearance, is presented. Now a possible objection is that on this picture, we have no idea about whether we are in the good case or not. Given our refusal of the KK principle, this objection is irrelevant. We can shrug our shoulders and reply to the sceptic: *why* do I have to know about whether I am in the good case in order for me to be in genuine perceptual contact with the world?

Now we are in a position to evaluate Blackburn's remarks quoted above. McDowell says: '[t]he uncontentiously legitimate category of things that are the same across the different cases is the category of how things *seem* to the subject' (ibid., p. 248; my emphasis). Phenomenal indistinguishability does imply there is something in common, but this 'something' is only *seeming*; after all, what guarantees it is *phenomenal* indistinguishability. And we have seen that for McDowell, this seeming should be taken disjunctively.

3. The problem of perceptual contact is in an important sense more fundamental than any problem in epistemology, for:

> Once we are gripped by the idea of self-contained subjective realm, in which things are as they are independently of external reality (if any), it is too late ... [O]ur problem is not now that our contact with the external world seems too *shaky* to count as knowledgeable, but that our picture seems to represent us as out of touch with the world altogether.
>
> ibid., p. 242

The inner space model insulates us from the external world, so the deepest problem is that we do not have any contact with the world *at all* if we are locked in the inner space. A reaction to the dreaming argument is to retreat from the outer realm to the inner, as the inner space theorist does, but the price it pays seems to be too high; in order to meet the challenge posed by the unreasonable KK principle, the inner space theorist loses the world altogether.

McDowell's disjunctive conception of experience leaves the plausible part of the inner space model intact:

> I approached this fully Cartesian picture of subjectivity by way of the thought, innocent in itself, that how things seem to one can be a fact, and is knowable in a way that is immune to familiar skeptical challenges. Short of the fully Cartesian picture, the infallibly knowable fact – its seeming to one that things are thus and

so – can be taken disjunctively, as constituted either by the fact that things are manifestly thus and so or by the fact that that merely seems to be the case.

ibid., p. 242[12]

But if we insulate ourselves in the inner space, then the innocent part is spoiled too, for if we never enjoy perceptual contact with the world, it soon becomes 'quite unclear that the fully Cartesian picture is entitled to characterize its inner facts in *content*-involving terms – in terms of its seeming to one that things are thus and so – at all' (ibid., pp. 242–3; my emphasis). On this miserable picture, subjectivity is 'blank or blind' (ibid., p. 243), which does not deserve to be called 'subjectivity' indeed.

Apart from the considerations about the dreaming argument, the inner space model might well be motivated by the rise of modern science, for '[i]t seems scarcely more than common sense that a science of the way organisms relate to their environment should look for states of the organisms whose intrinsic nature can be described independently of the environment' (ibid., p. 243). Worse still,

> [T]his intellectual impulse is gratified also in a modern way of purportedly bringing the mind within the scope of theory, in which the interiority of the inner realm is literally spatial; the autonomous explanatory states are in ultimate fact states of the nervous system, although, in order to protect the claim that the explanations they figure in are psychological, they are envisaged as conceptualized by theories of mind in something like functionalist terms. This conception of mind shares what I have suggested we should regard as the fundamental motivation of the classically Cartesian conception; and I think this is much more significant than the difference between them.
>
> ibid., p. 244

McDowell does not render his reply to this argument from science explicit, but what he would say is clear: we have good reasons for thinking that the mind as such should not be incorporated by any branch of natural science, for it lives in the space of reasons, a domain which cannot be reduced by natural sciences. If this is so, this motivation for the inner space model should be discarded from the very beginning. Sciences can help us understand the enabling conditions of various mental capacities, to be sure, but this should be distinguished from the constitutive questions of the mind.

Another possible motivation of the inner space model is to secure our first-person authority. In general cases, we know ourselves better than an outsider. The inner space model is sometimes thought to be a good explanation of this, for according to it the subject's introspection 'becomes the idea of an inner vision, scanning a region of reality that is wholly available to its gaze ...' (ibid., p. 245). But notice that what first-person authority says is that *generally* we ourselves have *better* knowledge; it does *not* say that we ourselves always know everything. However, what the inner space model delivers is the latter, which is blatantly too strong.[13] Moreover, the model 'puts in question the possibility of access to the inner realm from outside' (ibid., p. 245). If all of us are 'beetles in the box', to use the Wittgensteinian metaphor, how can we have *any* knowledge about other subjects' mental state? As McDowell asks, how can we 'perceive, in another person's facial expression or his behaviour, that he is ... in pain[?]' (1978b/1998b, p. 305)[14] This motivation for the inner space model is ill grounded, either way.[15]

A possible rejoinder runs like this. The inner space theorist might concede that the argument from self-knowledge does not work, and somehow render the picture and moderate (as opposed to omniscient) self-knowledge compatible. Now, 'subjectivity' may be taken as the next candidate for argument: 'the internal component of the composite picture ... irresistibly attracts the attributes that intuitively characterize the domain of subjectivity'. And here goes the alleged Fregean:

> It is in the internal component that we have to locate the difference Frege's constraint requires us to mark between pairs of (say) beliefs that in the full composite story would be described as involving the attribution of the same property to the same object, but that have to be distinguished because someone may without irrationality have one and not the other ... Frege's notion of a mode of presentation is supposed to have its use in characterizing the configurations of the interior ...
>
> 1986a/1998b, p. 251

This argument has some initial plausibility. Frege famously distinguishes between sense and reference, and presumably 'reference' should be located in the external world. Therefore, it is natural to identify 'sense' with the internal component. This line of thought is strengthened by the fact that sense is often seen as the constituent of the *cognitive* realm. Unfortunately, the 'difficulty is palpable':

> [H]ow can we be expected to acknowledge that our subjective way of being in the world is properly captured by this picture, when it portrays the domain of our subjectivity – our cognitive world – in such a way that, considered from its own point of view, that world has to be conceived as letting in no light from outside? The representational content apparently present in the composite story comes too late to meet the point.
>
> ibid., p. 251

So the argument from subjectivity fails also. If we regard subjectivity as something 'inner', we cannot make sense of the fact that we are beings *in the world*: not only our *bodies*, but our*selves*, are objective presences in the world. I shall come back to this in chapter 5 and 6.

4. Let's turn to McDowell's parallel story concerning knowledge, or more specifically, justification. Here McDowell begins with Sellars' thought that 'knowledge – at least as enjoyed by rational animals – is a certain sort of standing in the space of reasons' (1995b/1998b, p. 395). McDowell aims to disabuse a particular 'deformation' of the Sellarsian idea, namely 'an interiorization of the space of the reasons, a withdrawal of it from the external world' (ibid., p. 395). This putative 'deformation' is natural enough: 'reason' is often, if not always, treated as something 'subjective' and therefore 'internal'. But as we have seen in the above discussion, this seemingly natural thought is not really natural when thought through: if subjectivity belongs to the allegedly internal factor, the very idea of subjectivity as the *cognitive* space becomes unintelligible.

Since the general lesson in the case in epistemology is the same with that of perception, I shall concentrate on issues concerning justification specifically. To begin with, consider a traditional notion concerning knowledge – 'epistemic luck'. It is commonsensical that for something to be knowledge, it must at least be a true belief, and it is also commonsensical that this is not enough.[16] Not enough, because the two conditions do not rule out the possibility that a subject *happens to* have a true belief. This should be ruled out because we think that to have a piece of knowledge is to be in a normative status, and a true belief by luck does not give us this. The notion of 'justification' serves to bridge the normative gap: a subject has a piece of knowledge if and only if she holds the true belief in question with *good reasons*. Justification is thought to be a truth-conducive property; it is supposed to be something that *excludes* epistemic luck.[17]

The Gettier-style counterexamples end the good old days. The moral of those cases is that epistemic luck is unavoidable; the subjects in the examples have fairly good reasons to hold the beliefs in question, but those beliefs fail to be knowledge. The literatures in epistemology became a mess during the following few decades. It is not that there was no insightful proposal; the trouble is that it seems to become a dead issue before dampening the relevant misgivings: if some notion of 'justification' or some other conditions cannot preclude epistemic luck, then how is knowledge possible?

Now, a typical McDowellian move is to consider why a given question looks so urgent. Why, we should ask ourselves, do we think that knowledge requires the possessors of it manage to rule out epistemic luck completely? To answer this, imagine that somehow we do accomplish that flawless epistemic standing. It soon becomes clear that the picture is a version of the inner space model: the mental items are transparent or *luminous* through and through for the subject, for those items are self-standing, not beholden to any external conditions. Again, the fear about epistemic luck can be traced back to the argument from illusion, broadly construed. Consider the crucial step of it:

> If things are indeed thus and so when they seem to be, the world is doing me a favour. So if I want to restrict myself to standings in the space of reasons whose flawlessness I can ensure with external help, I must go no further than taking it that it *looks* to me as if things are thus and so.
>
> ibid., p. 396

The metaphor 'the world's favour' denotes epistemic luck. No one, including those who are faithful to traditional epistemology, can sensibly deny that they exist. The crucial question is what follows from this. The inner space model theorist thinks that we should 'restrict ourselves' to the inner space, for he assumes that epistemic luck is something to be avoided in order for us to have knowledge. This is the assumption McDowell disputes.

McDowell first lays out the desideratum – human subjects' *critical* reason. 'If it turns out to be an effect of interiorizing the space of reasons that we become unable to make sense of this critical function of reason, we ought to conclude that the very idea of the space of reasons has become unrecognizable' (ibid., p. 398). The strategy is to assume the inner space model for the sake of argument, and to see whether we can still make good sense of the very idea of the space of reasons. An obvious response is scepticism, which holds that in order to fulfil the demand of 'risk-free', we have to stay in the inner realm. But this means, at the same time, that we will never break the inner circle, hence scepticism. McDowell does not regard scepticism as the main opponent in the paper now I am concentrating on, but we have seen above how he responds to it: if we never have perceptual contact with the world, there is *no* reason to think that we can characterize the inner space with content-involving terms.[18]

Another response is to insist 'that there must be policies or habits of basing belief on appearance that *are* utterly risk-free' (ibid., p. 399). As McDowell points out, this looks attractive 'in the context of the threat of scepticism', but it is clear that it only 'express[es] a rather touching *a priori* faith in the power of human reason to devise fully effective protections against the deceptive capacities of appearance' (ibid., pp. 399–400). This response is *ad hoc*, for it clings on the original three-fold analysis of knowledge, and insists that they *must* be jointly sufficient for knowledge. Without any substantial argument for this position, we do not need to take it seriously.

The response McDowell considers in details is again the composite, or conjunctive, conception. In the context of knowledge, it goes like this:

> At least for rational animals, a satisfactory standing in the space of reasons is a necessary condition for knowledge. But since the positions one can reach by blameless moves in the space of reasons are not factive, as epistemically satisfactory positions are, a satisfactory standing in the space of reasons cannot be what knowledge is.
>
> ibid., p. 400

What does knowledge require in addition to a satisfactory standing in the space of reasons, according to the traditional picture? It is 'the familiar truth requirement for knowledge ... [conceived] as a necessary extra condition for knowledge, over and above the best one can have in the way of reliability in a policy or habit of basing belief on appearance' (ibid., p. 400). The notion of 'reliability' figures in the picture as the internal component, as opposed to its role in 'full-blown externalism', which 'reject[s] the Sellarsian idea' (ibid., p. 400) shared by all parties considered above. Thus the composite picture can be seen as combining internal reliability (blamelessness) with external truth.

To separate reliability and truth is the source of the problem, McDowell argues. On the one hand, the inner space theorist interiorizes the space of reasons, which means 'standings in the space [cannot] consist in a cognitive purchase on an objective fact ...'. But if that is so, then 'how can reason have the resources it would need in order to evaluate the reliability of belief-forming policies or habits' (ibid., pp. 402–3)? The 'interiorized Fregean sense' is unintelligible, as we have seen in the case of perception.

The epistemological version of the inner space model faces an additional challenge. Consider the reason why 'justification' is introduced in the first place. A true belief held by a subject accidentally does not count as knowledge, for knowledge requires *reasons*. Now we have a subject in the good case, the other in the subjectively indistinguishable bad case; one has knowledge, the other does not. McDowell then asks: 'if its being so is external to her operations in the space of reasons, how can it not be outside the reach of her rational powers' (ibid., p. 403)? Epistemologists introduce 'justification' in order to account for the *rational* element of knowledge, but when we consider the good case and the bad case with the inner space model, we realize that it is *epistemic luck* that make the difference. The subject in the good case has knowledge not because he has a better standing in the space of reasons, but because *he is lucky*. This is where the Gettier-style counterexamples come in. Epistemic luck does exist, but '[t]he hybrid view's concession to luck, tagged on to a picture of reason as self-sufficient within its own proper province, comes too late' (ibid., p. 405). What the existence of epistemic luck shows is *not* that we should confine ourselves to the flawless inner space and try to work out our ways to knowledge, but that our rational power has its limits.

As a result, justification is closer to the external world than we originally envisage. The space of reasons incorporates the worldly facts as its constituents:

> When someone enjoys such a position [of knowing], that involves, if you like, a stroke of good fortune, a kindness from the world; even so, the position is, in its own right, a satisfactory standing in the space of reasons, not a composite in which such a standing is combined with a condition external to the space of reasons. Whether we like it or not, we have to rely on favours from the world: not just that it presents us with appearances ... but that on occasion it actually is the way it appears to be.
>
> ibid., p. 406

In sum, we need to 'learn to live with' (ibid., p. 408) the fact that we are subject to epistemic luck, that is, our rational power has its limits. The inner space model strives to preserve the fantasy of human reason, but the resulting picture is quite implausible. Why is it so tempting to lapse into that picture then?

Again, consider the good case and the bad case. Intuitively, the BIV or the victim of the evil demon seems to have the same epistemic standing with normal subjects, for subjectively there is no difference. 'How can we blame the BIV for not having knowledge?' One might ask. But consider a parallel case in action. Someone may unintentionally kill others in a car accident. Now it may be true that he should not be blamed, but *is what he has done thereby justified*? It seems clear that the answer is negative. By the same token, the BIV is not to be blamed epistemically, but he is *not justified* in holding those empirical beliefs either. To be in a satisfying standing in the space of reasons, blamelessness is not enough. Justification is indeed an epistemically positive notion, while 'exculpation' is only negative.[19]

I opened this section with the notion of 'primeness'. It says that both perception and knowledge cannot be factorized into simpler elements; both of them involve external conditions *essentially*. Against the mainstream epistemology, primeness says that what the Gettier-style counterexamples show is *not* that we should engage further analyses for knowledge, but that knowledge is unanalysable.

I shall do some reprise before closing this section. In both the case of perception and knowledge, the (Cartesian) inner space model is motivated by phenomenal indistinguishability. From this indistinguishability, it is argued that there is a common internal factor – 'experience' for perception and 'justification' for knowledge (in different terms, 'phenomenal conception of evidence') – shared by the good case and the bad case. Since the factor is also present in the bad case, its relations to the external world must be extrinsic. They are free-floating items in the self-sustaining inner space. There are many problems with this picture, but the deepest one is that it makes cognition and rationality unintelligible: in order to account for subjectivity, the inner space theorist renders it as purely inner, but this makes the very idea of subjectivity unrecognizable: as our commonsense tells us, subjectivity is 'a vantage point on *the external world*' (1986a/1998b, p. 241).

Openness

1. We have seen how McDowell establishes the primeness claim. According to this view, the external world is incorporated into the space of reasons; the space of reasons has no outer boundary. This naturally brings us to the further stage of the argumentation: our 'openness' to the world.

The openness claim is the main theme of McDowell's Locke Lecture. His overall topic there, as he himself makes clear, 'is the way concepts mediate the relation between minds and the world' (1996a, p. 3). As the previous section shows, the world is embraced by the space of reasons; now McDowell's further claim is that the space of reasons *is* the space of concepts. It follows that the world is in the space of concept, hence the title of his second lecture, 'The Unboundedness of the Conceptual' (ibid., p. 24).

McDowell situates his discussion in the Kantian-Davidsonian background. Kant famously remarks that 'Thoughts without content are empty, intuitions without concepts are blind' (1998g/2008a, 1787/1998, A51/B75). He glosses this with Davidson's attack on scheme-content dualism (1974/2001).[20] 'Scheme' means 'conceptual scheme'; the opposite means 'nonconceptual content' or 'given'. When one uses the term nonconceptual 'content', she probably concerns the issues generated by the 'fineness-of-grained' argument and the argument from human infant and mere animals; this is the main theme of McDowell's third lecture. For our purposes, the term nonconceptual 'given' is better. What 'given' signifies is *passivity*, as opposed to scheme's *active* operations. From now on I will use 'dualism of scheme and Given' (1996a, p. 4) to denote McDowell's target.[21]

McDowell mentions that in the Kantian framework, 'the space of reasons is the realm of freedom' (ibid., p. 5). However, '[t]he more we play up the connection between reason and freedom, the more we risk losing our grip on how exercises of concepts can constitute warranted judgements about the world' (ibid., p. 5). The point is that we need 'external constraint on our freedom', otherwise our mentality will collapse into a 'self-contained game' (ibid., p. 6 and p. 5 respectively). The idea of the Given is supposed to undertake this external constraint. On this view, nonconceptual given can nevertheless serve as reasons, as McDowell describes, 'the space of reasons is made out to be more extensive than the space of concepts' (ibid., p. 6). Notice that the dialectics is primarily semantic; '[e]mpirical judgements in general ... had better have *content* of a sort that admits of empirical *justification* ...' ibid., p. 6). This is shown by the fact that McDowell never uses the label 'foundationalism' to identify his target. Starting with the recognition that there are close relations between reason and freedom, one is prone to accept coherentism, and if one also recognizes the need for external constraint, one tends to embrace the idea of the Given: the thought is that there must be something *given from outside*, in order for our thoughts to have directedness. In what I just said above, nothing directly concerns epistemological foundationalism.[22]

What we will be focussing on is McDowell's notion of the Myth of the Given, not Sellars'. However, since the term was appropriated from Sellars, it is better if we have some basic grasp of the Sellarsian usage. He introduces the 'framework of givenness' as follows:

> Many things have been said to be "given": sense contents, material objects, universals, propositions, real connections, first principles, even givenness itself. And there is, indeed, a certain way of construing the situations which philosophers analyze in these terms which can be said to be the framework of givenness.
> Sellars, 1956, p. 253

Sellars's obscure writings have generated a huge amount of secondary literature (e.g. deVries and Triplett, 2000; deVries, 2005; O'Shea, 2007), and reviewing it will take us too far. Another clue, which might not be too helpful, is his allusion to Hegel's notion of 'immediacy'. Basically, Sellars is attacking the idea of something being *given* without question. This is different from McDowell's notion, which hinges on rationality and conceptuality. I shall not go into the comparison between their notions of the Myth of the Given, and will focus on McDowell's notion only.

McDowell adumbrates the debate between coherentism and the Given as follows:

> It can be difficult to accept that the Myth of Given is a myth. It can seem that if we reject the Given, we merely reopen ourselves to the threat to which the idea of the Given is a response, the threat that our picture does not accommodate any external constraint on our activity in empirical thought and judgement... If our activity in empirical thought and judgement is to be recognizable as bearing on reality at all, there must be external constraint... Realizing this, we come under pressure to recoil back into the Given, only to see all over again that it cannot help. There is a danger of falling into an interminable oscillation.
>
> ibid., pp. 8–9

McDowell's metaphor for the situation is an oscillating 'seesaw' (ibid., p. 9). We can appreciate this more by comparing another position, 'bald naturalism'. As we have seen in Chapter 1, bald naturalism denies 'that the spontaneity of the understanding is *sui generis* in the way suggested by the link to the idea of freedom'; it 'opt[s] out of this area of philosophy altogether' (ibid., p. 67). The way bald naturalism dismounts from the see-saw is to reduce the space of reasons, to erase what is distinctively human. Coherentism and the Given are on the seesaw *precisely* because both of them recognize the *sui generis* character of the space of reasons. In addition, they (and bald naturalism) share the assumption that 'experience' is to be put on the Given side, as dualistically opposed to the scheme side, on the ground that experience is 'passive' (ibid., p. 10). For coherentism, since experiences are passive and hence confined in the realm of law, it cannot have rational relations with beliefs and judgements, which are denizens in the space of reasons. For the Given, though experiences are passive and hence confined in the realm of law, there must be rational relations between beliefs and judgements on the one hand, and experiences on the other, on pain of 'a frictionless spinning in a void' (ibid., p. 11). For bald naturalism, though experiences are passive and hence confined in the realm of law, there can be rational relations between beliefs/judgements and experiences, for beliefs and judgements are also in the realm of law. Thus, we get a clearer sense of the dialectical situations surrounding the see-saw metaphor.

Now we are in a position to understand McDowell's Kantian solution. We have seen that coherentism, the Given, and bald naturalism all assume that because experiences are passive, they are inhabitants of the realm of law. McDowell's key move is to argue that the inference here is a *non sequitur*:

> The original Kantian thought was that empirical knowledge results from a co-operation between receptivity and spontaneity. (Here "spontaneity" can be simply a label for the involvement of conceptual capacities.) We can dismount from the seesaw if we can achieve a firm grip on this thought: receptivity does not make an even notionally separable contribution to the co-operation.
>
> The relevant conceptual capacities are drawn on *in* receptivity... It is not that they are exercised *on* an extra-conceptual deliverance of receptivity... In experience one takes in, for instance sees, *that things are thus and so*. That is the sort of thing one can also, for instance, judge.
>
> ibid., p. 9

The passivity of experiences is a plain fact; indeed, this passivity is what distinguishes experiences from judgements. 'In experience one finds oneself *saddled* with content' (ibid., p. 10). McDowell admits. It does not follow, however, that experiences are not inhabitants of the space of reasons: experiences can be *at the same time conceptual and passive*. In judgements, we *exercise* conceptual capacities; in experiences, conceptual capacities are *operative*.[23]

2. An immediate doubt is that if conceptual capacities are operative *only passively* in experiences, how can we ensure that they are *conceptual*? After all, conceptual capacities are often seen as constituents of judgements, and judgements are active if anything is. McDowell agrees that '[the putative conceptual capacities] would not be recognizable as conceptual capacities at all unless they could also be exercised in active thinking...' (ibid., p. 11). Judgements are indeed the paradigmatic locus for conceptual capacities, but it does not mean that they cannot be operative in other cases. Recall how McDowell reaches his Kantian conclusion: if we think experiences are not in the space of reasons, we will face a quandary illustrated by the stalemate between coherentism, the Myth of the Given, and bald naturalism. The quandary is that all of the three positions make intentionality unintelligible. So we should uncover and reject the ungrounded assumption shared by them. The assumption in question is the thought that experiences are in the realm of law because they are passive. McDowell's conclusion that experiences are participants of the space of reasons follows from the rejection of that assumption. This is a transcendental argument: the possibility of intentionality requires that the space of reasons incorporate experiences, and intentionality does present in human activities, therefore experiences are in the space of reasons. To say that it is hard to conceive passively operative conceptual capacities does not touch the transcendental argument directly.

It is instructive to note that 'synthesis' is an important notion in Kant. For him, human understanding synthesizes the products of sensibility by applying concepts to form cognitions of objects. For Husserl, both active and passive syntheses are operative in the constitution of objects of consciousness (1920–1926/2001). As a dedicated Kantian, McDowell always has *active* synthesis in mind when developing his case for his version of conceptualism. This makes it difficult for him to answer several worries from his critics, for example the worry that McDowellian experiences are too idealistic to guarantee objectivity ('the unboundedness of the conceptual'), and 'intuitional content' from his later philosophy fares worse than Travisian no-content view (2004; for more on intuitional content, see Chapter 7). Husserlian *passive* synthesis opens up a new possibility to understand experiences without diverging too much from McDowell's ideas on the content view and the Myth of the Given.[24]

But in any case, there is still a gap between the conclusion of the transcendental argument and McDowell's actual conclusion, namely that conceptual capacities are operative all the way out in experiences, for one might hold that the space of reasons are *not* exhausted by conceptual capacities. Many philosophers think that there are nonconceptual content in play in our experiences, but this does not relegate experiences out of the space of reasons. They maintain this position for many different reasons, notably the fineness-of-grained/richness argument, the argument from human infant and mere animals, and the argument from concept-formation, amongst others. This is the main theme of McDowell's third lecture, but for the main line we can bypass this for the moment: what concerns us in this essay is how McDowell identifies a model of subjectivity that is responsible for various puzzlements concerning human subject as perceiver, knower, thinker, speaker, agent, person and (self-) conscious animal, and further, how he manages to develop a positive account that makes our direct contact with the world intelligible. For this specific purpose, the discursivity of experience is relevant, but by far not in the main thread.[25]

So let's cling onto the main thread. The primeness claim, as discussed in the previous section, has it that the space of reasons incorporates the external world: in the case of knowledge and veridical experience, the worldly facts themselves are unfactorizable parts of the states. This repels the composite picture, which regards the worldly facts as only extrinsically related to the states in question even in the case of knowledge and veridical perception, which means that there is a common inner factor shared by the good case and the bad case. The primeness claim goes with the disjunctive conception and the composite/conjunctive claim goes with the common factor conception. Now McDowell takes up this aspect of his thought again in *Mind and World*:

> I insist ... that when we acknowledge the possibility of being misled, we do not deprive ourselves of "taking in how things are" as a description of what happens when one is not misled ... *That things are thus and so* is the content of the [veridical] experience, and it can also be the content of a judgment ... So it is conceptual content. But *that things are thus and so* is also, if one is not misled, as aspect of the layout of the world: it is how things are. Thus the idea of conceptually structured operations of receptivity puts us in a position to speak of experience as openness to the layout of reality. Experience enables the layout of reality itself to exert a rational influence on what a subject thinks.
>
> 1996a, p. 26

In this passage, McDowell combines the primeness claim and the conceptuality thesis: the worldly facts that figure in the content of experience are characterized by 'that things are thus and so'. 'That things are thus and so' is both the conceptual content of veridical experiences and an aspect of the layout of reality. This radically changes the traditional picture: on the traditional, composite picture, the conceptual content of experiences is 'in the head', or at least 'in the subject', and that inner conceptual content 'represents' outer, worldly facts. On McDowell's openness view, by contrast, the conceptual content of experience is identical with an aspect of the world.

The following passage is another expression of the same line of thought:

> [T]here is no ontological gap between the sort of thing one can mean, or generally the sort of thing one can think, and the sort of thing that can be the case. When one thinks truly, what one thinks *is* what is the case. So since the world is everything that is the case ... there is no gap between thought, as such, and the world.
>
> ibid., p. 27

As McDowell himself notices, nevertheless, an obvious and strong objection to this 'unboundedness of the conceptual' is the charge of 'idealism' (ibid., pp. 25–6). The line of thought is quite simple: concepts are mental, so if the conceptual has no outer boundary, then the 'external' world becomes mental. How does McDowell respond to this fairly straightforward argument?

McDowell invokes the act/content distinction in reply:

> "Thought" can mean the *act* of thinking; but it can also mean the *content* of a piece of thinking: what someone thinks. Now if we are to give due acknowledgement to the independence of reality, what we need is a constraint from outside *thinking* and *judging*, our exercises of spontaneity. The constraint does not need to be from outside *thinkable contents*.
>
> ibid., p. 28[26]

The identity McDowell commits to is between thinkable contents, i.e. *what* one thinks, and worldly facts. Read like this, it becomes a tautology. As Wittgenstein says, the openness claim 'has the form of a truism', quoted by McDowell (ibid., p. 27; also see his 1989a, 2005c). But if it is indeed a truism, what is the point of insisting on it? The answer should be clear when we consider the inner space model. On this view, there are self-standing items populated in the mental inner space, and these items somehow 'represent' outer states of affairs. The items function as *inner* representations that are distinct from aspects of the *outer* world. Since this inner space model is very popular in contemporary philosophy, McDowell's insistence on that truism has a real point.

3. I almost finish the exposition of McDowell's conception of perceiver and knower. Before closing this chapter, however, I would like to consider a larger objection to McDowell's overall position. In arguing for primeness cum openness, the notion of 'experience' plays a crucial role for McDowell. This reflects his 'minimal empiricism: the idea that *experience* must constitute a tribunal, mediating the way our thinking is answerable to how things are …' (1996a, p. xii; my emphasis). But not everyone accepts this claim (e.g. Gupta, 2019). Recall that coherentism, in recognizing that the Given is a myth, only acknowledges experiences' causal role. In repudiating scheme-content dualism, the third dogma of empiricism, Davidson asserts that 'if we give it up it is not clear that there is anything distinctive left to call empiricism' (1974/2001b, pp. 189–90). Robert Brandom follows this and writes:

> [W]hen we are properly wired up and trained, and favorable circumstances, the perceptible facts wring from us perceptual judgments. In order to *explain* how this is possible – quite a different enterprise from *justifying* the resulting judgments – we postulate the existence of something like sense impressions, whose properties systematically covary with the contents of the judgments they causally elicit from us. But these sense impressions are features of the physiology

of perception. They are not something we are aware of, and they do not themselves have conceptual content.

1996, pp. 253–4

Similar line of thought can also be found in other authors who take experience more seriously, for example Charles Travis (2004) and Anil Gupta (2006). I shall confine myself to the criticisms raised by Brandom, for his principal argument is from the *social, public* character of intentionality, which is very important throughout this essay.

In his positive project, Brandom elaborates '[a] *social*, linguistic account of intentionality' (1994, p. xv; my emphasis). He complains that '[t]he social nature of spontaneity ... is acknowledged [by McDowell], but only belatedly, in the discussion of the need for knowers and agents to be properly brought up in order to be sensitive to various sorts of norms' (1996, p. 256). In short, Brandom argues that McDowell's emphasis on experience betrays a 'residual *individualism*' (ibid., p. 258). In what follows I shall argue for the opposite.

No one will deny that experiences *in some way* mediate the relations between mind and world, but McDowell and Brandom have very different view about the way in question. For McDowell, experiences have both semantic and causal roles to play; for Brandom, experiences are like sense impressions in old empiricism's sense. Before evaluating these two views, it would be helpful to know more about their conceptions of the world and the mind-world relation generally.

Brandom urges, in a Fregean vein, that 'facts are just true claims' (1994, p. 327). 'Fact' presumably refers to a constituent of 'world'. He further distinguishes 'what is claim*ed*' and 'the claim*ing* of it' (ibid., p. 327):

> To say that facts are just true claims does not commit one to treating the facts as somehow dependent on our claimings; it does not, for instance, have the consequence that had there never been any claimers, there would have been no facts ... Talk of facts as what *makes* claims true is confused if it is thought of as relating two distinct things – a true claim and the fact in virtue of which it is true ...

ibid., p. 328

For Brandom, facts are true contents, not truth-makers. In other words, Brandom also accepts the openness thesis that the world is in the realm of the conceptual.[27] The only discernable difference between him and McDowell in this context is that where Brandom uses 'claimings', McDowell uses 'experience' (1996, p. 26). As I have said, Brandom avoids 'experience' because he thinks that implies individualism, which has it that social elements are not essential to the constitution of intentionality in general. In principle, a normal individual will do, so to speak. Does McDowell unwittingly commit this implausible picture?

Brandom quotes McDowell: '*The world* itself must exert a rational constraint on our thinking' (1996, p. 253) and goes on to argue that 'in his positive suggestions, McDowell looks to rational constraint, not by the *facts*, but by *experience* of the facts' (ibid., p. 253). Brandom then makes two claims: first, what McDowell really has in mind here is 'experience', but his insistence on 'the need for conceptually structured pre-judgmental experiences that warrant our perceptual judgment is a *non sequitur*' (ibid., p. 255). Second, as we just briefly described, 'the aetiology of [McDowell's] blindness to alternatives should be traced to a residual *individualism* ... [which is] a systematic underestimation of the significance of the fact that talk of the space of reasons is an abstraction from concrete, essential *social* practices of giving and asking for reasons' (ibid., p. 258). Against this, I shall argue that actually McDowell never slides from world to experience, and his talk of experience by no means commits him individualism.

Brandom is not alone in noticing McDowell's putative oscillation between experience and world. Hannah Ginsborg, for example, questions:

> If the streets are wet and, recognizing that fact, I come to believe that it has rained, is my reason for believing that it has rained my belief that the streets are wet or the fact that the streets are wet? If, as some philosophers hold, the right answer in these cases is that it is the fact rather than the belief which serves as a reason, then Davidson [and McDowell are] mistaken about something more fundamental...
>
> 2006, p. 287[28]

Their worry seems to be this: McDowell is not determinate (or worse, consistent) about the ultimate step in his picture; sometimes he thinks it is the world that fits the bill, but on other occasions he retreats that claim and lets experience play the role. Brandom, in particular, provides a diagnosis for this oscillation: he thinks in regarding experience as the final step for both intentionality and justification, McDowell betrays his residual individualism, which is inherited from his 'predecessor' C. I. Lewis' (Brandom, 1996, p. 256). The correctness of this diagnosis aside, Brandom's move shows that he thinks individualism and the emphasis on the role of experience goes hand in hand. To be sure, he does not claim that there is any implicative connection between the two, but at least he takes the emphasis on experience as a symptom of individualism.

Granting this point for the sake of argument, I would like to suggest that the above doubt cast by Brandom, Ginsborg and Ayers presupposes a gap firmly and reasonably rejected by McDowell: the gap between experiences and the facts they take in.

'*Experience enables the layout of reality itself* to exert a rational influence on what a subject thinks' (1996a, p. 26; my emphasis), McDowell remarks; he makes clear that it is the layout of reality *itself*, rather than our experiences of it, that serves the rational constraint required. 'But if that is so,' one might ask, 'why does McDowell sometimes talk as if it is experiences that do the trick?' Recall the act/content distinction discussed above. The distinction is invoked to explicate the openness of thought, but for McDowell, this can be naturally generalized to the openness of experience. The 'act' of experience is what makes facts available to us; the 'content' of experience is the fact itself when we are not misled. There is no extra item for McDowell to 'lapse into': the act is not a 'thing' that can exert the rational constraint; it is a way to make the true content available to us and therefore able to exert constraint on us; the content, when veridical, is the fact itself, which exerts rational constraint. Individualism will not strike back in McDowell's picture, for he does not commit to the existence of a thing called 'experience' whose individuation condition excludes the world. Brandom's worry applies only to the picture McDowell objects to: if one postulates mental representations representing the world, he *does* need to make a choice between 'experience' and the world. McDowell, in repudiating this picture, should be exempt from the kind of charge made by Brandom, Ginsborg and Ayers.

In defence of Davidson's claim that 'nothing can count as a reason for holding a belief except another belief' (1983/2001c, p. 141) against Ayers' charge, McDowell writes: 'Davidson's claim is obviously not that one bases a belief on *one's believing* something else... It is *what* one believes, not one's believing it, that is one's reason in the sense Davidson is concerned with' (2005b/2008a, p. 138). There is no problem for Davidson and McDowell here; what justifies our beliefs is a given fact, not its 'psychological surrogate' (2006a, p. 135). But we need some way to make the fact available to us, hence the crucial role of experience, conceived as an act: '[i]t is not ... that the fact itself, as opposed to the fact that one experiences its obtaining, is one's reason for believing what one believes' (ibid., p. 135). This looks like a 'narrow content' theory only on the assumption that experience is something internal and whose individuation condition excludes the fact it takes in. This is in no way McDowell's conception of 'experience'.[29]

This is not the end of the story between McDowell and Brandom, to be sure, but for my purposes this should be enough. Brandom's argument from social elements against McDowell's use of experience fails. But one might still tend to think that McDowell does not take social elements or publicity seriously enough. In the next chapter I will spell out this aspect of McDowell's philosophy by considering his view of thinker and speaker. The main interlocutors are Saul Kripke and Donald Davidson, both of whom stress the social aspects of language painstakingly.

4

Thinker and Speaker

Custom

1. In his preface of the celebrated *Word and Object*, Quine says, 'Language is a social art' (1960, p. ix). Most, if not all, contemporary philosophers regard the publicity of meaning as basically uncontroversial. Even John Searle, as a dedicated 'internalist', says that '[l]anguage is indeed public ...' (1987/2002, p. 250). Other key players like Davidson, Putnam, Burge, amongst others, have their own ways to conceive the crucial social elements. The idea often traces back to Wittgenstein, in particular his notion of 'custom' (1953/2001, §198). How this notion is relevant to McDowell's conception of thinker and speaker will become clear later on. As we shall see, Heidegger's ideas on interpretation and understanding, and Gadamer's ideas on language and linguistic community, are both crucial elements in McDowell's picture.

> *In interpretation, understanding does not become something different. It becomes itself. Such interpretation is grounded existentially in understanding; the latter does not arise from the former.*
>
> Martin Heidegger, *Being and Time*

> *[L]anguage maintains a kind of independent life vis-à-vis the individual member of a linguistic community; and as he grows into it, it introduces him into a particular orientation and relationship to the world as well.*
>
> Hans-Georg Gadamer, *Truth and Method*

The guiding question in the present chapter is this: how does McDowell conceive the social/public elements of intentionality, and how does this conception connect to his diagnosis and treatment of the inner space model, as discussed in the previous chapter? I answer this question by considering McDowell's criticisms against Saul Kripke's reading of Wittgenstein (1982). As we shall see, in formulating the 'sceptical paradox' of meaning, Kripke tacitly presupposes the inner space model. This may be somewhat surprising, for Kripke is often read as a critic of our *residual Cartesianism* about meaning, as we shall see. One of McDowell's main tasks here is to persuade us that Kripke's anti-Cartesianism does not go to the root.

So here goes Kripke's Wittgenstein, or 'Kripkenstein'.[1] Kripke attempts to shed light on the issue about meaning by discussing and elaborating Ludwig Wittgenstein's 'rule-following considerations'. We normally think that our linguistic behaviours are rule-governed: a concept is a rule; when we use it we need to follow the rule given by its content. This is where *normativity* comes in. The rule determines *correct and incorrect* uses of the concept in question. The Kripkenstein paradox challenges this conception of language. Kripke summarizes the paradox as follows:

> The sceptic doubts whether any instructions I gave myself in the past compel (or justify) the answer "125" rather than "5." He puts the challenge in terms of a sceptical hypothesis about a change in my usage. Perhaps when I used the term 'plus' in the *past*, I always mean quus: by hypothesis I never gave myself any explicit directions that were incompatible with such a hypothesis.
>
> 1982, p. 13

The problem is this: one's past performances are *finite*, and we can always fit them into more than one rule, however deviant they might be. But if that is so, then the normativity vanishes, for it goes with rules. Given a set of past behaviours or intentions, including linguistic ones, the sceptic claims that we can always *interpret* them as confirming *infinitely* different rules. There is no principle to prevent him from doing so.

Kripke goes on to envisage a reply to the sceptic:

> [S]uppose we wish to add x and y. Take a huge bunch of marbles. First count out x marbles in one heap. Then count out y marbles in another. Put the two heaps together and count out the number of marbles in the union thus formed. The result is $x + y$. This set of directions, I may suppose, I explicitly gave myself at some earlier time. It is engraved on my mind as on a slate. It is incompatible with the hypothesis that I mean quus. It is this set of directions, not the finite list of particular additions I performed in the past, that justifies and determines my present response.
>
> ibid., pp. 15–16

And Kripke launches a Wittgensteinian rejoinder to this reply:

> True, if "count," as I used the word in the past, referred to the act of counting ..., then "plus" must have stood for addition. But I applied "count," like "plus," to only finitely many past cases. Thus the sceptic can question my present interpretation of my past usage of "count" as he did with "plus." In particular, he can claim that by "count" I formerly meant *quount*, where to "quount" a heap is to count it in the ordinary sense, unless the heap was formed as the union of two heaps, one of which has 57 or more items, in which case one must automatically give the answer "5."
>
> ibid., p. 16

Here Kripke is applying again the *infinite* regress of *interpreting* rules. This time the regress is not within a single symbol, say '+', but between different symbols. The basic insight, if any, is the same: a rule is never *self-interpreting*; we can always assign infinite interpretations to it, and if we attempt to interpret it with other rules, the series of interpretation are also infinite. Hence the paradox.[2]

Let me now briefly introduce Kripke's 'sceptical solution'. He says this kind of solution 'begins on the contrary by conceding that the sceptic's negative assertions are unanswerable. Nevertheless our ordinary practice or belief is justified because ... it need not require the justification the sceptic has shown to be untenable' (ibid., p. 66). He goes on to say that 'Wittgenstein proposes a picture of language based, not on *truth conditions,* but on *assertability conditions* or *justification conditions*: under what circumstances are we allowed to make a given assertion' (ibid., p. 74)? He then concludes by saying that '[t]he success of the practices ... depends on the brute empirical fact that *we agree with each other in our responses*' (ibid., p. 109; my emphasis). This is the general guise of Kripke's sceptical solution.[3]

2. As we have seen, the first principle of the Kripkenstein paradox is the infinite regress of interpreting rule. We can equally interpret the '+' sign to mean 'plus' or 'quus', and if we attempt to determine its meaning by invoking another notion, say 'count', the sceptic can still interpret it as 'quount', which again is a deviant interpretation. This infinite regress seems to be the hardstand of the paradox. But is it well grounded?

At the early stage of his argumentation, Kripke identifies the sceptical paradox with the first paragraph of *Philosophical Investigations* §201:

> This was our paradox: no course of action could be determined by a rule, because every course of action can be made out to accord with the rule. The answer was:

if everything can be made out to *accord* with the rule, then it can also be made out to *conflict* with it. And so there would be neither accord nor conflict here.[4]

But as McDowell notices, '§201 goes on with a passage for which Kripke's reading makes no room' (1984b/1998a, p. 229):

> It can be seen that there is a misunderstanding here from the mere fact that in the course of our argument we give one interpretation after another; as if each one contented us at least for a moment, until we thought of yet another standing behind it. What this shews is that there is a way of grasping a rule which is *not an interpretation*, but which is exhibited in what we call 'obeying the rule' and 'going against it' in actual cases.
>
> Wittgenstein, 1953/2001, §201

The problem identified in the first paragraph is the 'infinite regress of interpretations', which is even clearer in *PI* §198: 'any interpretation still hangs in the air along with what it interprets, and cannot give it any support' (ibid., §198). Now a natural way to respond to the regress is this:

> What one wants to say is: "Every sign is capable of interpretation; but the meaning mustn't be capable of interpretation. It is the last interpretation."
>
> 1958, p. 34

But it should be clear that this will not work, for if we let the chain of interpretations get started, on what ground are we entitled to stop it at any point? To simply insist that there will be 'the last interpretation' is ad hoc and dogmatic. McDowell's metaphor for this is 'a super-rigid yet (or perhaps we should say "hence") ethereal machine' (1984b/1998a). It is super-rigid because it sustains all other interpretations without being itself interpretable; it is therefore ('hence') ethereal because actually it cannot sustain anything: if every interpretation itself can be further interpreted but the supposed 'last' interpretation cannot, it is disqualified as 'interpretation' anyway.

The way Wittgenstein confronts the paradox is not, *pace* Kripke, to be acquiesce to the 'paradox' introduced in the first paragraph of *PI* §201; on the contrary, he asserts that 'there is a way of grasping a rule which is *not an interpretation* ...' Although so far we have no idea about the general shape of a solution, we can be sure that for Wittgenstein, it will *not* be a Humean 'sceptical solution', which 'begins ... by conceding that the sceptic's negative assertions are unanswerable' (1982, p. 66). But does it follow that what Wittgenstein has in mind is a 'straight solution'? It depends on how we conceive the straightness. Kripke first introduces the notion of a straight solution like this: 'a straight solution ... shows that on closer examination the scepticism proves to be unwarranted...' (ibid., p. 66), but he later adds that a straight solution 'point[s] out to the silly sceptic a hidden fact he overlooked, a condition in the world which constitutes my meaning addition by 'plus' (ibid., p. 69). If we stick to the earlier formulation, Wittgenstein's solution is indeed a straight one, for he attempts to show that 'the scepticism proves to be unwarranted' by elaborating how there can be 'a way of grasping a rule which is *not an interpretation*'. If we adopt the later qualification, however, it is not clear that Wittgenstein would admit that he is providing a straight solution, for the second formulation presupposes certain *reductionism* about meaning and understanding: as Jerry Fodor famously declares, '[i]f aboutness is real, it must be really something else' (1989, p. 97). Maybe we can accept certain supervenience thesis about meaning, but to ask us to 'cite the fact' is asking something more than that. 'Supervenience' is an ontological relation; it does not further require that we are able to *cite* the very fact. I cannot go into the reductionism debate here, but it seems plausible to reply to the sceptic that the requirement of 'citing the fact' commits reductionism, and we have no reason to accept it without further arguments from the sceptic. What is important for our present purposes is to recognize that though Wittgenstein is not offering a sceptical solution here, he is not offering a straight solution either, understood in the second formulation. As we shall see, he does *not* cite a fact and identify it with meaning; his talks about 'customs' and other related notion are not like that.[5]

Before going into the positive account, McDowell further quotes Wittgenstein for his denial of the thought that understanding is always a matter of interpretation:

> How can the word "Slab" indicate what I have to do, when after all I can bring any action into accord with any interpretation?
>
> How can I follow a rule, when after all whatever I do can be interpreted as following it?
>
> 1956/1978, VI-38[6]

If we accept McDowell's suggestion to read Wittgenstein as arguing against the thought that understanding is always interpretation, the question '[h]ow can there be a way of grasping a rule which is not an interpretation?' becomes urgent (1984b/1998a, p. 238). McDowell submits that we should turn to Wittgenstein's notion of 'practice' for the answer:

> And *hence also* "obeying a rule" is a practice. And to *think* one is obeying a rule is not to obey a rule. Hence it not possible to obey a rule "privately": otherwise thinking one was obeying a rule would be the same thing as obeying it.
>
> 1953/2001, §202, my emphasis

The ground for regarding the notion of practice as the answer is the 'hence also' in the first line of the above quotation: 'we have to realize that obeying a rule is a practice *if* we are to find it intelligible that there is a way of grasping a rule which is not an interpretation' (McDowell, 1984b/1998a, p. 238; my emphasis). The same line of thought goes further:

> "Then can whatever I do be brought into accord with the rule?" – Let me ask this: what has the expression of a rule – say a sign-post – got to do with my actions? What sort of connexion is there here? – Well, perhaps this one: I have been trained to react [to] this sign in a particular way, and now I do so react to it.
>
> "But that is only to give a causal connexion: to tell how it has come about that we go by the sign-post; not what this going-by-the sign really consists in." – On the contrary; I have further indicated that a person goes by a sign-post only in so far as there exists a regular use of sign-posts, a *custom*.
>
> 1953/2001, §198, my emphasis

When one goes by a sign-post in normal cases, what guides her is not an interpretation of the sign; she just does it in the way the relevant customs dictate. Consider *PI* §506: '[t]he absent-minded man who at the order "Right turn!" turns left, and then, clutching his forehead, says "Oh! Right turn" and does a right turn. – What has struck him? *An interpretation*?' It seems clear that there is no interpretation in play here. True, we do from time to time interpret man-made or natural signs, but that is *not* the general case.[7] Normally, we just do it in the way were trained. A natural objection, anticipated by Wittgenstein, is that this answer is also a '*causal* explanation' (1984b/1998a, p. 239); or worse, a *behaviouristic* explanation. In response, McDowell reminds us that for Wittgenstein, 'the training in question is initiation into a custom' (ibid., p. 239). If the subject being trained is not a human being, but instead a mere animal, we would not say that in the training it has been initiated into a custom. The crucial difference is whether one has a language or not; I shall come back to this later.

Let's consider some of Kripke's remarks in details. The sceptics asks, '[h]ow do I know that "68 + 57," as I *meant* "plus" in the *past*, should denote 125' (1982, p. 12)? He goes on to ask that 'why I now believe that by "plus" in the past, I meant addition rather than quaddition' (ibid., p. 12)? A page later he asks, '[b]ut I can doubt that my past usage of "plus" denoted plus' (ibid., p. 13).[8] An assumption underlying all these queries is that we need to offer justifications here, but why should we think so? Wittgenstein writes 'That is not agreement in opinions but in form of life' (1953/2001, §241). If what in play here are opinions, it might be reasonable to ask for justifications, but 'what is at issue here is below that level –

the "bedrock" where "I have exhausted the justifications" and "my spade is turned" (*PI* §217)' (1984b/1998a, p. 240). Also see this passage:

> Giving grounds, however, justifying the evidence, comes to an end; – but the end is not certain proposition' striking us immediately as true, i.e. it is not a kind of *seeing* on our part; it is our *acting*, which lies at the bottom of the language-game.
>
> 1969, §204

We can appreciate this move by comparing this with the debate about the structure of empirical knowledge. Foundationalism is one of the responses to the infinite regress of justification; it attempts to stop the regress by postulating so-called 'basic beliefs', beliefs with certain special status. Now many have cast doubt on the cogency of this response, for after all, basic beliefs are *beliefs*. If they are beliefs, it is hard to see how they can be exempted from being in need of justification in one way or another. Now in our context, if what sustains all the understandings are themselves opinions or propositions, there seems to be little reason for thinking that they are not themselves in need of justifications. So the notion of customs and the like are *not* to be conceived as explicitly codified articles; instead, they are our forms of life pertaining to our language-games. At the level of 'bedrock' (1953/2001, §217) we just carry out actions without a justification, but 'without a justification does not mean ... without right' (ibid., §289).

In introducing the notion of 'bedrock', Wittgenstein is not embracing one horn of the dilemma, i.e. 'the last interpretation'. Rather, he is trying 'to steer a course between a Scylla and a Charybdis. Scylla is the idea that understanding is always interpretation', but if we avoid this by insisting that at the 'bedrock' level, no justification is needed, 'then we risk steering on to Charybdis – the picture of a basic level at which there are no norms' (1984b/1998a, p. 242). But as McDowell warns, '[u]ntil more is said about how exactly the appeal to communal practice makes the middle course available, this is only a programme for a solution to Wittgenstein's problem' (ibid., p. 242).

3. One might wonder why the practices in question have to be *communal* ones. Can't an individual form her own form of life so as to sustain linguistic abilities?[9] To this McDowell replies that 'one must search one's conscience to be sure that what one has in mind is not really, after all, the picture of a private interpretation... [one is] resigning oneself to Scylla...' (1984b/1998a, p. 246). McDowell's remarks here are not very clear; I understand him as saying this: how can an individual carry out actions with normativity, all by one's own? It appears that all one can do here is to launch one interpretation after another; as Kripke points out to us, this does not work.

But if McDowell's Wittgenstein invokes *communal* practice to the rescue, what distinguishes this picture from Kripkenstein's one? Recall that at the outset of this chapter, I said that almost all philosophers nowadays regard the social elements as essential to or at least important for intentionality. 'But it makes a difference how we conceive the requirement of publicity to emerge' (ibid., p. 243). McDowell argues that Kripke (and Crispin Wright):

> Picture a community as a collection of individuals presenting to one another exteriors that match in certain respects. They hope to humanize this bleak picture by claiming that what meaning consists in lies on those exteriors as they conceive them. But ... if regularities in the verbal behaviour of an isolated individual, described in norm-free terms, do not add up to meaning, it is quite obscure how it could somehow make all the difference if there are several individuals with matching regularities. The picture of a linguistic community degenerates ... into a picture of a mere aggregate of individuals whom we have no convincing reason not to conceive as opaque to one another.
>
> ibid., pp. 252–3

The picture McDowell recommends, by contrast, is that

> [S]hared membership in a linguistic community is not just a matter of matching in aspects of an exterior that we present to anyone whatever, but equips us to make our minds available to one another, by confronting one another with a different exterior from that which we present to outsiders ... [S]hared command of a language equips us to know one another's meaning without needing to arrive at that knowledge by interpretation, because it equips us to hear someone else's meaning in his words ... [A] linguistic community is conceived as bound together, not by a match in mere externals (facts accessible to just anyone), but by a capacity for a meeting of minds.
>
> ibid., p. 253

The above two passages convey one and the same thought from opposite angles. The negative part says that community in the relevant sense is *not just* aggregations of individual: there is no reason why quantity can explain the emergence of meaning. The positive part invokes the notion of 'membership', meaning that individuals need to be *initiated* into customs. The second line mentions 'anyone'. If we do not consider the *membership* of the individuals, then meaning is available to *anyone*. This collapses into behaviourism, or to use Simon Blackburn's phrase, 'a *wooden* picture of the use of language' (1981, p. 183).

Without the constraint of membership, anyone can access the meaning fact, but what is available to anyone regardless their customs? Answer: behaviours. But this is obviously *not* what Wittgenstein has in mind, and not a good picture to have anyway.

Recall that in Chapter 3, I discussed Brandom's accusation of residual individualism in McDowell's picture. Now it is interesting to learn that McDowell's counterargument against Brandom echoes his criticisms to Kripke and Wright:

> Within the putative observer's perspective, as opposed to the interpreter's, the fact is not in view as calling for a rational response. It is not in view as something to be taken into account in building a picture of the world. But that seems indistinguishable from saying it is not in view as the fact that it is ... How could multiplying what are, *considered by themselves, blind responses*, to include blind responses to how the blind responses of one's fellows are related to the circumstances to which they are blind responses, somehow bring it about that the responses are after all not blind?
>
> 1995b/1998b, pp. 408–9; my emphasis

McDowell's thought here is connected to his view about the other-mind problem. He argues that we can 'literally perceive, in another person's facial expression or his behaviour, that he is ... in pain ...' (1978b/1998b, p. 305). We are mind-readers, but in knowing others' minds, we are not conducting interpretations in normal cases; rather, we just *see* that they are in pain or other mental states. A general tendency of analytic philosophy is to start with meaningless noises and behaviours, and try to regain meaningfulness from those dead building blocks. The gist of McDowell's interpretation of Wittgenstein is that we need to start in the midst of meaning, or what we get is only an aggregate of individuals.[10] Those who read Wittgenstein as a reductionist ignore the following remark from him: '[h]earing a word in a particular sense. How queer that there should be such a thing' (1953/2001, §534).

Hopefully, the cogency of McDowell's case against the assimilation of understanding to interpretation has been generally established. But even if some readers agree with this, they might still wonder what the relation between this reflection on rule-following considerations and the inner space model is. McDowell provides the connection in another work on Wittgenstein:

> The conception is one according to which such regions of reality are populated exclusively with items that, considered in themselves, do not sort things out side the mind, including specifically bits of behaviour, into those that are correct or

incorrect in the light of those items. According to this conception, the contents of minds are items that, considered in themselves, just "stand there like a sign-post," as Wittgenstein puts it (*PI* §85). Consider in itself, a sign-post is just a board or something similar, perhaps bearing an inscription, on a post ... What does sort behaviour into what counts as following the sign-post and what does not is not an inscribed board affixed to a post, considered in itself, but such an object *under a certain interpretation* ...

1993b/1998a, pp. 264–5[11]

The first half of the passage is a characterization of the inner space, which is populated by inert, self-standing items that only extrinsically relate to external states of affairs. The second half is to connect the assimilation of understanding to interpretation (the 'master thesis', ibid., p. 270) to the inner space model: *self-standing* items need to be *interpreted* to be about something else; considered in themselves, they are 'normatively inert' (ibid., p. 265). In constructing the sceptical paradox, Kripke seldom talks about the mind directly, but his assimilation of understanding to interpretation betrays that he implicitly commits the inner space model. But if we abandon that way of conceiving ourselves, the regress of interpretations cannot get off the ground, and we can thereby shrug our shoulders to the meaning sceptics.[12]

Kripke does talk about the mind at the early stage of his discussions. He says that a set of directions 'is engraved on my mind as on a slate' (1982, p. 15). Not many people think there is anything crucial around, but I think Kripke's metaphor here is indeed disastrous: to conceive our minds as slates is to *distance* ourselves to our mental items, treat them as *objects*, so as to *make room for* deviant interpretations. The picture Kripke offers suggests that when someone entertains a thought, she needs to *consult her own past intentions* in using that symbol. The falsity of this way of thinking is that this makes *ownership* (or 'first-person character') of thoughts a myth. If one needs to consult her mental history whenever she entertains relevant thoughts, the difference between spontaneously entertaining one's own thoughts and attributing thoughts to our fellow speakers vanishes. This does not seem right.[13] And again we can see the rebuttal of this in Wittgenstein:

> We are tempted to think that the action of language consists of two parts; an inorganic part, the handling of signs, and an organic part, which we may call understanding these signs, meaning them, *interpreting* them, thinking.
>
> 1958, p. 3; my emphasis[14]

It is helpful to think this in Searle's terms: sometimes interpretations do constitute meanings, but that kind of intentionality is merely 'derivative', i.e. 'observer-relative'. I am not here defending Searle's distinction between original and derivative intentionality, but it is quite clear that to think that human intentionality is universally derivative is straightforwardly wrong (Searle, 1983).[15]

4. I shall turn to some objections to McDowell's position. Actually Kripke himself anticipates and comments on this kind of position:

> Perhaps we may try to recoup, by arguing that meaning addition by "plus" is a state even more *sui generic* than we have argued before. Perhaps it is simply a primitive state, not to be assimilated to sensations or headaches or any "qualitative" states, nor to be assimilated to dispositions, but a state of a unique kind of its own.
>
> 1982, p. 51

And he goes on to criticize this unclear approach right away:

> Such a move may in a sense be irrefutable, and if it is taken in an appropriate way Wittgenstein may even accept it. But it seems desperate: it leaves the nature of this postulated primitive state ... completely mysterious. It is not supposed to be an introspectible state, yet we supposedly are aware of it with some fair degree of certainty whenever it occurs.
>
> ibid., p. 51

Kripke does not spell out in what sense it is irrefutable, and the word 'irrefutable' is ambiguous. Sometimes it is taken to be a positive word, but in philosophy and science most of the time it is a dirty word. Since Kripke leaves the meaning of the word totally undetermined, I shall not focus on this remark. The same problem plagues the following sentence. What does he mean by 'appropriate'? This is especially important because if we spell it out, the opponent here may succeed in answering the paradox. Disappointingly enough, Kripke does not say anything specific here. I think we can think of McDowell's view as an attempt to find this appropriate way. Kripke then says that this approach is 'desperate', for it leaves the nature of this kind of state 'mysterious'. Indeed, given the characterizations in the above quotation, the nature of the state is mysterious so the proponents of it do make a desperate move. But notice that Kripke does not even try to give a fair construal to this position, as presented above. What is really mysterious is why Kripke picks an empty opponent to belabour. Thus there are some latitudes for anti-sceptics to freely envisage varieties of possibility here.

Kripke thinks this sort of state is not supposed to be introspectible, but this description is unmotivated. Maybe he thinks only experiential states which he previously considered are introspectible, but this is not true. I can introspect to my beliefs, though many of my beliefs do not give me any *qualitative* feels.[16]

Kripke has another line of objection. He thinks there is a logical difficulty inherited in primitivism, and again he attributes this view to Wittgenstein:

> Even more important is the logical difficulty implicit in Wittgenstein's sceptical argument ... Such a state would have to be a finite object, contains in our finite minds ... Can we conceive of a finite state which could not be interpreted in a quus-like way?
>
> ibid., pp. 51–2

The problem of infinite deviant interpretations strikes back, but since we have rejected the model generating the regress, it should be seen as an innocuous remark now. Another thing to be said is that the infinity can be explained by *compositionality*. The 'plus' sign is a piece of language, so it can be used in infinitely different ways thanks to compositionality. I cannot see why there is any puzzle about it. Besides, the infinity objection is not particular for the present proposal anyway: anti-sceptics are finding certain facts to sustain meaning, and supposedly most facts are finite – maybe dispositions are not, if they turn out to be relevant facts. So even if this is indeed a problem, this is not a particular problem for primitivism. The logical difficulty amounts to nothing.

Kripke's own objections to primitivism are not very impressive; in what follows I shall consider objections raised by one of his major defenders, Martin Kusch, who proposes a systematic defence of Kripke's Wittgenstein (2006).

Kusch is sceptical about McDowell's starting point, that is, Kripke's sceptical case utterly relies on the infinite regress of interpretation. He argues:

> In all these cases, the meaning sceptic counters the proposal with the observation that the proposed items (past behaviours, formulae, qualia, intentions and Fregean ideas) can be interpreted in many different ways. In all these cases Kripke does indeed work with the regress of interpretations. Note, however, that the same is not true in the case of reductive dispositionalism. It seems as though the dispositionalist is, in a way, doing precisely what McDowell's Wittgenstein urges us to do: get rid of any mental items that just "stand there like sign-post." Moreover, the arguments that Kripke marshals against dispositionalism on Wittgenstein's behalf – the normativity considerations, the finitude objection, the mistake objection – do not make use of the regress of interpretations. Given the central place of dispositionalism in Chapter 2 of *WRPL* this should make us cautious about McDowell's reading of the book.
>
> ibid., pp. 225–6

Kusch attempts to show that Kripke's objections to dispositionalism do *not* rely on the infinite regress of interpretation. However, McDowell's criticisms against Kripke presuppose that the regress is the backbone of Kripke's whole argumentations. It follows that McDowell's reading of Kripke is biased or even wrong. Furthermore, this shows that McDowell's view is more like dispositionalism, a position that cannot accommodate normativity.

Even if Kusch is right about Kripke's objections against dispositionalism – which I will later show that it is not – it is not clear why this should be a reason for assimilating McDowell's position to dispositionalism. Given Kusch's interpretation, maybe they have similar consequences – both of them have no regress problem, for example – but that does not mean they are similar to each other in crucial respects. Whether dispositionalism succeeds in preserving normativity, it does not incorporate this property in its starting point; it starts rather with the finitude problem. McDowell, on the contrary, starts with normativity. We can see this in his insistence on membership. Dispositionalism and McDowell's position are just different.

And Kripke's objections to dispositionalism include the infinite regress of interpretation anyway.

The regress problem implicitly resides in the 'finitude objection'. Kripke gives a rejoinder to dispositionalist's attempt to overcome the finitude problem:

> The dispositional theory attempts to avoid the problem of finiteness of my actual past performance by appealing to a disposition. But in doing so, it ignores an obvious fact: not only my actual performance, but also the totality of my dispositions, is finite ... Let "quaddition" be redefined so as to be a function which agrees with addition thereafter (say, it is 5). Then, just as the sceptic previously proposed the hypothesis that I meant quaddition in the old sense, now he proposes the hypothesis that I meant quaddition in the new sense. A dispositional account will be impotent to refute him. As before, there are infinitely many candidates the sceptic can propose for the role of quaddition.
>
> 1982, pp. 26–7

Now we should ask why finitude would be a problem at the very beginning. We non-sceptics want some way to get a determined rule from past behaviours, but we fail if we let the infinite regress of interpretation get going. No matter how many past intentions or behaviours we have, *since they are finite, the sceptic can always find some ways to give deviant interpretations.* Finitude is a problem precisely because it generates vicious infinite regress. The regress nightmare is with dispositionalism anyway, at least according to Kripke.

Kusch then says actually Kripke can accommodate McDowell's concern:

> [T]here is also reason to doubt McDowell's claim according to which Kripke's fails to recognize Wittgenstein's crucial third position: a primitivism about meaning and rules that is centred around the ideas of training, acting blindly, agreement, custom, practice and institution.
>
> 2006, p. 226

He then goes on to give plenty of textual evidence from Kripke to support his complaint here. First thing to be noted is that Kusch seems to contradict himself here, for he formerly says that McDowell's position is rather like dispositionalism. Now he commits himself to the thought that Kripke's sceptical solution is similar to dispositionalism. This might not be intrinsically problematic, but in any case let's turn to Kusch's concern here in some details, that Kripke's solution can accommodate what McDowell is driving at.

We can resist this assimilation by the distinction between the 'insulated-individuals conception' and the 'intimate-individuals conception'; the former refers to the position shared by Kripke, Wright and Brandom; the later refers to McDowell and McDowell's Wittgenstein. There is no denying that Kripke's solution does have some Wittgensteinian flavour. This is recognized by McDowell in the very paper Kusch is considering:

> Wittgenstein's point is that we have to situate our conception of meaning and understanding within a framework of communal practice. Kripke's reading credits Wittgenstein with the thesis that the notion of meaning something by one's word is "inapplicable to a single person considered in isolation" (p. 79). The upshot is similar, then; and it cannot be denied that the insistence on publicity in Kripke's reading corresponds broadly with a Wittgensteinian thought. But it makes a difference how we conceive the requirement of publicity to emerge.
>
> 1984b/1998a, p. 243

Indeed, who can sensibly deny that Kripke's picture is in a sense social, and it incorporates Wittgenstein's insistence on the importance of practice and custom? The problem is, to repeat, his conception of a community is *only* an aggregation of individuals, regardless of their memberships. The fact that Kripke also underscores the importance of practice and custom does not justify Kusch's attempted assimilation.

Another attempt to assimilate McDowell with Kripke can be found in another passage from Kusch:

> McDowell's Wittgenstein's opposition to "constructive philosophical accounts" is really an opposition to, and "diagnostic deconstruction" of, all forms of reductivism. Kripke's Wittgenstein would obviously sympathize. His only proviso would be that reductionism is not the only candidate for "diagnostic deconstruction." Semantic and intentional reductivism is a natural upshot of meaning determinism, and unless we cure ourselves of the latter, we can never be sure that we are free of the inclination to be tempted by the former.
>
> 2006, p. 227

This passage seems puzzling. I cannot see why Kripke's Wittgenstein would oppose to reductionism, let alone 'obviously' does so. Kusch does not give clear justification as far as I can tell. Moreover, it is not true that there is a close relation between meaning determinism and reductionism. When Kripke demands us to find some facts to sustain meaning, he constrains us with a reductive requirement. Quine is another prominent example of reductionist about meaning, but he is the last one who will accept meaning determinism.[17]

The last objection from Kusch is not very clear. He seems to say that McDowell's position is not a stable one:

> Can we read McDowell differently? Can we perhaps read him as proposing an improved version of meaning determinism: meaning determinism without the master thesis? I doubt that this reading can be squared with McDowell's commitments. McDowell's position questions or rejects almost all meaning-determinist assumptions... This rules out immediate knowledge, privacy, and the individualistic contractual of semantic normativity... As far as objectivity goes, McDowell seeks to find a middle way between "platonistic autonomy" and "ratification dependence"... This is weaker than the meaning determinist's objectivity, which seems to be precisely a form of the autonomy thesis. Finally, McDowell does not advocate full-blown classical realism with its inflationary factualism.
>
> 2006, pp. 227–8

McDowell is obviously not an indeterminist, and he rejects Kripke's master thesis, that understanding is a species of interpretation. Therefore, to read him as proposing a version of meaning determinism without the master thesis is definitely a natural reading. Kusch nevertheless thinks this is a 'different' reading of McDowell, which seems to me a misunderstanding. What is more, all the above descriptions of McDowell's position just show that his determinism is quite unique, without traditional determinisms' assumptions. McDowell's overall philosophical concern is to make meaning and understanding unproblematic, so he should be read as a determinist, though with various delicate provisos.

5. Why do Kripke and Wright (probably not Brandom) want a picture that starts from meaningless noises and behaviours? To answer this diagnostic question, I shall turn to the well-known dichotomy between psychologism and behaviourism, between the Cartesian and the Rylean.[18] Kripke starts with a Cartesian model in formulating the paradox, and that makes mental states idle with respect to meaning. This leads him to end up with a Rylean conception of meaning and understanding. His solution is Rylean in the sense that he does not have a place for membership in his picture. The insulated-individuals conception of community does *not* allow people to make contact with one another's meaning. The source of the paradox, then, is that he cannot get rid of the dichotomy between psychologism and behaviourism.

The dichotomy is deeply rooted in the analytic tradition. Traditional empiricisms and rationalisms share the psychologistic conception of language, and from the early twentieth century the behaviouristic atmosphere took over. Philosophers struggle between the two seemingly mutually exhaustive options.

Kripke is not alone in the framework between the Cartesian and the Rylean. In *Word and Object*, Quine notices this dichotomy and happily endorses behaviourism. Quine writes:

> One may accept the Brentano thesis either as showing the indispensability of intentional idioms and the importance of an autonomous science of intention, or as showing the baselessness of intentional idioms and the emptiness of a science of intention. My attitude, unlike Brentano's, is the second.
>
> 1960, p. 221[19]

I am not here attacking behaviourism; I just want to stress that the dichotomy is often seen in important philosophers' thinking. Many of them never question the dichotomy, however. Now Kripke's case is more complicated. On the one hand, one of his main points is to challenge a version of Cartesianism: he argues that one's confidence about one's own meaning – one's self-knowledge – is an illusion. On the other, he explicitly distances himself from behaviourism.[20] He seems to be aware of the predicament followed from the dichotomy, but nevertheless ends up with a Rylean picture unintentionally. Now Michael Dummett also wants to find a middle course between the two extremes. McDowell argues that Dummett commits to similar mistakes in the sense that he is also too close to behaviourism. This debate between Dummett and McDowell is not in the context of rule-following, so I shall briefly describe it and relate it to the present discussion.[21]

The locus of their disagreement is Davidson's truth-theoretic view of meaning (2001b).[22] Details aside, the main question here is about what we should expect in our theory of meaning. Dummett thinks that our meaning theory should be 'full-blooded': intentional notions are 'of no use in giving an account of the language as from the outside' (1981, p. 40). McDowell, by contrast, thinks that our theory of meaning should be modest. This is a debate between reductionism and non-reductionism, which is highly relevant to the main topic of the present chapter. Kripke imposes reductionist's requirement when he demands anti-sceptics to cite facts that does not themselves involve meaning, and primitivism is a version of non-reductionism, for it insists on the *sui generis* character of meaning.[23]

Dummett thinks, following Quine, that modesty is inevitably psychologistic.[24] McDowell summarizes this as follows:

> Now one strand in Dummett's objection to modesty is the view that modesty necessarily involves this conception of language as a code [that is, psychologism.] ... [A modest theory] is intelligible only on the supposition that adherents of modesty imagine the task ... delegated to a prior and independent theory of *thought*.
>
> 1987b/1998b, pp. 93–4. Also see his 1997b/1998b

And Dummett thinks psychologism is objectionable:

> [I]f communication is to be possible, that in which our understanding of the language we speak consists must "lie open to view, as Frege maintained that it does, in our use of the language, in our participation in a common practice."
>
> ibid., p. 94

We should credit Dummett in insisting that meaning should *not* be considered as lying behind behaviours. But the question is how he can achieve this given his requirement of full-bloodedness. 'How, then can a description of the practice of speaking a language "as from outside" content succeed in registering the role of mind? How can it be more than a mere description of outward behaviour, with the mental (inner) aspect of language use left out of account' (ibid., p. 94)?

Now one particular objection from McDowell is especially relevant. It is about Dummett's example of attribution of the concept square. McDowell argues:

> Can implicit knowledge that that is how *square* things are to be treated be manifested in behaviour, characterized "as from outside" content? It may seem that nothing could be simpler: the manifestation would be someone's treating a square thing in whatever way is in question. But any such performance would be an equally good manifestation of any of an indefinite number of different pieces of such implicit knowledge ... If we assume a stable propensity, guided by an

unchanging piece of implicit knowledge, we can use further behaviour to rule out some of these competing candidates. But no finite set of performances would eliminate them all; and finite sets of performances are all we get.

ibid., p. 96

Under this construal, Dummett's position is strikingly similar to Quine's.[25] Both of them think modesty – non-reductionism – goes hand in hand with psychologism. Both of them think somehow behaviours or dispositions of behaviour can manifest meaning (if any). Quine famously shows that meaning is underdetermined with respect to behaviours. If we combine this with reductive behaviourism, indeterminacy is home and dry. Now, Dummett rejects this and attempts to steer between psychologism and behaviourism. However, his insistence on full-bloodedness commits him to the Quinean line of reasoning. It is not clear how he can block this route given the requirement of full-bloodedness.

Now how does McDowell steer the middle course? Since psychologism is not desirable, our mindedness must somehow manifest in our behaviours. But if we insist that the characterization must be 'as from outside', we fall in the trap of behaviourism, and thereby commit Quinean indeterminacy. The solution is to insist that meaning does manifest in behaviours, *but* characterizations of them must be modest: we should not expect we could characterize behaviours in meaning-free terms. McDowell writes:

> Steering that middle course requires the difficult idea that competence in a language is an ability to embody one's mind – the cast of one's thoughts – in words that one speaks, and to hear others' thoughts in their words ... [W]e have to entitle ourselves to the idea that acquiring a first language is, not learning a behavioural outlet for antecedent states of mind, but becoming *minded* in ways that the language is anyway able to express. We have to equip ourselves to see how our ability to have dealings with content can be, not a mere natural endowment (something we can take for granted), but an achievement, which an individual attains by acquiring membership in a linguistic community.

ibid., pp. 104–5

We have seen that in the picture McDowell recommends, the notion of 'custom' plays an indispensably crucial role: to be a genuine thinker, one has to be initiated into relevant customs. And to be initiated into customs is to acquire a language:

> Now it is not even clearly intelligible to suppose a creature might be born at home in the space of reasons. Human beings are not: they are born mere animals, and they are transformed into *thinkers* and intentional agents in the course of coming

to maturity. This transformation risks looking mysterious. But we can take it in our stride if, in our conception of the *Bildung* that is a central element in the normal maturation of human beings, we give pride of place to the learning of *language*. In being initiated into a language, a human being is introduced into something that already embodies putatively rational linkages between concepts, putatively constitutive of the layout of *the space of reasons*, before she comes on the scene.

1996a, p. 125; my emphasis

So the notion of 'a language' is indeed vital for McDowell's overall picture. Given this, it is interesting to learn that Davidson famously remarks that 'there is no such thing as *a language*, not if a language is anything like what many philosophers and linguists have supposed' (1986/2005, p. 107). A more intimate relation can be found in Davidson's negative attitude towards Kripkenstein's ways of thinking:

> What would matter [for communication] ... is that we should each provide the other with something understandable as a language. This is an intention speakers must have; but carrying out this intention ... does *not involve following shared rules* or conventions.
>
> 1992/2001c, p. 114; my emphasis[26]

If Davidson is right, then the whole discussion of rule-following is misguided. Is this also a knockdown objection to McDowell's proposal? I shall respond to this concern in my next section.

Bildung

1. When he first tackles the relevant issues, Davidson formulates the question like this: 'could there be *communication* by language without convention' (1984/2001b, p. 265)?[27] His main opponent Dummett also regards 'communication' as one of the principal functions of language (1989).[28] Given this common ground, the debate is about the primary status of a shared language, as Davidson puts: '[w]hich is conceptually primary, the idiolect or the language' (1994/2005, p. 109)? He opts for the former:

> [I]n learning a language, a person acquires the ability to operate in accord with a precise and specifiable set of syntactic and semantic rules; verbal communication depends on speaker and hearer sharing such an ability, and it requires no more than this. I argued that sharing such a previously mastered ability was neither necessary nor sufficient for successful linguistic communication.
>
> ibid., p. 110

On the face of it, Davidson's main argument for his case is based on counterexamples, notably *malapropism*.[29] A malapropism is a wrong use of one word instead of another because they sound similar to each other, and what is interesting is that the occurrences of malapropism often do *not* prevent successful communication. One of Davidson's examples is between 'a nice arrangement of epithets' and 'a nice derangement of epitaphs' (1986/2005, p. 103). Davidson thinks that in this kind of case, speaker and hearer can understand each other without sharing any common understanding of the contingent usages of the words involved. If this is right, to approach the issues of linguistic meaning with the rule-following considerations is wrongheaded, for linguistic behaviours are not *essentially* rule-governed practices; 'shared linguistic practice' has merely practical utility (McDowell, 2002c/2008b, p. 143).

McDowell does not dispute this; as he says, '[m]alapropisms provide *clear* counterexamples – cases where understanding is not disrupted by mismatches between speaker and hearer in respect of anything we might see as rules to which they conform their linguistic behavior' (ibid., p. 143). Where Davidson denies 'portable interpreting machine' (1986/2005, p. 107), Gadamer contemns 'method'. What McDowell objects to is the following inference:

> Now to make a leap. There seems to me to be no reason, in theory at least, why speakers who understand each other *ever* need to speak, or to *have* spoken, as anyone else speaks, much less as each other speaks.
>
> 1994/2005, p. 115

This is indeed a 'leap', for cases like malapropisms (or 'two monoglot survivors' scenario, 2002c/2008b, p. 143) do not warrant a 'perfective' claim. Davidson of course knows this, so his ground for the further claim is not those examples, but the argument from 'absence of negative reason'. McDowell's response to this challenge is in effect providing a reason against that perfective claim. He writes,

> Davidson's claims commit him to denying that one needs to learn to speak as others do, in the ordinary sense, in order to become a *human subject*, a potential party to an encounter with another that leads to mutual understanding, at all.
>
> ibid., p. 144; my emphasis

McDowell doubts that 'Davidson ever considers the thought that shared languages might matter for the constitution of subjects of understanding', for '[h]is target is always the conception of a sharing that would suffice of itself for *communication*' (ibid., p. 145; my emphasis) as we have seen at the beginning of this section. But if McDowell is right about the rule-following discussions, as discussed in the previous section, then to be a thinker is to be initiated into relevant customs, and to start the initiation is to be a speaker. A shared language is indispensable *not* because linguistic practices are *essentially* rule-following behaviours – they are not, as shown by malapropisms and the like – but because it is responsible for the constitution of a genuine thinker. Davidson makes the unfortunate leap, for he overlooks the possibility McDowell argues for in the context of the rule-following considerations.[30]

McDowell agrees with Davidson that 'familiarity with a human way of life [is] surely not just aids to arriving at understanding', but he adds that a form of life is 'conditions for being potential subjects of understanding at all' (ibid., p. 145). Relatedly, Davidson is hostile to the idea of 'non-linguistic institution' (1994/2005, p. 119) and to this McDowell replies:

> A "language-game" cannot be confined to bursts of speech. It is a whole in which verbal behavior is integrated into a form of life, including practices that if considered on their own would have to be counted as nonlinguistic.
>
> 2002b/2008b, pp. 145–6; 1980c/1998b

2. It is helpful to take stock before I close the present chapter. The discussions of rule-following have been very heated for about four decades, since the publication of Kripke's *Wittgenstein on Rules and Private Language* (1982). Most participants do not accept Kripke's interpretation of Wittgenstein, including the 'paradox' part and the 'solution' part. Nevertheless, most (if not all) of them assume with Kripke that linguistic behaviours are essentially rule-following practices. Now as we have seen, Davidson is sceptical about this idea; he attempts to *resolve* the debate by arguing against the essentialist claim. Now McDowell concurs with Davidson at this point, but he refuses to accept Davidson's further 'leap', namely the 'perfective' claim. So we can say that Davidson gestures the right direction but unfortunately goes too far. Therefore it is potentially misleading to regard McDowell as a player in the rule-following battlefield: though he rejects Davidson's excessive move, he nonetheless sides with Davidson in thinking that the 'rule-following considerations' generated by Kripke's interpretation of Wittgenstein is misguided, philosophically speaking. Communication *per se* does not, *contra* many philosophers' convictions, involve shared rules essentially, but being able to understanding does, *pace* Davidson.

In Chapter 1, I explained how McDowell's Locke Lecture relies on Gadamer's thinking about *Bildung*. Now we see more intimate connections between this notion and a central issue in analytic philosophy. 'The idea of inheriting a *tradition* helps us to understand what is involved in possessing conceptual capacities ...' (2002c/2008b, p. 134; my emphasis). Through a careful reading of Wittgenstein's notions of 'custom' and 'form of life', McDowell shows us how the resources from Continental thinkers can after all shed light on central concerns in the analytic tradition. I shall finally conclude this chapter with the following passage:

> Human beings mature into being at home in the space of reasons or, what comes to the same thing, living their lives in the world; we can make sense of that by noticing that the *language* into which a human being is first initiated stands over against her as a prior embodiment of mindedness, of the possibility of an orientation to the world.
>
> 1996a, p. 125; my emphasis

Some readers might still wonder what *exactly* McDowell's positive proposal is after the above long journey. I am afraid that here is where McDowellian-cum-Wittgensteinian quietism would come in: at these crucial moments, McDowell tends to shy away like this; later we will see this again in the context of 'causation in the space of reasons' in the Epilogue. I will myself be more constructive and seek to say something more positive at these points, but in interpreting McDowell I can only say that he has been consistent with regard to his quietist methodology.

5

Agent and Person

Embodiment

1. In the quotation at the end of the previous chapter, McDowell uses the notion of 'mindedness' in passing. Presumably, this is to prevent the *reification* of our mental phenomena. Same consideration appears in the replacement of 'meaning' with 'meaningfulness' in the literatures of philosophy of language. For McDowell, mindedness is '*conceptual* mindedness' (2007c/2008b, p. 316) As I briefly mentioned in Chapter 3, this claim is very controversial and there are many negative arguments from different considerations. In the present chapter I take up this debate in the context of action and agency. In particular, the debate between McDowell and Hubert Dreyfus will be considered in detail. But before that, let me say more about McDowell's conceptualism, especially its application to action. To anticipate, in the previous chapter we have seen elements from German phenomenology, and in the current chapter we will see elements from French phenomenology, as the quotations below of Merleau-Ponty and from Sartre show:

> *If habit is neither a form of knowledge nor an involuntary action, what then is it? It is knowledge in the hands, which is forthcoming only when bodily effort is made, and cannot be formulated in detachment from that effort.*
>
> Maurice Merleau-Ponty,
> *Phenomenology of Perception*

> *The environment can act on the subject only to the exact extent that he comprehends it; that is, transforms it into a situation.*
>
> Sean-Paul Sartre, *Being and Nothingness*

In understanding conceptual capacities, McDowell relates it to the idea of rationality:

> The notion of rationality I mean to invoke here is the notion exploited in a traditional line of thought to make a special place in the animal kingdom for rational animals. It is a notion of responsiveness to reasons *as such*.
>
> 2005b/2008a, p. 128[1]

As McDowell immediately says, this 'wording leaves room for responsiveness to reasons ... on the other side of the division drawn by this notion of rationality between rational animals and animals that are not rational' (ibid., p. 128). For example, when we observe a dog fleeing from potential danger, we are justified in saying that he is responsive to danger as a *reason* to flee, without attributing him a belief *that he is in danger*, i.e. the reason *as such*.

Things are quite different in the case of human being. As McDowell says, we have the ability to 'step back from an inclination to flee, elicited from her by an apparent danger, and raise the question whether she *should* be so inclined – whether the apparent danger is, here and now, a sufficient reason for fleeing' (ibid., p. 128). If she then decides to act on the reason, her action exhibit 'self-determining subjectivity' (ibid., p. 128).[2]

Recall that in experiences, conceptual capacities are *operative*, rather than *exercised*, for we do not normally actively decide which concepts to apply, contrary to the case of judgements.[3] Similarly, in the case of actions we do not usually pay attention to what we are doing or going to do, but if we can regard them as *intentional* actions, we need to connect it to the idea of rationality.[4] McDowell reminds:

> Acting for a reason, which one is responding to as such, does not require that one reflects about whether some consideration is a sufficient rational warrant for something it seems to recommend. It is enough that one could.
>
> ibid., p. 129

This is the way McDowell conceives the relation between conceptual capacities and rationality. This also responds to a usual query: how can McDowell put a heavy weight on the notion of 'conceptual capacities' without saying anything about the metaphysics of concept? To this McDowell would reply that his invocation of the notion of 'concept' is a matter of 'stipulation: conceptual capacities in the relevant sense belong essentially to their possessor's rationality in the sense I am working with, responsiveness to reasons as such' (ibid., p. 129).[5] He further works out this stipulation with his interpretation of Fregean sense (1996a, p. 107). But in any case, he can leave open the nature of concept, as long as we do not regard it as normatively inert items populated in the inner space.

There is another important point about the exercise/operative distinction. In the case of judgements, we exercise conceptual capacities through conducting inferences; in experiences it is not the case. As McDowell explains, '[t]he content that the explanation attributes to the experience is *the same* as the content of the belief explained, not *a premise* from which it would make sense to think of the subject as having reached the belief by an inferential step' (2005b/2008a, p. 131). And something analogous can be said about action.

After setting the stage, McDowell then offers his case for conceptualism:

> [I]f our notion of an experience is to be capable of playing the role it plays when we explain perceptually based beliefs as manifestations of rationality, we must understand having such an experience – being in possession of such an entitlement – as itself, already, an actualization of the conceptual capacities that would be exercised by someone who explicitly adopted a belief with that content.
>
> ibid., p. 132

Again, something parallel can be said about actions. Simply put, the thought is that human experiences and actions are integral parts of human rationality, so given McDowell's stipulation of conceptual capacities, the 'pervasiveness of *conceptual* rationality' follows (2007c/2008b, p. 321; my emphasis).

Notice that in the above stipulation, McDowell says nothing about language. It is definitely McDowell's view that language is a crucial precondition of rationality; as he puts it, 'the ability to step back from considerations and raise the question whether they constitute reasons for action or belief ... is coeval with command of a language' (2005b/2008a, p. 135) but he never argues that conceptual capacities are linguistic or 'quasi-linguistic' in Michael Ayers' term (2004, p. 249; see also his 2019) – whatever that means. This makes room for the thought that 'experience as actualization of conceptual capacities *in sensory consciousness*' (2005b/2008a, p. 135). This dampens a similar worry raised by Arthur Collins (1998), that McDowell is 'committ[ing] to a picture in which our experience comes as it were with subtitles' (ibid., p. 135). This is important in the present context, for if the sense of the conceptual is indeed 'quasi-linguistic', the Ayers-Collins line of objection will appear again. To be sure, so far McDowell does not say anything positive about the sensory aspect of experience, but the objection was that McDowell *cannot* make room for that. It is enough for now to say that the room has been made, though the accommodation has not been prepared.

As usual, McDowell has a diagnosis for the misfire. Here it goes:

> In disallowing my proposal that actualizations of conceptual capacities can present things in a sensory way, Ayers assumes a sharp separation between the sensory and the intellectual, as I shall put it to avoid that tendentious implication.
> 2005b/2008a, p. 136; also see his 1998i

The dualism of intellect and sensory is only assumed, without any argument. And McDowell's above argument for conceptualism provides some reason for not believing it. As acknowledged above, he does not have a positive account about the way the conceptual and the sensory can merge together, but at least he depicts a way to understand the conceptual without precluding the sensory. Again, we can draw a parallel for actions. Experiences are of course sensory; actions are of course bodily. But without arguments, we should not simply assume that the sensory and the bodily are incompatible with the conceptual. Later we will see that Dreyfus is attempting to provide arguments for the dualism in question, but I shall complete my exposition of McDowell before evaluating Dreyfus's case.

For McDowell, conceptual capacities, freedom and self-determining subjectivity come in the same package.[6] But we should not forget that we are not unconditionally free, both in experiences and in actions (see also 1996a, p. 96). As McDowell says, 'there is a sense in which perceptual experience can compel belief' (2005b/2008a, p. 139). There is also a sense in which the world, together with affordances and solicitations, can compel actions.[7] The passivity in perceptions and actions is of course acknowledged. The issue is how we should understand the relations between freedom and passivity. Again, this is the focal disagreement between McDowell and Dreyfus.

Let me adumbrate what I have said before getting into the debate. McDowell first stipulates the sense in which rational animals possess conceptual capacities. This is the capacity to be responsive to reasons *as such*. He then rehearses a distinction between exercised and operative conceptual capacities. In experiences, the capacities are passively at work. The main argument for the conceptuality is that experiences are integrated into the larger framework of rationality, and this (together with other thoughts not presenting here) implies that experiences are conceptual through and through. This does not, *contra* many critics, mean that experiences are quasi-linguistic. To think otherwise is to embrace the dualism of intellect and sensory, without arguments. Experiences belong to the realm of self-determining subjectivity, but there is indeed a sense in which perceptions can compel beliefs, for it is in a significant sense passive. Now, everything said above has a place in the parallel story of actions. In actions, conceptual capacities are passively at work. They are conceptual because they are integral parts of the larger framework of rationality. They are passive because we are constrained by affordances, solicitations and the world. We should not, however, conceive the conceptual and the passive aspects of action with the dualism of intellect and bodily.[8] This is the general McDowellian picture.[9]

Like experiences, actions also mediate mind and world, though with different 'directions of fit' (Searle, 1983, p. 7). Perceptions reflect the world, actions change the world; perceptions sustain beliefs, actions carry out intentions. To expect a parallel story for actions is not unnatural at least. In his Locke Lecture, McDowell claims that 'intentions without overt activity are idle, and movements of limbs without concepts are mere happenings, not expressions of agency' (1996a, p. 89).[10] And some philosophers start to envisage what McDowell would say, or should say, about action, Jonathan Dancy (2006; also McDowell's reply in the same volume, 2006a, and 2013a) for example. Some other philosophers go even further to criticize the envisaged McDowellian account of action; as mentioned, Hubert Dreyfus is one amongst them.[11] In presenting his picture, as we have seen, McDowell invokes plenty of resources from big names in Western philosophy, including Aristotle, Kant, Hegel, Wittgenstein and Gadamer.[12] A blatant feature of this list is that phenomenologists are absent: Husserl, Heidegger and Merleau-Ponty are not in the list. Dreyfus suggests that McDowell's position is defective exactly in this respect.[13]

2. In considering Dreyfus's objections, McDowell adumbrates his relevant thoughts as follows:

> I have urged that our perceptual relation to the world is conceptual all the way out to the world's impacts on our receptive capacities. The idea of the conceptual that I mean to be invoking is to be understood in close connection with the idea of rationality, in the sense that is in play in the traditional separation of mature human beings, as rational animals, from the rest of the animal kingdom. Conceptual capacities are capacities that belong to their subject's rationality. So another way of putting my claim is to say that our perceptual experience is permeated with rationality. I have also suggested, in passing, that something parallel should be said about our agency.[14]
>
> 2007c/2008b, p. 308

We will see that McDowell and Dreyfus have very different notions of the main concepts appearing in the above passage, such as 'perception', 'concept', 'receptive capacities', 'rationality', 'animals' and 'agency'.[15] But first let's go back to where the story began. In his editorial introduction to Samuel Todes' *Body and World* (2001), Dreyfus briefly takes issue with McDowell. He writes:

> Neither Davidson nor McDowell tries to describe *perceptual objects as they are in themselves* and how they become the objects of thought. By calling attention to the structure of nonconceptual, practical perception and showing how its judgments can be transformed into the judgments of detached thought, Todes is able to provide a framework in which to explain how the content of perception, while not itself conceptual, can provide the basis for *conception*. Thus, Todes's *Body and World* can be read as a significant anticipatory response to McDowell's *Mind and World*.
>
> 2001, p. xvi; my emphasis

Here Dreyfus separates perception from conception. He thinks that there is something called 'perception as they are in themselves, independent of conception'. This seems to beg the question against McDowell, but I think Dreyfus is not blamable at this point, for what he did there is to introduce Todes' seminal work, situating it into certain philosophical contexts by contrasting it with McDowell's thoughts. Although it will be better if he provides substantive arguments for the claim, I think we can be more charitable here.[16] What I mainly concern here is a series of debates where Dreyfus and McDowell engage with each other seriously.

A few words about my strategy: the debate between McDowell and Dreyfus appears like continuous conversations: Dreyfus's Presidential Address was responding to McDowell's earlier works, and later on in *Inquiry* they responded to each other twice. In addition, Dreyfus did not reach his stable framework until the final response. Therefore, it would be onerous and ineffective for us to go through the discussions with the original sequence. Hence I shall offer a two-stage presentation of Dreyfus's objections. First its general structure, and then its details. This means that sometimes I will fit Dreyfus's earlier points and examples into his later, stable framework. The motivation is to present Dreyfus at his best. In what follows I will discuss how Dreyfus reaches his stable framework first.

Dreyfus seriously argues against McDowell in his 2005 APA Presidential Address. He starts his argumentation by posing this rhetoric question: '[c]an we accept McDowell's Sellarsian claim that perception is conceptual "all the way out," thereby denying the more basic perceptual capacities we seem to share with prelinguistic infants and higher animal' (2006)? The positive statement of the position goes like this: 'in assuming that all intelligibility, even perception and skillful coping, *must be, at least implicitly, conceptual* ... Sellars and McDowell join Kant in endorsing what we might call *the Myth of the Mental* (ibid., p. 46; my emphasis). In supporting this claim, he brings in a distinction that is crucial to his argumentations:

> The actual phenomenon [i.e. expertise] suggests that to become experts we must switch from *detached rule-following* to a more *involved and situation specific way of coping*... Such emotional involvement seems to be necessary to facilitate the switchover from *detached, analytical rule following* to an entirely different *engaged, holistic mode of experience*...
>
> ibid., p. 46; my emphasis

Dreyfus uses some other distinctions to supplement this one, including detached theoretical perspective/engaged situation in the world (ibid., p. 44), calculate/involve (ibid., p. 47), and knowing-that/knowing-how (ibid., p. 48). I shall focus on the one appearing in the quotation. Dreyfus assumes that McDowell regards actions as detached rule-following, but he never tells us why he thinks that. Moreover, we have positive reasons to think otherwise. Recall that McDowell painstakingly disabuses this detached conception of rule-following in his critique of Kripke's Wittgenstein, as discussed in Chapter 4. For example, he writes:

> [Kripke's] line of interpretation gets off on the wrong foot, when it credits Wittgenstein with acceptance of a "skeptical paradox" ... the reasoning that would lead to this "skeptical paradox" starts with something Wittgenstein aims to show up as a mistake: the assumption, in this case, that the understanding on which I act when I obey an order *must be an interpretation*.
>
> 1984b/1998a, p. 236

To rehearse, Kripke conceives understanding as a species of interpretation, so whenever I use the 'plus' function, I can interpret my past usages of it so as to conform other deviant functions, hence the paradox. McDowell urges that the source of the paradox is the *detached* conception of rule-following: we *have to do interpretation* when our understanding is functioning. The problematic inner space model has it that there are some freestanding mental items that have no intrinsic normative relations with the external world, so we need interpretations to build up these relations. It is this *detached* picture, McDowell submits, that generates the sceptical paradox. He further connects his critique to Wittgenstein's notions of 'practice', 'custom' and 'form of life'; I shall not here repeat the discussions of Chapter 4. It is not clear, then, why Dreyfus does not regard McDowell as an ally at least in this respect.

The distinction between detached rule-following and involved skillful coping seems to be dubious; moreover, it is precisely what McDowell disagrees with when he writes that '[w]e find ourselves *always already engaging* with the world' (1996a, p. 34; my emphasis). Dreyfus's distinction is actually congenial to McDowell.

Dreyfus admits this misunderstanding in his reply: 'I did assume, accepting the traditional understanding, that McDowell understood rationality and *conceptuality* as *general*. I should have known better. I'm sorry that I attributed to McDowell the view of rationality he explicitly rejects in his papers on Aristotle' (2007a, p. 353).[17] Unfortunately, Dreyfus lapses again, ten pages later, when he contrasts 'detached conceptual intentionality' with 'involved motor intentionality' (ibid., p. 363). This is puzzling: Dreyfus first claims, rightly, that he and McDowell agree that conceptuality is situation-dependent; that is, not general or detached. But after that he, in the very same paper, describes conceptual intentionality as detached. It is hard to know what to make of this. In his rejoinder, McDowell observes:

> Dreyfus acknowledges that he was wrong to think practical intelligence, as I conceive it, is situation-independent. But he still thinks my view of mindedness can be characterized in terms of "detached conceptual intentionality."
>
> 2007d/2008b, p. 324

Here McDowell writes as if Dreyfus only admits that practical intelligence is situation-dependent in McDowell's sense, but in fact, he confesses that he should not understand McDowell's notions of 'rationality', 'conceptuality' and related notions as situation-independent. Therefore, I cannot see any decisive progress in Dreyfus's first reply. I am not saying that there is no progress at all, but Dreyfus still preserves the general structure from his Presidential Address. It can be dubbed the 'detachment/involvement' distinction.

Dreyfus replaces this structure with a new one in his second reply. Now the crucial distinction is constituted by 'subjectivity' and 'absorption':

> [There is] a deep issue dividing us – an issue that is obscured by my failure to distinguish explicitly *absorption* and involvement.
>
> I should have argued that *subjectivity* (not detachment) is the lingering ghost of the mental ...
>
> 2007b, p. 373; my emphasis

In this final response, Dreyfus realizes that it is inappropriate to saddle McDowell with the notion of 'detachment', and he proposes that it is 'subjectivity', by which he means the operation of 'subject' or 'agent', that is at fault. Besides, realizing that McDowell can accommodate the phenomena of 'involvement', Dreyfus submits that it is 'absorption', that is, 'involved coping *at its best*' (ibid., p. 373; my emphasis), that shows the falsity of conceptualism.[18] This completes my characterization of Dreyfus's stable framework. Now I turn to the details of his objections.

3. The final version of the general framework is the 'subjectivity/absorption' distinction. By 'subjectivity' Dreyfus means 'agency', which is 'the lingering ghost of the mental' (ibid., p. 373) according to him. As to 'absorption', he writes that '[i]n fully absorbed coping, there is no immersed *ego*, not even an implicit one' (ibid., p. 374; my emphasis). He further adds that 'in *attentive, deliberate* ... action an ego is always involved' (ibid., p. 374; my emphasis). Notice that before Dreyfus reaches this final version, the notion of 'attention' and the like has occupied a central place in his objections, including his favourite example from Chuck Knoblauch:

> As second baseman for the New York Yankees, Knoblauch was so successful he was voted best infielder of the year, but one day, rather than simply fielding a hit and throwing the ball to first base, it seems he *stepped back* and took up a "free, distanced orientation" towards the ball and how he was throwing it – to the mechanics of it, as he put it. After that, he couldn't recover his former absorption and often – though not always – threw the ball to first base erratically – once into the face of a spectator.
>
> Interestingly, even after he seemed unable to resist stepping back and being mindful, Knoblauch could still play brilliant baseball in difficult situations – catching a hard-hit ground ball and throwing it to first faster than thought. What he couldn't do was field an easy routine grounder directly to second base, because that gave him time to think before throwing to first.
>
> 2007a, p. 354

The notion of 'attention' and the like play a heavy role in Dreyfus's objections throughout the whole debate. Here is another example:

> [We] are only part-time rational animals. We can, when necessary, step back and put ourselves into a free-distanced relation to the world. We can also monitor our activity while performing it ... But *monitoring* what we are doing as we are doing it ... leads to performance which is at best competent.
>
> ibid., p. 354–5; see also p. 363

This line of argumentation, nevertheless, is both uncharitable as an interpretation and ungrounded as a thesis. Consider the passage McDowell first invokes the notion of 'stepping back':

> Consider someone following a marked trail, who at a crossing of paths goes to the right in response to a signpost pointing that way. It would be absurd to say that for going to the right to be a rational response to the signpost, it must issue from the subject's making an explicit determination that the way the signpost points gives her a reason for going to the right. What matters is just that she acts as she does because (this is a reason-introducing "because") the signpost points to the right. (This explanation competes with, for instance, supposing she goes to the right at random, without noticing the signpost, or noticing it but not understanding it.) What shows that she goes to the right in rational response to the way the signpost points might be just that she can *afterwards* answer the question why she went to the right – a request for her reason for doing that – by saying "There was a signpost pointing to the right." She need not have adverted to that reason and decided on that basis to go to the right.
>
> 2005b/2008a, p. 129[19]

First of all, notice that the subject in this scenario steps back and reflects on her *reason* for the action *retrospectively*, as opposed to Dreyfus's subject who steps back and reflects on his *mechanics* of the action when he *is carrying out the action*. So the fact that the stepping-back messed up the expertise is simply irrelevant. Secondly, it is clear that 'mindedness' never means 'attention' in McDowell's writings[20]: it would be insane to hold that our perceptual experiences (and actions) are *attentive* all the way out; if that were the claim, Mind and World would be easily refuted. Dreyfus's reading of McDowell strikes me as uncharitable.

Dreyfus reminds us that absorbed coping is involved *coping* at its best. He should have acknowledged that, by similar considerations, attention, deliberation and monitoring are *mindedness* at its best. This means that mindedness is *not* exhausted by attention and the like. To claim otherwise, Dreyfus needs to establish that attention is the mark of the mental. I see every reason to oppose to this proposition.[21]

McDowell never claims that there is an immersed or implicit self in actions, if we understand self with attention and the like. Self *does* accompany intentional actions in a weaker sense that actions are within the realm of the conceptual or the rational. But Dreyfus disagrees. He urges that cases like the chess Grandmaster show that absorbed coping is in no sense rational (2007b, p. 374). I suggest we compare that case with the case like alien hand or reflexive behaviours. Dreyfus is not willing to identify absorbed coping with mere reflexive behaviours,[22] so presumably it still has to do with our agency. Dreyfus is hostile to this idea, for he persistently confines mindedness to the realm of the attentive. But as I just said, McDowell never claims that, and the claim itself is simply wrong: when you are not paying attention to one of your beliefs, that does not disqualify that belief's status as a *mental* state. To concentrate on the notion of 'attention' is a red herring of the whole discussion.

In identifying the minded with the attentive, Dreyfus cannot make sense of McDowell's proposal:

> This pervasiveness claim, however, seems to be based on a *category mistake*. Capacities are *exercised* on occasion, but that does not allow one to conclude that, even when they are not exercised, they are, nonetheless, "*operative*" and thus pervade all our activities.
>
> ibid., p. 372; my emphasis

We are not allowed to make that conclusion, according to Dreyfus, for to claim that conceptuality is operative involves a category mistake. But that is not so. To say that conceptuality or mindedness is operative is to insist that conceptual capacities can be activated *passively*. This may sound strange for Dreyfus or some others, but they need to tell us why that is incoherent or at least problematic. McDowell offers reasons for this claim in his Locke Lecture, as we have seen above.

Dreyfus acknowledges that 'mindedness' is a technical term on McDowell's part (ibid., p. 374), but he does not really respect this point: he opens his response to McDowell by classifying 'conceptuality' and 'mindedness' as *mentalist* notions (ibid., p. 371). 'Mentalism' is a very vague term, to be sure, but to my knowledge none of its meanings fits McDowell's usage: the term can be seen in Quine's attack on old theories of meaning, and recent epistemology of perception, for example.

Dreyfus would presumably press this question: 'if mindedness is not identical to a monitoring self, then what is it?' To this McDowell has an answer:

> It is a matter of an "I do" ... Conceiving action in terms of the "I do" is a way of registering *the essential first-person character* of the realization of practical rational capacities that acting is.
>
> 2007d/2008b, p. 325

Dreyfus objects to this, but again on the false assumption that this first-person character is attention etc. (2007b, p. 375). What McDowell does mean, however, is that our absorbed coping, involved coping at its best, is not like cases such as alien hand syndrome. By contrast, in repudiating this first-person character, it is unclear how Dreyfus can leave room for the crucial distinction between absorbed coping and mere reflexive behaviours.

Dreyfus sets a dilemma between 'a meaninglessly bodily movement' and 'an action done by a subject for a reason' to McDowell (ibid., p. 374). McDowell would escape this dilemma by insisting that (intentional) bodily movements are *meaningful*. Dreyfus would agree on this point, but it should be clear that this 'motor intentionality' can be appropriately understood only by those who respect the distinction between absorbed coping and mere reflexive behaviours.

About this ownership consideration, Dreyfus says:

> Of course, the coping going on *is* mine in the sense that the coping can be interrupted at any moment by a transformation that results in an experience of stepping back from the flow of current coping. I then retrospectively attach an "I think" to the coping and take responsibility for my actions.
>
> 2007a, p. 356[23]

McDowell's explanation of this is the pervasiveness claim, but Dreyfus's is not convinced. His alternative explanation is, surprisingly enough, purely physiological (2007b, p. 374). But this is problematic. For one thing, this physiological claim is compatible with all camps in this debate; for another, if it is the whole story for Dreyfus, then how can the notion of 'responsibility' mentioned in the quotation above be explained?

Later Dreyfus seems to radicalize his answer. In describing McDowell's view he disagrees with, he writes that: 'to the question "who act?" [McDowell] responds: "the answer is 'I do'"' (ibid., p. 373). But if this is an answer Dreyfus objects to, he seems to have no alternative but commit that the answer is 'this body does'. That is why McDowell argues that '[t]he real myth in this neighborhood is ... *the Myth of the Disembodied Intellect*' (2007c/2008b. p. 322; my emphasis).[24] Dreyfus replies that this Myth is more like Gadamer's and McDowell's view, for '[i]t assumes that human beings are defined by their capacity to distance themselves from their involved coping' (2007a, p. 355). This does not seem right. Even if one holds this definition of human beings, it does not follow immediately that our mindedness is disembodied. Dreyfus rejects this because he mistakenly identifies mindedness with attention or deliberation. And McDowell attributes that Myth to Dreyfus because '[i]f you distinguish me from my body, and give my body that person-like character, you have too many person-like things in the picture ...' (2007d/2008b, p. 328). That is to say, if both the self and 'this body' are person-like things and the self is not this body, than it must be a disembodied person. Dreyfus does not address this objection at all.

Dreyfus thinks our animal nature has no philosophically interesting differences from other animals. This is backed up by what McDowell identifies as the 'quick argument': from the premise that we share basic perceptual capacities and embodied coping skills to the conclusion that 'those capacities and skills, as we have them, cannot be permeated with rationality, since other animals are not rational' (2007c/2008b, p. 313). 'But the quick argument does not work'. McDowell continues,

> [t]he claim that the capacities and skills are shared comes to no more that this: there are descriptions of things we can do that apply also to things other animals can do... But the truth about a human being's exercise of competence in making her around, in a performance that can be described like that, need not be *exhausted* by the match with what can be said about, say, a cat's correspondingly describable response to a corresponding affordance. The human being's response is, if you like, indistinguishable from the cat's response *qua* response to an affordance describable in those terms. But it does not follow that the human being's response cannot be unlike the cat's response in being the human being's rationality at work.[25]
>
> ibid., p. 313

This reflects a central thought of McDowell's thinking: when two phenomena share something, we are not forced to regard this 'something' as a *discrete* thing, 'a core' shared by these two phenomena. 'It is not compulsory', as he likes to put it. And he further argues that 'if we do take this line, there is no satisfactory way to understand the role of the supposed core in our perceptual lives' (1996a, p. 64). Here 'perceptual lives' is of course just an example. This central thought is two-staged: first, the factorizing way is not compulsory, and second, it will lead to in principle an irresolvable quandary. In the case of passivity, the devastating problem is the infamous Myth of the Given. I have discussed this in Chapter 3, but since it is highly relevant to the present debate between McDowell and Dreyfus, I shall enter into this again, though from a different angle.[26]

4. 'The Myth of the Given', to rehearse, was introduced and criticized by Wilfrid Sellars in his celebrated 'Empiricism and the Philosophy of Mind' (1956). Most contemporary philosophers identify the myth with indubitability, but that is not Sellars's original formulation.[27] Dreyfus is not aware of this:

> Given its structural similarity to empiricism, we need to make clear that existential phenomenology does not assume an *indubitable* Given on which to base empirical certainties. As with all forms of intentionality, solicitations can be *misleading* and in responding to such solicitations one can be misled.
>
> 2007a, p. 362; my emphasis

Notice that Dreyfus distances himself from the Myth of the Given by stressing that the foundations in his picture are not indubitable, but this does not respond to the mystical part of the Given identified by McDowell. Notice that when McDowell diagnoses the oscillating see-saw in modern philosophy, he never mentions 'foundationalism'. Foundationalism, at least in its stronger form, often implies indubitability, but that is *not* the problem McDowell (and Sellars) is identifying. The McDowellian problematic is constituted by coherentism and *the Myth of the Given*, not foundationalism.

The worse thing is that later Dreyfus says something which exactly falls prey to the Myth of the Given:

> The world of solicitations, then, is not foundational in the sense that it is indubitable and grounds our empirical claims, but it is the self-sufficient, constant, and pervasive background that provides the base for our dependent, intermittent, activity of stepping back, subjecting our activity to rational scrutiny, and spelling out the objective world's rational structure.
>
> ibid., p. 363

It is not clear that what the 'base-providing' claim amounts to, but obviously Dreyfus thinks solicitations have to do with our rational structures. Now how does he characterize solicitations as such? In the figure that he invokes to contrast McDowell's notion of 'world' with Merleau-Ponty's one, he writes that for phenomenologists the world is '[s]olicitations to act; [a] web of attractions and repulsions' (ibid., p. 357). Later in contrasting with 'affordance', he binds solicitations with the notion of 'drawing' (ibid., p. 361). Now solicitations sound like something in the realm of law: in this realm there is no freedom; we are just drawn into these or those movements of limbs, or 'expertise' in Dreyfus sense. Freedom kicks in when we step back and reflect, so it does not belong to solicitations, in Dreyfus's sense. Dreyfus says that solicitations 'can be misled' (ibid., p. 362), and this makes the Merleau-Pontyan world 'normative' (ibid., p. 357). But solicitations in this sense are just attractions and repulsions constituted by relations between objects and our bodies, which subject to the realm of law, so 'being misled' can be only a metaphor. By contrast, McDowell's world deserves to be called 'normative', for he argues that the world is encompassed by the realm of the conceptual, and conceptual relations are normative connectedness.

In this way, Dreyfus unwittingly commits to a version of the Myth of the Given: solicitations are inhabitants in the realm of law, but they are supposed to 'provide the base' for the space of reasons: '[t]hese solicitations have a systematic order that ... works in the background to *make rationality possible*' (ibid., p. 358; my emphasis). Given that Dreyfus is not a bald naturalist, who are willing to bite the bullet of reducing the space of reasons to the realm of law, his picture ultimately falls prey to the Myth of the Given.

I find Dreyfus's notion of 'the body' peculiar. On the one hand, he attributes the body person-like characters; on the other, the body responds to only solicitations conceived as inhabitants in the realm of law. I see no way to reconcile these two elements in his picture.

Dreyfus recognizes a problem similar to the one we are discussing: '[the existential phenomenologist] owes an account of how our absorbed, situated experience comes to be *transformed* so that we experience context-free, self-sufficient substances with detachable properties ...' (ibid., p. 364; my emphasis). But the problem is much more serious than this. Given that Dreyfus presumably accepts the *sui generis* character of the space of reasons, and given that his understanding of solicitations commits him to putting them in the realm of law, the 'owing an account' acknowledgement does not touch the real and deep problem. He goes on to accuse that 'the conceptualists can't give an account of how we are absorbed in the world ...' (ibid., p. 364). But this is not so. Given that McDowell never identifies conceptuality and mindedness with a monitoring self, cases like Knoblauch and Grandmaster are simply irrelevant. Dreyfus prefers the phenomenological approach because it 'accepts the challenge of relating the preconceptual world to the conceptual world ...' (ibid., p. 364), but what we should say is that the phenomenologist accepts the challenge *before he really appreciates it*. On the contrary, while the conceptualist also accepts the *sui generis* character of the space of reasons, he puts solicitations in the realm of the conceptual, and this avoids the Myth of the Given and intellectualism at the same time (since conceptuality is not in the realm of law, and is not identical to a monitoring self either).[28]

5. If what I have said so far is correct in general outlines, I side with McDowell that many of Heidegger's, Merleau-Ponty's and Dreyfus's thoughts should be regard as supplementations, as opposed to corrections, to the conceptualist picture (2007c/2008b). Although the cases of Knoblauch and Grandmaster are compatible with McDowell's view, more can be, and should be, said on these or other interesting cases. I conclude that though Dreyfus's objections raise interesting questions for us to think about, his case against McDowell nevertheless cuts no ice.

Before closing this section, I want to remind my readers of the relation between Dreyfus's picture criticized by McDowell and the *inner space model*. According to McDowell, Dreyfus unwittingly commits to the Myth of the Disembodied Intellect in depicting his picture of agency. This Myth, as I mentioned in passing, is parallel to the dualism of intellect and sensory lurking in Michael Ayers' thinking. Now we should further recognize that the Myth of the Disembodied Intellect is a special version of the inner space model. Originally, the inner space is defined by a self as an inner eye directing at self-standing mental items. Now in the context of bodily agency, the self-standing mental items are replaced by automaton-like bodily movements, independent of a detached self. There is a *distance* between the intellect and mindless bodily movements; with this picture at hand, 'it is too late to try to fix things by talking about the former *merging into* the latter' (ibid., p. 322; my emphasis). Dreyfus fiercely argues against any detached conception of embodied agency, but his unconscious commitment to the inner space model makes the very idea of 'embodiment' unavailable to him.

Consequently, McDowell's own position binds the subject and its bodily capacities together:

> The fact is that there is nothing for me to mean by "I," even though what I mean by "I" is correctly specified as *the thinking thing I am*, except the very thing I would be reefing to (a bit strangely) if I said "this body"...
>
> ibid., p. 322–3

And McDowell identifies 'I' with 'person' (2007d/2008b). It seems to follow that person is *identical with its living body*. This raises important issues about personhood. In the next section I discuss how McDowell conceives personhood and the mind-body relation.

There is a potential complication here. For Husserl, the *Body* (Leib) is the 'animated flesh of an animal or human being', i.e. a bodily self, while a *mere body* (Körper) is simply 'inanimate physical matter' (1913/1982, p. xiv). The Body presents itself as 'a bearer of sensations' (ibid., p. 168). A similar distinction emerges in Merleau-Ponty's work between the *phenomenal/lived* body and the *objective* body that is made of muscles, bones, and nerves (1945/2013). There is a debate over whether the distinction should be interpreted as between different entities or different perspectives of the same entity, which I will discuss (Baldwin,

1988). For Merleau-Ponty, '[t]he body is not one more among external objects' (1945/2013, p. 92). One can only be aware of oneself as the phenomenal self in one's pre-reflective awareness. This is in tension with McDowell's idea that one can 'conceive itself, the subject of its experience, as a bodily element in objective reality – as a bodily presence in the world' (1996a, p. 103). For Merleau-Ponty, '[t]he body is not one more among external objects' (1945/2013, p. 92). One can only be aware of oneself as the phenomenal self in one's pre-reflective awareness. As Frederique de Vignemont explains,

> [T]he lived body is not an object that can be perceived from various perspectives, left aside or localized in objective space. More fundamentally, the lived body cannot be an object at all because it is what makes our awareness of objects possible ... The objectified body could then no longer anchor the way we perceive the world ... The lived body is understood in terms of its practical *engagement* with the world ... [Merleau-Ponty] illustrates his view with a series of dissociations between the lived body and the objective body. For instance, the patient Schneider was unable to scratch his leg where he was stung.
>
> 2018, pp. 17–18, emphasis added

Another gloss is that the lived body is 'the location of bodily sensation' (Smith 2016, p. 148, original emphasis; cf. Merleau-Ponty, 'sensible sentient', 1964/1969, p. 137). Compare Quassim Cassam's characterisation of the physical or material body as the 'bearer of primary qualities' (2002, p. 331). Merleau-Ponty also writes, 'I observe external objects with my body, I handle them, inspect them, and walk around them. But when it comes to my body, I never observe it itself. I would need a second body to be able to do so, which would itself be unobservable' (1945/2013, p. 93). The McDowell-Cassam line is also at odds with Sartre's idea that one's body is either 'a thing among other things, or it is that by which things are revealed to me. But it cannot be both at the same time' (1943/2003, p. 304). These are all difficult and intriguing questions that are in need of further investigations. Merleau-Ponty's 'Subject-Object' (1945/2013), and Husserl's intriguing idea that the human body is 'simultaneously a spatial externality and a subjective internality' (1913/1982), can potentially shed lights on this area.[29]

Embedment

1. McDowell starts with John Locke's definition of personhood: a person is 'a thinking intelligent being, that has reason and reflection, and consider itself as itself, the same thinking being, in different time and places' (1689/1999, 3.27.9). The crux here is a person's 'inner angle' on its own persistence' (1997c/1998a, p. 359). Locke's sketchy characterization permits different ways of development. Derek Parfit thinks the only legitimate way to cash out this Lockean idea is to accept a version of 'reductionism' (1984). According to McDowell, Parfit's line of thinking presupposes a dubious dualism between 'purely mental' and 'purely material', the assumption 'that there is no alternative to reduce except to commit ourselves to continuants whose persistence through time would consist in nothing but the continuity of "consciousness" itself' (1997c/1998a, p. 360).[30] In other words, 'Locke's phenomenon must be understood in isolation' (ibid., p. 361).

McDowell introduces Gareth Evans' discussions of 'identification-freedom' at this point. McDowell comments:

> In continuity of "consciousness," there is what appears to be knowledge of an identity, the persistence of the same subject through time, without any need to take care that attention stays fixed on the same thing. Contrast keeping one's thought focused on an ordinary object of perception over a period; this requires a skill, the ability to keep track of something, whose exercise we can conceive as a practical substitute for the explicit allocation of a criterion of identity. Continuity of "consciousness" involves no analogue to this – no keeping track of the persisting self that nevertheless seems to figure in its content.
>
> ibid., p. 361–2[31]

So far, the description is pretty innocent indeed. But there is a common Cartesian response to it.[32] The response assumes that:

> [T]he content of that awareness must be provided for completely within the flow of "consciousness"; and to conclude, from the fact that no criteria for persistence through time are in play in the field to which that assumption restricts us, that what continuing to exist consists in for the continuant in question must be peculiarly simple, something that does not go beyond the flow of "consciousness" itself. In particular, this line of thought rules out the idea that the continuant in question might be a human being.
>
> ibid., p. 362

This condensed passage cries out for exposition. I think here the argument contains two premises; one is the 'narrow assumption' (within the flow of 'consciousness')[33], and the other is the 'identification-freedom'. However, it is not at all obvious that they can jointly imply the conclusion that the constituent is 'simple', and in particular, not a human being. First of all, it is not clear what 'simple' is supposed to mean, so I am going to focus on the notion of 'human being'. In the context of personal identity, 'human being' usually means human *animal*. So the conclusion is saying that the conception of the subject ('person' in this context) is at odds with a human animal. This partially explains McDowell's usage of 'simple': a human animal is constitutive of divergent parts, so it is by no means simple (i.e. it is composite).[34] Now, what does the combination of the narrow assumption and the identification-freedom amount to? I begin with the later. If we can keep track with the persistence of a given object without any effort, it follows that the object does not have 'hidden aspect', that is, *simple*. It seems to follow that we, as human animals, cannot have this power of identification-freedom. The role of the narrow assumption, however, is just to ensure this power: if all we are considering is 'within the flow of "consciousness"', which 'can hold [things] together in a single survey seem to figure within its purview' (ibid., p. 361), then the troublemaker identification-freedom is forced on us. But this does not sit well with the fact that we are human beings.

This is of course unacceptable from a naturalist point of view. According to McDowell, this motivates Parfit's reductionist response:[35]

> [T]his line of thought purports to force on us ... to revise our view of the content of the flow of "consciousness" in a Reductionist direction: to conclude that "consciousness" does not, after all, present the temporally separated states and occurrences over which it plays as belonging to the career of a single continuant, but rather as linked by a conceptually simpler relation of serial co-consciousness, which might subsequently enter into the construction of a derivative notion of a persisting subject if such a notion seems called for.
>
> ibid., p. 363

This reductionism preserves both the identification-freedom and the narrow assumption, but avoids the conclusion by *deflating* the notion of 'consciousness' involved in the narrow assumption. Since the two premises can deduce the Cartesian-flavour ego *only* on the assumption of the *ego* theory, Parfit purports to avoid the unpalatable conclusion by replacing the ego theory with the *bundle* theory.[36]

2. Rather than arguing against this reductionism immediately, McDowell proposes another line of thought in response to the original argument.

> The alternative is to leave in place the idea that continuity of "consciousness" constitutes awareness of an identity through time, but reject the assumption that

that fact needs to be provided for within a self-contained conception of the continuity of "consciousness." On the contrary, we can say: continuous "consciousness" is intelligible (even "from within") only as a subjective angle on something that has more to it than the subjective angle reveals, namely the career of an objective continuant with which the subject of the continuous "consciousness" identifies itself. The subjective angle does not contain within itself any analogue to keeping track of something ... this is thanks to its being situated in a wider context, which provides for an understanding that the persisting referent is also a third person, something whose career is substantially traceable continuity in the objective world.

ibid., p. 363

Again, the remarks here are not crystal clear. I shall understand it with the above framework. The key point here is to situate the subjective angle in a wider context, to insist that the persisting referent is also a third person. This amounts to renouncing the narrow assumption. Now how does this move discard the 'purely mental' stuff? Recall the identification-freedom condition. This condition implies that the object in question is simple, i.e. with no hidden aspects. But this is incompatible with the fact that we are human beings. We can avoid this, McDowell proposes, by recognizing that the freedom of identification in question is not freedom *simpliciter*: a subject is embedded in a wider context, as a third person. With this recognition, the identification-freedom does not imply the purely mental stuff.

Now we have two pictures competing with each other, and McDowell says that 'it should seem doubtful that Reductionism deserves respect on the ground of its opposition to Cartesian philosophy' (ibid., p. 363). Notice that reductionism is in effect 'bald naturalism' in McDowell's phrase, and McDowell's stance towards it is always to dislodge its motivation and to provide a more satisfying alternative. What he tries to point out is that Parfit's reasoning is driven by the purely mental/ purely material dichotomy. But as McDowell shows, there is a way to avoid Cartesian purely mental stuff without reducing 'consciousness': to recognize that the identification-freedom condition does *not* imply the unpalatable conclusion, for a subjective angle is also a third person, embedded in a wider context.

One might wonder in what respect McDowell's picture is a more satisfying one. Indeed, many people may prefer Parfit's solution, for reductionism seems to be a straightforward consequence of the scientific worldview. To see how McDowell promotes his position, recall that the main motivation of Parfit's position is its 'anti-Cartesian credentials' (ibid., p. 361). So if it turns out that Parfit's anti-Cartesianism does not go to the root, its plausibility will thereby be debased. According to Parfit, and indeed many others,[37] the ultimate goal here is to avoid Cartesian immaterialism. Now of course McDowell does not accept the immaterialism, but that does not mean that there is no deeper mistake to be avoided. As we have seen in Chapter 3, the deepest Cartesian mistake is the commitment to the inner space model. This is Cartesian because it asserts that our inner realms can be 'stripped of all objective context[s] by the Method of Doubt' (ibid., p. 365). This method presupposes the absolute metaphysical independence of the inner realm, and this presupposition generates all kinds of problems concerning human subject. If the immaterialism is the deeper problem, its renunciation should give us peace in philosophy. But it does not. Blackburn, Kripke and Parfit reject immaterialism, but their pictures still make intentionality and other kinds of mentality unavailable to us. The deepest Cartesian mistake, to repeat, is the inner space model, which is intimately connected to the narrow assumption. We should notice that the narrow assumption is even stronger than the inner space model, for the former can be refuted by the broadness claim, which is weaker than primeness, as indicated in Chapter 3. In urging reductionism, Parfit retains the real root of Cartesianism, the narrow assumption.

McDowell thinks Locke sometimes lapses into the Cartesian problem too, when he divides a human being 'into merely animal functions on the one hand and operations of "consciousness" on the other' (ibid., p. 367; also see Locke's 3.27.27) though he 'carefully distances himself from Descartes' (ibid., p. 369; see Locke's 3.27.10–14). Against this, McDowell thinks that we should not '[disallow] any help in understanding personal identity from the continuity of human (or, if you like, dolphin or Martian) life' (ibid., p. 369). The parenthesis is crucial. It means that here by 'human' McDowell means human *animal*. This classifies McDowell into the 'animalism' camp, but McDowell is cautious concerning the label:

> My so-called "animalism" is nothing but the Lockean conception of what a person is, freed from Locke's extra assumption so that the continuation of a certain individual life can emerge as a condition for a person to continue to exist.
> 2006b, p. 115

Normally, the label 'animalism' is for the thought that repudiates psychological continuity altogether; hence the sub-title of Eric Olson's famous book (1999). McDowell's position, by contrast, regards Locke's basic thinking as central, with the proviso that the 'consciousness' can also be instantiated by a human animal. Therefore his position is also been called 'the hybrid view' or 'the compatibilist position' (Noonan, 2019; Johansson, 2007). When we get away from the narrow assumption, we find a way to see how a subjective angle with 'identification-freedom' can be a human being.[38] 'The capacity to think, considered as including the capacity to consider oneself as oneself, [is not separable] from the capacities whose actualization constitutes a human life' (2006b, p. 114).

McDowell deepens his diagnosis by focusing on 'memory', 'the capacity to retain knowledge of one's own past' (1997c/1998a, p. 370).[39] Clearly, this is a notion reductionism cannot make use of, so its espousers need to construct a similar but 'more innocent' (from their point of view) notion. The most popular version of their *Ersatz* memory is called 'quasi-memory'.[40] 'The only difference', between real memory and this *Ersatz* one, 'is that there is no requirement that the remembering subject is identical with the subject from whose point of view the past occurrences are recaptured' (ibid., p. 370). Given this definition, it follows that 'ordinary memories are quasi-memories that satisfy that extra condition' (ibid., p. 370). This appears to be innocuous, but we need to dig deeper.

In science fiction, we often see scenarios in which memory-copying occurs. We need to notice that in those cases the copied memories are *merely quasi-memories*, for they do not 'constitute *knowledge*'; in effect, quasi-memories are '*illusions* of ordinary memory' (ibid., p. 372; my emphasis). Memories are knowledge, for they are factive, amongst other things. Quasi-memories have 'epistemic potential', but 'using [them] as a basis for knowledge would require "consciousness" to draw explicitly on information extraneous to its own contents'. In this sense, 'quasi-memory is intelligible only derivatively' (ibid., pp. 372–3).

After these elaborations, the problem behind the notion of 'quasi-memory' should be clear: given that memory is a species of knowledge, quasi-memory is the corresponding species of illusion (or even hallucination). The basic spirit of Parfit's manoeuvre here is the same as that of 'the Argument from Illusion'.[41] As McDowell observes, 'we may be tempted to think, the concept with fewer requirements must be simpler and therefore independently graspable' (ibid., p. 373). He continues,

> Well, there is no reason to assume that what is left when the requirement is dropped will stand on its own as an adequate explication of a concept. That need not be so, even though the result is admitted to be a set of necessary and sufficient conditions for the concept's application. It takes more than an arithmetic of subtracting necessary conditions to guarantee us an autonomously intelligible concept.
>
> ibid., p. 374

Again, this is a warning against the temptation to *factorize* things into simpler components. In understanding a given phenomenon, analysis is a good, if not the only, method, but that does *not* follow that every component after breaking down can stand on its own, ontological speaking. To start with quasi-memory, reductionists need to face the challenge parallel to the one posed by the Gettier-style counterexamples (1963).

In a word, '[r]eductionism is wrong, not because personal identity is a further fact, but because there is no conceptually simpler substratum for personal identity to be further to' (1997c/1998a, p. 378). McDowell illustrates this with an example:

> Not that a person should be identified with his brain and (the rest of) his body, anymore than a house should be identified with the bricks, and so forth, of which it is composed; but there is no commitment to some peculiar extra ingredient, which would ensure determinateness of identity, in a person's make-up.
>
> ibid., p. 378–9

There are some delicacies here. I think McDowell is quite right in urging that personal identity, like a house, is not a further entity, and this does not mean that it can be identified with its components. I am hesitant, however, to conclude with McDowell that there is *no further fact*. Consider the house example; is it wrong to say that being a house is a further fact, further than being composed by those bricks? This concerns our views on the nature of social reality, and I believe considerations in the case of the house can shed light on our reflections of personhood. But I shall stop myself at this point.[42]

The investigations on personal identity help us give a more satisfying answer to Dreyfus's challenge. I *am* this living body, but the 'am' here does not stand for strict identity. 'I' is not a further entity, like Cartesian soul, but it is *not* a disembodied intellect either. The satisfying picture should deliver the consequence that we are human animals, not, as Dreyfus's one does, that our bodies are intentional automata.

3. The above discussions bring us into 'the midst of the philosophy of mind' (1998a, p. viii). One might wonder where McDowell's place in the mind-body problem is. He never devotes to this issue in full length, but I shall connect those suggestive remarks to the present context.[43] A natural impression is that McDowell's position here is pretty close to Davidson's anomalous monism. McDowell admires Davidson's insistence on the 'constitutive ideal of rationality', which implies the anomalism of the mental. And this is also congenial to McDowell's insistence on the distinction between the space of reasons and the

realm of law. Nevertheless, it should be clear that McDowell would *not* agree on everything in Davidson's picture, for anomalous monism is a version of mind-brain token identity theory. As the above discussions show, McDowell opposes to strict identity between mind and brain. But now the problem arises: Davidson's version of the identity theory is already a relaxed naturalism. How can McDowell further relax it without lapsing into bad versions of dualism? The question is reminiscent of the leading question dealt with at the outset of this project. Here that deep question reappears in the context of the mind-body problem.

To understand McDowell's own position, it is helpful to see how he distinguishes himself from Davidson. McDowell has three lines of objection to Davidson's monism; the first is to question the theoretical motivations, the second is to deny one of the premises of Davidson's principal argument, and the third is to point out the problem of the conclusion. McDowell first identifies two motivations, 'the ideal of the unity of science' and 'avoidance of Cartesian dualism' (1985b/1998a, p. 339). The first is not available to Davidson, for '[a]nomalism itself, or what sustains it, neutralizes this putative motivation' (ibid., p. 339). And Cartesian dualism is irrelevant:

> [S]ince it is not events but substances that are composed of stuff, one can refuse to accept that all the events there are can be described in "physical" terms, without thereby committing oneself to a non-"physical" stuff, or compromising the thesis that persons are composed of nothing but matter.[44]
>
> ibid., p. 339

Now to the argument itself. For our purposes, we can focus solely on the premise McDowell aims to dispute, namely 'the Principle of the Nomological Character of Causality' (1985b/1998a, p. 340). It says that any causal relation is an instantiation of a strict law.[45] This understanding of causality is distinctively Humean, and Hume's argument was that 'since singular causal relations are not given in experience, there is nothing for causation to consist in but a suitable kind of generality' (ibid., p. 340). McDowell rejects this, for he has a much richer conception of experience. He concludes that the Principle of the Nomological Character of Causality is a 'fourth dogma of empiricism' (ibid., p. 340).[46] Without this dogma, Davidson's event monism does not follow.

Finally, McDowell objects to the intelligibility of the conclusion itself. As I briefly indicated above, Davidson secures the psycho-physical interactions by locating the causal relations in the physical world. But if we take this idea seriously, we find that mental properties become epiphenomena, for according to the nomological view, they are *not* in the realm of causality. As McDowell alludes to, '[a]ccording to the ontological thesis, the items that instantiate the *sui generis* spontaneity-related concepts have a location in the realm of law. But the concepts are *sui generis* precisely in that it is not by virtue of their location in the realm of law that things instantiate those concepts' (1996a, p. 75–6). That is, according to Davidson, mental properties, *qua* mental, are epiphenomena, for *qua* mental they are not in the realm of law. This is contrary to Davidson's own insistence on the psycho-physical interactions.

In pointing out the irrelevance of the avoidance Cartesian dualism, together with the inadequacy of Davidson's event monism, as we have seen, McDowell seems to accept substance monism cum *event dualism*: mental events are causally effective, for they enjoys *sui generis* 'space of reasons causations'. It is not difficult to understand why he would say this, but I am not in a position to defend it in this essay.[47]

6

Apperceiver and *Homo sentiens*

Those who believe in the forms came to this belief because they became convinced of the truth of the Heracleitean view that all sense-perceptible things are always flowing. So that if there is to be explanatory knowledge and wisdom about anything, there must be certain other natures . . . the Platonists [thereby] make them separate, and such beings they called "ideas."
Aristotle, Metaphysics, Book XIII

Self-Consciousness exists in and for itself when, and by the fact that, it so exists for another; that is, it exists only in being acknowledged.
G. W. F. Hegel, Phenomenology of Spirit

Objectivity

1. Earlier in Chapter 5, we saw how the embedment of subjectivity can set us straight about the very idea of 'the subjective angle'. Now we shall see another application of the same argument – the application on Kant's thinking about the relation between consciousness and self-consciousness. After this, I will introduce McDowell's criticisms against the dualism of scheme and content, connecting it to the present topic, and to many previous discussions in earlier chapters.

McDowell begins by venturing an interpretation of the Transcendental Deduction. Following Strawson, he thinks that in the Deduction,

> Kant seems to offer a thesis on these lines: the possibility of understanding experiences, "from within," as glimpses of objective reality is interdependent with the subject's being able to ascribe experiences to herself; hence, with the subject's being self-conscious.
>
> 1996a, p. 99

McDowell is not aiming to argue for the legitimacy of the interpretation here; instead, he argues that other parts of Kant's thinking render the interdependence thesis not satisfying. Here it goes:

> When he introduces the self-consciousness that he argues to be correlative with awareness of objective reality, he writes of the "I think" that must be able "to accompany all my representations." In the Paralogisms of Pure Reason, he claims that if we credit this "I" with a persisting referent, the relevant idea of identity through time is only formal.
>
> Ibid., p. 99. *Critique of Pure Reason*, 1787/1998, B131 and A363, respectively

Kant uses 'I think' and 'apperception' interchangeably. 'Apperception' is a term coined by Leibniz (1765/1999). He defines apperception as 'consciousness or reflective knowledge of this inner state itself and which is not given to all souls or to any souls all of the time' (1714/1991, p. 637). Although with complications, Kant's usage of this notion is basically the same. We can simply understand it as 'self-consciousness' for our purposes. I shall illustrate this with an example. Suppose that I think that the present essay will not have a great success. Now I can hold this without consciously entertaining the thought all the time. But if I say to someone, or even myself, 'I think that the present essay will not have a great success', I have a piece of 'reflective knowledge' concerning the thought. So Kant's 'I think' and Locke's 'consciousness' are generally the same notion; this is, of course, not to deny that they have extremely different theories behind their notions.

According to McDowell, Kant supplements this with an unhappy thought that the 'I think' is only 'formal'. How does Kant arrive at this dim conclusion? The situations are somewhat complicated, for this involves how Kant conceives the reasoning of Descartes. I shall quote McDowell first and explain:

> Kant's point in the Paralogisms is that the flow of what Locke calls "consciousness" does not involve applying, or otherwise ensuring conformity with, a criterion of identity ... when a subject makes this application of the idea of persistence, she needs no effort to ensure that her attention stays fixed on the same thing. For a contrast, consider keeping one's thought focused on an ordinary object of perception over a period. That requires the ability to keep track of things, a skill whose exercise we can conceive as a practical substitute for the explicit application of a criterion of identity.
>
> 1996a, p. 100

This is essentially the same line of thought as the one applied to Parfit. But here the player is Descartes:

> If the topic of the thought is a substantial continuant, what its continuing to exist consists in must be peculiarly simple. The notion of persistence applies itself effortlessly; there is nothing to it except the flow of "consciousness" itself. This looks like a recipe for arriving at the conception, or supposed conception, of the referent of "I" that figures in Descartes.
>
> ibid., p. 101

We have seen that Parfit avoids this reasoning by reducing 'consciousness' to a series of co-consciousness. This is a way to *deflate* the very idea of self-consciousness. Now Kant does not share the reductionist agenda, so he attempts to deflate 'consciousness' in another way, as McDowell observes, 'it can easily seem that we had better draw Kant's conclusion: the idea of persistence that figures in the flow of 'consciousness' had better be only formal' (ibid., p. 101). McDowell's response here, again, is virtually the same as his treatment to Parfit's problem:

> It is true that the continuity within the subjective take does not involve keeping track of a persisting thing, but this effortlessness does not require us to agree with Kant that the idea of identity here is only formal. Even "from within," the subjective take is understood as situated in a wider context; so there can be more content to the idea of persistence it embodies. The wider context makes it possible to understand that the first person, the continuing referent of the "I" in the "I think" that can "accompany all my representations," is also a third person, something whose career is a substantial continuity in the *objective* world: something such that other modes of continuing thought about it would indeed require keeping track of it.
>
> ibid., p. 101–2, my emphasis

Although this argument has been explained in Chapter 5, let me say something more in line with the present context. The 'identification-freedom' is the shared starting point of all camps. The Cartesian explains this by substance dualism: within this realm of mental substance, everything is transparent or luminous, so one does not need to keep track of her mental phenomena. Kant resists this reasoning by insisting that the 'I think', apperception, is only formal: the fact that we enjoy effortlessness when it comes to our own mental phenomena implies that the 'I think' is only formal, that is, does not have any hidden aspect.

But McDowell points out that this argument does not go through, for it involves two different senses of *effortless*. What the 'accompanying' idea implies is 'first-person effortless', but what implies the 'formal' idea is 'effortless *simpliciter*': if we get effortless all the way out, then the subject matter in question is indeed insubstantial. But we need to remember that from a third-person point of view, any 'I think' need to be kept track if the idea of persistence is to be applied. Every 'I think' is also a third person, embedded in the objective world.

After pinpointing the fault of Kant's argument, McDowell goes on to explain why Kant's picture is unsatisfying. First the characterization:

> The result of Kant's move is that the subjective continuity he appeals to, as part of what it is for experience to bear on objective reality, cannot be equated with the continuing life of a perceiving animal. It shrinks, as I said, to the continuity of a mere point of view: something that need not have anything to do with a body, so far as the claim of interdependence is concerned.
>
> ibid., p. 102

And then the criticism:

> If we begin with a free-standing notion of an experiential route through objective reality, a temporally extended point of view that might be bodiless so far as the connection between subjectivity and objectivity goes, there seems to be no prospect of building up from there to the notion of a substantial presence in the world. If something starts out conceiving itself as a merely formal referent of "I" (which is already a peculiar notion), how could it come to appropriate a body, so that it might identify itself with a particular living thing?
>
> ibid., pp. 102–3

The argument here is that it comes too late to do justice to the fact that every one of us, 'the subject of its experience, [is] a bodily element in *objective* reality – [is] a *bodily presence* in the world' (ibid., p. 103; my emphasis). It is too late, because

> [I]t leaves us with what look like descendants of those problems [i.e. the familiar Cartesian problems about the relation between a peculiar substance and the rest of reality]. If we start from a putative sense of self as at most geometrically in the world, how can we work up from there to the sense of self we actually have, as a bodily presence in the world?
>
> ibid., p. 104

The general thought is this. It is a fact that we are bodily presences in the objective world; we are subjects, to be sure, but we are also *objects*. It is *not* the case that only our bodies, our behaviours, are objects in the world, objects of other subjects' experiences. What we should say is that it is *we*, not our bodies and behaviours conceived in behaviouristic terms, are objects in the objective world. We are *not mere points of view* in the geometrical realm. Any conception of subjectivity has to respect this, but Kant's picture seems to fail exactly at this point. The acceptance of the narrow assumption betrays Kant's residual Cartesianism.[1]

Kant is always hostile to the Cartesian philosophy, so officially he rejects the narrow assumption – '*I think* is thus the sole text of rational psychology, from which it is to develop its entire wisdom'. (1787/1998, A343/B401) – pointing out that it is not warranted by 'first-person effortless'; however, his failure to distinguish between 'first-person effortless' and 'effortless *simpliciter*' betrays his unwitting commitment to that very assumption, as in Parfit's case.

2. The issue about 'identification-freedom' is itself a big topic, and here is not the place to get involved too much. However, since McDowell's argument is aiming at Kant, I must take care of this exegesis aspect to some extent. My way of doing this is to consider objections from Maximilian de Gaynesford, who thinks McDowell's, and indeed Strawson's, presentation of Kant's argument is unfair.[2]

De Gaynesford first reconstructs McDowell's argument as follows:

(1) The *I* of the "I think" refers.
(2) There is no Cartesian ego (rational psychologism's immaterial substance) for the *I* of the "I think" to refer to.
(3) The narrow assumption holds for the "I think."
(4) Criterionless self-ascription holds for the "I think."
(5) So the referent of the *I* of the "I think" must be merely formal (if it were a substantial subject, then it could only be an immaterial one, *pace* (2); for only so could the idea of its persistence be provided for in accord with (3) and (4) – i.e. effortlessly and entirely from within the flow of self-consciousness).

2003, p. 158

I disagree with several points in this reconstruction, but I shall present them in replying to de Gaynesford's particular objections. The only thing I want to say before going into the details is that in the above reconstruction de Gaynesford never refers to specific passages from McDowell, and this makes it hard to take issue with this detailed reconstruction. Even before the reconstruction, de Gaynesford refers to *Mind and World* only seldom. Generally, I think his reconstruction over-complicates the matter, but let me show this with de Gaynesford's framework.

The first objection from him is about (1) and (5) that 'Kant is careful not to commit himself to the claim that the *I* of the "I think" refers' (ibid., p. 158). We can agree on this to some extent, but with a proviso: though Strawson, Evans and McDowell frame the issue with terms such as 'reference', we need to remember that Kant was *not* doing philosophy of language in the contemporary sense, and Strawson et al. certainly know this. I believe a charitable understanding of their interpretation of Kant should recognize this, and try to understand their interpretation without regarding those terms in philosophy of language as central. Now I think my way of reconstructing the argument is better in this respect; to rehearse: Kant points out that the 'I think' must be able to accompany all my representations, which implies the effortless in our own case, and this effortless in turn implies that the 'I think' must be a formal condition. Nothing in this line of reasoning, as far as I can tell, invokes notions such as 'reference'. So I think this first objection can be answered by pointing out that notions from philosophy of language in the contemporary sense are not essential to interpretations offered by Strawson et al.

The second objection is against (2). De Gaynesford argues that 'Kant does not reject the rational psychologist's conception of the ego as one of his premises in the Paralogisms' (ibid., p. 159). As he reminds, the falsity of a given paralogism is due to its form 'whatever its content may otherwise be' (1787/1998, A341/B399). Indeed, everyone who is familiar to the *First Critique* to some extent knows that in Paralogisms Kant's aim is to expose bad *reasoning*, not bad theses. Now how could McDowell miss this? Or better, how could de Gaynesford think that McDowell misses this? Again, McDowell's reconstruction of Kant's argument is from the 'accompanying' idea to the 'effortless' and finally to the 'formal condition'. Nothing here involves a blank rejection of Cartesian substance dualism. That is why what McDowell says is that 'it can easily seem that we *had better* draw Kant's conclusion' (1996a, p. 101; my emphasis). McDowell of course notices that Kant is pointing out that rational psychologist's inference is *not compulsory*.

The third objection is also not difficult to answer. 'The narrow assumption is Kant's *target* in the Paralogisms, not his tenet' (De Gaynesford, 2003, p. 159), *pace* (3). As I have said earlier, the residual Cartesianism accusation is that Kant *tacitly* assumes a central Cartesian assumption, not that he happily endorses that. In failing to distinguish first-person effortless and effortless *simpliciter*, Kant's argument for his own position nevertheless involves the narrow assumption. De Gaynesford quotes Kant's declaration of the denial, but he does not notice that without the narrow assumption, Kant's original argument cannot go through.

The following two objections from de Gaynesford are closely related, so I shall answer them together. Against (4), he argues that the 'criterionless self-ascription' may be correct, but 'Strawson fails to show that Kant held it', and 'it would be oddly inconsistent for Kant to hold it' (ibid., p. 159, 160).[3] De Gaynesford first points out that Strawson and McDowell are 'almost alone among Kant's commentators in even mentioning the thesis... in relation to Kant', and they do 'not cite texts where the thesis is adopted by Kant, either explicitly or implicitly' (ibid., p. 159, 160). And he further presents how Kant himself conceives the situation. This raises important exegetic issues, but I tend to think that we can say Kant *implicitly* adopts that thesis in connecting his positive and negative thoughts: his claim that *I* of the apperception must be able to accompany all one's representations, and that rational psychologist's reasoning to the substantial *Cogito* is a *non sequitur*. To make sense of the relation between the Transcendental Deduction and Paralogisms, it seems reasonable to say that Kant commits the 'criterionless of self-ascription' tacitly. The thesis as such is harmless; the trouble lies rather in the narrow assumption. De Gaynesford's presentation of Kant's relevant texts is helpful, but it does not undermine the Strawson-McDowell diagnosis.

The issue concerning McDowell's interpretation of Kant is enormous, and to give a satisfying defence is going beyond the current purposes. But I hope my discussions of the above objections from de Gaynesford can at least dampen some initial worries about the exegetic aspect of McDowell's thinking.

3. At this stage I would like to connect the present discussion to a larger concern of McDowell, that is, his attacks on the dualism of scheme and content. I want to do so because that larger concern also underlies most, if not all, of McDowell's thinking, which has been discussed throughout the essay. Let me start with the very idea of that dualism.

'Scheme-content dualism' was first introduced by Donald Davidson as a critical target (1974/2001b). In a later paper he comments that '[t]his picture of mind and its place in nature has defined many of the problems modern philosophy has thought it had to solve' (1988/2001c, p. 41) This theme was subsequently taken up by McDowell in various writings, as we shall see. Both of them are hostile to this dualism, but they also find each other's characterization of it problematic: both of them present the dualism as a conception of the relation between mind and world, but while Davidson construes it in *evidential* terms, McDowell thinks it does not go to the root of the problem and presents his version in *intentional* terms. Let me start with Davidson. The opening paragraph of his 1974 paper goes like this:

> Philosophers of many persuasions are prone to talk of conceptual schemes. Conceptual schemes, we are told, are ways of organizing experience; they are systems of categories that give form to the data of sensation; they are points of view from which individuals, cultures or periods survey the passing scene. There may be no *translation* from one scheme to another, in which case the beliefs, desires, hopes, and bits of knowledge that characterize one person have no true counterparts for the subscriber to another scheme. Reality itself is relative to a scheme: what counts as real in one system may not in another.
>
> 1974/2001b, p. 183

Here we can see that the dualism itself has many faces and to a large extent metaphorical, but we can see that in characterizing it, Davidson uses 'translation', a *semantic* notion. So one would not be surprised when Davidson says this in response to McDowell:

> I was clear from the start that unconceptualized "experience," sense data, sensations, Hume's impressions and ideas, could not coherently serve as *evidence* for beliefs: only something with propositional content could do this.
>
> 1999, p. 105

For Davidson, the target to be criticized is 'conceptual relativism', as he makes clear at the beginning of the 1974 paper. And for A to be relative to B, both of them must be *contentful* in the first place. Now, given that both of them are contentful, 'evidence' is the only thing that can determine whether they are commensurable or not. So it seems natural for Davidson to grant contents to the alleged conceptual schemes and to focus on the notion of 'evidence'.

McDowell objects to this. He thinks Davidson grants too much to the opponent. He writes:

> The dualism, on my reading, generates a much more radical anxiety about whether we are in touch with reality. Within the dualism, it becomes unintelligible that we have a world view at all.
>
> 1999b/2008b, p. 121

McDowell further argues that on the one hand, his understanding and diagnosis of the dualism are more basic, since Davidson leaves the *contentfulness* of the conceptual scheme unquestioned; on the other hand, Davidson gives up too much when he renounces 'minimal empiricism', the idea that experiences constitute the tribunal for human rationality. But I shall leave this aside and turn to McDowell's analysis of the dualism. McDowell's main thought is that since it is a kind of dualism, the two elements must be 'dualistically set over against' each other (1996a, p. 3). Thus, the content side should be 'non-conceptual content', and the scheme side 'non-contentful scheme'. But this generates a problem immediately:

> If abstracting it from content leaves a scheme empty, what can be the point of identifying this side of the dualism as *the conceptual*? It is not a routine idea that concepts and their exercises, considered in themselves, are empty, and it is not obvious why it should seem that we can abstract them away from what makes the embracing of beliefs or theories non-empty, but still have concepts and their exercises – what they essentially are – in view.
>
> 1999b/2008b, p. 116

The problem is this: scheme-content dualism is supposed to be an extraordinarily tempting view, for it sets out the agenda of modern philosophy, both Davidson and McDowell argue. But if the scheme side denotes 'non-contentful scheme', or more annoyingly, 'non-contentful *concept*', it is not clear that this dualism has any initial plausibility at all. McDowell dampens this doubt in this way:

> First, that the linkage between concepts that constitute the shape, so to speak, of a conceptual scheme are linkages that pertain to what is a reason for what. Second, that if matter, in this application of the form-matter contrast, is supplied by the deliverances of the sense, then the structure of reason must lie on the other side of the matter-form contrast, and hence must be formal; reason is set over against the senses.
>
> ibid., p. 116

As McDowell understands it, the scheme side should be understood as 'reason', or more precisely, '*pure* reason', as opposed to '*empirical* content'. It is our rational structure, as opposed to sense content. This, I believe, makes the dualism more plausible. And this looks like Kant's insistence that the *I* of apperception is only 'formal', so as to be able to 'accompany all one's representations'. We have seen how McDowell criticizes Kant's argument for this position, and now I suggest that this can be further related to McDowell's denial of the dualism.

As we shall see presently, McDowell applies his diagnosis of this dualism to many issues, and I will take care of them one by one. In the present case, we can see the dualism as an instantiation of the inner space model, constituted by the formal *I* and its representations. This model is a nonstarter, for it makes intentionality unavailable to us. And given Kant's thesis of the interdependence between self-consciousness and consciousness of the world, the model also makes apperception unavailable.

We can also see the connection between scheme-content dualism and the inner space model in the context of knowledge. In Chapter 3, we have seen that McDowell thinks epistemology in the twentieth century suffers the 'interiorisation of the space of reasons'. After identifying the space of reasons with the space of concepts, he suggests that:

> [W]e can see the interiorization of the space of reasons as a form of a familiar tendency in philosophy: the tendency to picture the objective world as set over against a "conceptual scheme" that has withdrawn into a kind of self-sufficiency The fantasy of a sphere within which reason is in full autonomous control is one element in the complex aetiology of this dualism. The dualism yields a picture in which the realm of matter, which is, in so far as it impinges on us, the Given, confronts the realm of forms, which is the realm of thought, the realm in which subjectivity has its being.
>
> 1995b/1998b, p. 408

McDowell also calls this dualism the 'dualism of subjective and objective – or inner and outer' (ibid., p. 409). Once we conceive our inner world as under full autonomous control, our reach to the external world becomes problematic.

A related discussion can be found in the relation between German Idealism and the inner world conceived by Wittgenstein. German idealism gives up the 'in itself' talk, arguing that 'world and thought are constitutively made for one another' (1991a/1998a, pp. 306–7). In this context, one may want to rebut this by saying that 'in the inner life the "in itself," brutely alien to concepts, insistently makes its presence felt. The inner world is a lived refutation of idealism' (ibid., p. 307). But as we have seen, the retreat from the external world makes the external world totally unavailable to us.

Another prominent example is the conceptuality of experience. Again, in the opening of his Locke Lecture, McDowell mentions Kant's famous slogan: 'Thoughts without content are empty, intuitions without concepts are blind' (1787/1998, A51/B75). This can be read with the dualism of scheme and content, that is, frictionless scheme and nonconceptual given. If one recognizes that nonconceptual given cannot bring us intentionality and justification, one is prone to accept coherentism; if by contrast, one insists on the crucial role of nonconceptual, experiential intake, one commits to the Myth of the Given.[4] We have seen the inadequacy of both positions in Chapter 3, and McDowell's alternative, as I discussed in Chapter 5, is that experiences are conceptual all the way down; scheme and content do not dualistically oppose to each other. In this way, McDowell applies the diagnosis of scheme-content dualism to the topic of 'experience'. This can also be related to the inner space model: 'pure' empirical content, 'uncontaminated' by reasons, can serve to sustain intentionality. This does not work, for 'experiences' so conceived just 'stand there like a sign-post' (Wittgenstein, 1953/2001, §85).[5] This normatively inert thing cannot do any work for intentionality. In addition, though we often concentrate on 'outer' experience, 'the dualism ought to be equally wrong about purely "inner" experiences: pains, tickles, and the like' (1989c/1998a, p. 279). McDowell explains further:

> What is essential is to avoid the temptation to suppose that when, say, a cat, or a human infant, is in pain, what constitutes the relevant kind of episode in our inner lives is *all there* in the cat's, or infant's, consciousness, barring only the ability to talk...
>
> ibid., p. 294

Here McDowell connects scheme-content dualism to the factorization approach: it is tempting to think of animals' or human infants' inner experiences in a factorized way, but that generates hopeless problems as we have seen in other cases. Although it is the easiest for us to lapse in this domain, we should hold firm to the lessons we have learned elsewhere.

The final example I want to discuss is McDowell case against Hume's conception of causality, briefly discussed at the end of Chapter 5. For Hume, 'singular causal relations are not given in experience', and 'this recommendation seems inextricably bound up with a "dualism of scheme and content, of organizing system and something waiting to be organized" ...' (1985b/1998a, p. 340). For Hume and his followers, experience is unorganized, but this falls into the guilty dualism. As mentioned earlier, this 'Nomological Character of Causality' is accused by McDowell as 'the fourth dogma of empiricism'. This is, nevertheless, accepted by Davidson and most contemporary empiricists.

Although McDowell disputes Davidson's exact formulation of the dualism, he definitely agrees with Davidson that:

> In giving up the dualism of scheme and world, we do not give up the world, but re-establish unmediated touch with the familiar objects whose antics make our sentences and opinion true or false.
>
> 1974/2001b, p. 198

And the recapitulation above shows how this repudiation of the dualism can be done in different regions of philosophy. If we want real *objectivity*, we must acknowledge the 'interpenetration of the subjective and the objective',[6] *contra* most philosophical outlooks.

Subjectivity

1. The title of the essay is *John McDowell on Worldly Subjectivity*, and the title for Chapter 1 is 'The Many Faces of Human Subject'. So far I have been exploring aspects of subject through discussing McDowell's philosophy, and my working hypothesis, as I said in Chapter 1, is that the best way to understand subjectivity is to understand various *aspects* of it. Now I come close to the core of this project, that is, subjectivity *per se*. By this I mean the narrow sense of subjectivity – the 'what-it-is-like' aspect. Any conception of subjectivity should not content itself if it does not offer any account of consciousness.

However, 'consciousness' is never a main theme of McDowell's thinking. He does talk about it from time to time, but always only in passing. The reason is that what he concerns is the direct *contact* between mind and world, and the problem of *sentience* is less central than *sapience* relative to this goal, at least on the face of it. Therefore, in this section I need to elaborate and extrapolate, as opposed to merely interpret and evaluate, McDowell's line of thought. This requires me to say something not directly about McDowell, but the digression will prove fruitful.

I shall begin by an observation from Ned Block:

> The greatest chasm in the philosophy of mind – maybe even all of philosophy – divides two perspectives on consciousness. The two perspectives differ on whether there is anything in the phenomenal character of conscious experience that goes beyond the intentional, the cognitive, and the functional . . . Those who think that the phenomenal character of conscious experience goes beyond the intentional, the cognitive, and the functional believe in qualia.
>
> 2003/2007b, p. 533[7]

Let me explain. Almost everyone agrees that there are two main aspects of the mental, the phenomenal and the intentional. The former refers to the 'what-it-is-like' aspect; the latter refers to 'what-it-is-about'. Some mental states sustain both aspects, such as perception, some others might sustain only one of them, like pain (phenomenal) and belief (intentional).[8] What is at issue is that whether the phenomenal 'goes beyond' the intentional, as Block puts. Those who hold the positive answer commit the existence of 'qualia'. 'Qualia' is the plural of 'quale', which has been heavily theory-laden, but we can learn its essential traits by considering the positions that deny its existence. As Block succinctly summarizes above, qualia is non-intentional, non-functional, and non-cognitive qualities of experience. I slightly change Block's order, for we can understand 'non-intentional' and 'non-functional' with the notion of 'non-relational', that is, 'intrinsic'.[9] Therefore, we can identify qualia as 'non-cognitive' and 'intrinsic' qualities of experience.[10] Now those who think intentional properties exhaust phenomenal characters deny the existence of any 'non-cognitive', 'intrinsic' quality of experience. This denial of qualia has been called the 'intentional theory of consciousness', or simply 'intentionalism'.[11] Intentionalism maintains that there is no intrinsic quality of experience, and experiences are cognitive through and through. I shall argue that McDowell holds a form of intentionalism.[12]

Let me begin by McDowell's own words:

> I urge that we could not recognize capacities operative in experience as conceptual at all were it not for the way they are *integrated into a rationally organized network of capacities* for active adjustment of one's thinking to the deliverances of experience. That is what a repertoire of empirical concepts is. The integration serves to place even the most immediate judgements of experience as possible elements in a world-view.
>
> 1996a, p. 29; my emphasis

He extends this claim even to 'concepts of secondary qualities', though they are only '*minimally* integrated into the active business of accommodating one's thinking to the continuing deliverances of experience ...' (ibid., pp. 29–30; my emphasis). The main reason for this, not surprisingly, is *transcendental*: intentionality and rational entitlement are *possible only if* every bit of mentality is *integrated* into a *cognitive* net. Suppose, for the sake of argument, that I am struck by a bunch of blue qualia. By definition, it follows that I am struck by a bunch of blue *non-cognitive* qualities of experience. Now how could these qualities, given that they are non-cognitive, have any intentional and rational bearings with my thoughts? How can I, for example, refer to my non-cognitive blue qualia to *justify* my experiential judgements? Philosophers who commit the existence of qualia seldom address, or even recognize, this puzzle. Although McDowell never makes clear about his attitude towards qualia, it is reasonable to conjecture that he holds a version of intentionalism.

A similar consideration is from his rebuttal of the dualism of scheme and content. The scheme side is constituted by rational connectedness; the content side is thereby populated by items that do not have any rational relations with each other. It seems clear that the qualia theory is a variant of scheme-content dualism, and we have also seen why we should resist it.

So far I have concentrated on the 'non-cognitive' aspect, but the argument can be naturally extended to 'intrinsicality': the *cognitive* net is constituted by rational *relations*, so 'non-cognitive' and 'intrinsic' go hand in hand. If we accept the two lines of argument presented above by McDowell, the two essential traits of qualia are thereby rejected. It should be clear, then, that McDowell is an intentionalist about consciousness.

2. Since the present essay is not primarily about consciousness, I have omitted lots of complications surrounding this heated topic. However, there is one issue that I must deal with: the issue about the compatibility between *intentionalism* and *disjunctivism*. I cannot ignore this concern because my goal in this essay is to present McDowell's philosophy, and consistency is arguably the minimal requirement. Readers shall find that the situation is extremely convoluted, and the needed clarifications will be lengthy. I will explain why these two views seem to be incompatible at the first blush, but first consider this passage from Tim Crane:

> I [argue] that there is a large chasm in the philosophy of perception, but that is created by the dispute about whether experience is *relational*. It is this dispute – between "intentionalists" and "disjunctivists" – which contains the most recalcitrant problems of perception. The major theories of perception in contemporary analytic philosophy line up on either side of this dispute.
>
> 2006, p. 128

In saying this, Crane has Block in mind as his main opponent:

> I [argue] that as far as the philosophy of perception is concerned, the dispute over the existence of qualia is not very significant at all ...It may be that in other parts of philosophy of mind ... the existence of qualia is a chasm-creating question. (Actually, I doubt this too ...)
>
> ibid., p. 127

In his footnote, Crane says that Chalmers and Block 'express the problem of consciousness in terms of the notion of qualia', but 'their dispute is not over the existence of qualia, but over whether they can be physicalistically explained' (ibid., p. 127). Crane's choice of example strikes me as apt: Block is a physicalist, while Chalmers is not. Now, since here our topic is perception, I shall leave this to my readers and focus on theories of perception instead.

Crane claims that the debate between intentionalism and disjunctivism creates *the* chasm in philosophy of perception. If this is so, my attribution of intentionalism to McDowell is problematic, for he is a self-deemed disjunctivist. I will argue, however, that Crane chasm-creating claim is based on a false conception of issues concerning perception, and that there is a much deeper problem concerning the notion of 'intentionalism' accepted by Crane and many others. Without these two failures, one can consistently hold intentionalism and disjunctivism at the same time. But before that, I need to say something more about disjunctivism, and McDowell's version of it.

According to Adrian Haddock and Fiona Macpherson (2008), disjunctivism about perception can be roughly divided into three versions. They are J. M. Hinton's and Paul Snowdon's 'experiential disjunctivism', John McDowell's 'epistemological disjunctivism', and M. G. F. Martin's 'phenomenal disjunctivism'.[13] The experiential version is about 'the nature of experience' (ibid., p. 1), more precisely, about perceptual 'state'.[14] Therefore I suggest that we call this version '*state* disjunctivism', in order to highlight its difference from the phenomenal version. The epistemological version is about 'the epistemic warrant' (ibid., p. 1) provided by experiences. The phenomenal version concerns 'experience's phenomenal character' (ibid., p. 1). There might be another version of disjunctivism, which maintains that 'a veridical experience shares no content with its corresponding hallucination' (Byrne, 2001, p. 202). I shall call this 'content disjunctivism'. Haddock and Macpherson regard state (experiential) and phenomenal disjunctivism as 'two sub-varieties of *metaphysical* disjunctivism' (ibid., p. 21; my emphasis), as opposed to McDowell's epistemological version. I find this way of putting things potentially misleading: presumably, phenomenal disjunctivism can be seen as a kind of metaphysical disjunctivism because it is about the *nature*, the *metaphysics* of phenomenal character. By the same token, state and content disjunctivism are metaphysical in the sense that they are about the nature, the metaphysics of state and content, respectively. But if so, the so-called 'epistemological' disjunctivism is metaphysical in the same sense, for it is about the nature, the metaphysics, as opposed to the *epistemology* of reason. So I suggest that we replace the label 'epistemological disjunctivism' with '*reason* disjunctivism': it is *not* the case that we have the same reason in subjectively indistinguishable veridical experience and its deceptive counterpart; instead, in the good case we have an *indefeasible* reason, which is absent in the bad case. So according to my way of labelling, we have four versions of disjunctivism about perception: Hinton's and Snowdon's *state* version, McDowell's *reason* version, Martin's *phenomenal* version, and Byrne's *content* version.[15]

What version(s) of disjunctivism does Crane have in mind when he makes the chasm-creating claim? There he mentions most representatives, including Hinton, Snowdon, McDowell, Martin, Putnam and Williamson, so we cannot find out the answer through the player list. Fortunately, later he says that disjunctivism '[denies] that the hallucination and the subjectively indistinguishable perception are *states* of the same fundamental psychological kind' (2006, p. 139; my emphasis). Therefore we can reasonably think that he locates the battlefield within the 'state' view. Now a quick argument on McDowell's behalf might be suggested: since McDowell's disjunctivism is the *reason* view, the putative inconsistency between *state* disjunctivism and intentionalism is simply irrelevant. This does not work, unfortunately, because according to my interpretation McDowell also holds *state* disjunctivism. Consider McDowell's main target in his overall thinking, the inner space model. This putative inner space is constituted by self-standing mental *items*. Items are things, and McDowell's alternative is that mental things – mental *state*s – are prime, that is, *inextricably* involved *external* conditions.[16] The inner space is a metaphysical position, and McDowell's anti-Cartesian alternative, i.e. disjunctivism, must have some metaphysical flavour too. In particular, the inner space theory is wrong about the nature of mental *states*, i.e. as free-floating items, so its opponent disjunctivism should be about mental *states* also.[17] This is not to fly in the face of the obvious fact that in his papers on epistemology McDowell argues for the reason version of disjunctivism; it is just that in responding to different challenges, he defends different versions of the doctrine.

What is the relation between the state and the reason version of disjunctivism? In their co-authored paper, Alex Byrne and Heather Logue (2008) argue that the former implies the latter, but not *vice versa*.[18] I shall not take issue with this claim, but dispute their claim that McDowell denies state disjunctivism. They offer two textual evidences, from 'Criteria, Defeasibility, and Knowledge' (1982b/1998b) and 'The Disjunctive Conception of Experience as Material for a Transcendental Argument' (2006c/2008b) respectively. First, '[i]t 'look[s] to one exactly as if things [are] a certain way' in the good case and the illusory cases, and there is the strong suggestion that this is a perfectly proper mental respect of similarity' (Byrne and Logue, 2008, p. 67). I do not understand. Here McDowell only says 'it *looks* to one exactly as if . . .', but this is no more than a description of subjective indistinguishability. Maybe by this remark McDowell rejects strong *phenomenal* disjunctivism, as I shall explain presently, but that is irrelevant to *state* disjunctivism. Let's turn to the second quotation. There McDowell says that the 'difference in epistemic significance is of course consistent with all sorts of commonalities between the disjuncts. For instance, on both sides of the disjunction it appears to one that, say, there is a red cube in front of one' (2006c/2008b, p. 232). Again, I do not see how the quoted remarks help establish their point. For one thing, 'it *appears* to one that . . .' is again phenomenal[19]; for another, to say that the difference in epistemic significance is consistent with all sorts of commonalities is not to say that other forms of disjunctivism are precluded. It is just that reason disjunctivism does not expel the common kind theory in other domains. Byrne and Logue's case for the claim that McDowell refuses to accept state disjunctivism seems to fail. McDowell argues against self-standing mental *items* in the 'singular thought' paper. Byrne and Logue does cite the paper, but for some other purposes.

So we need to respond to Crane's challenge after all, given that McDowell is a state disjunctivist. But again before this, I hope to say more about McDowell's relations to two other versions of disjunctivism. Sometimes McDowell writes as if he thinks a veridical experience and its deceptive counterpart can share the same content, for example he says that 'a kind of actualization of conceptual capacities [are operative in] cases of *perceiving*, or at least *seeming* to perceive, that things are thus and so' (2005b/2008a, p. 132).[20] But I think it is better to say that he also holds *content* disjunctivism, which says that in the good case and in the bad case there is no shared content in play. Let me explain. There is a sense in which there is one and the same content shared by a veridical experience and its deceptive counterpart: that both of them can be characterized by 'that things are thus and so'. I think this is what McDowell insists on. But in a more important sense, those episodes do not share the same content, for in the good case the contents of experience are *facts*, and facts do not present in the bad case. We can say that those episodes share the same content, 'that things are thus and so', and in the good case the content is true, in the bad case the content is false. This is plain, but we need to remember that for McDowell, true contents are facts. When the content is true, the nature of this very content has been transformed from 'mere appearance' (1982b/1998b, p. 386) to 'fact'. For McDowell, we cannot *factorize* facts into truth-value and contents. So I think it is better to say that McDowell is a *content* disjunctivist, with the proviso that he does not deny that a veridical experience and its deceptive counterpart can have the same propositional structure, 'that things are thus and so'.

How about phenomenal disjunctivism? This version of disjunctivism itself comes with two sub-versions. The weak one leaves subjective indistinguishability in place, but argues that the explanations of the phenomenal characters in veridical experiences and deceptive ones are different.[21] The strong one challenges the indistinguishability itself.[22] Now we have seen that McDowell always starts his argumentation against the inner space with the acknowledgement of subjective indistinguishability; maybe he does this for the sake of argument, but anyway there is no reason to saddle him with strong phenomenal disjunctivism.

How about the weak version? This weaker one says that though a veridical experience and its deceptive counterpart can share the same phenomenal characters, we need to have different explanations for the good case and the bad case respectively. Since McDowell is an intentionalist, he would invoke the intentional part of experience to explain its phenomenology. And since for him in the good case and in the bad case we do not have the same content, we can have different explanations for phenomenal characters in the good case and in the bad case respectively.[23] Just how this can be done exactly is not clear. But I think it is safe to say that McDowell is a weak phenomenal disjunctivist: as a philosopher who abandons the Cartesian inner/outer divide by externalizing reasons, mental states and mental contents, there seems to be no reason for him to stop in the case of phenomenology.[24] However, I must admit that so far I see no clue to pursue this line. I shall leave this to other occasions, and come back to Crane's challenge that the controversy between disjunctivism and intentionalism creates a large chasm in philosophy of perception.

3. Philosophy of perception, like other philosophical enterprises, consists in plenty of intertwined questions. But most if not all practitioners agree that arguably the most central question is our perceptual *contact* with the world, challenged by the argument from illusion and from hallucination, amongst others.[25] Crane echoes this point by saying that '[w]ithout challenges like this [i.e. those which are raised by the argument from illusion and related arguments], it is somewhat hard to see why we would need a philosophical theory of perception at all' (2006, p. 142). I agree with this, but I have reservations concerning Crane's claim that he has shown 'how the main theories of perception are best seen as responding to these problems' (ibid., p. 142). To see this, we must consider the argument from illusion as such.[26]

Here I adopt A. D. Smith's formulation. Schematically, it runs as follows:

P1. The Possibility of Illusion
P2. The Sense-Datum Inference
P3. Leibniz Law
P4. The Generalizing Step.

P1 is true because 'any sense involves the functioning of sense receptors that can, in principle, malfunction' (2002, p. 25). And we are entitled to ask if illusions do occur, what do we perceive or experience in those cases? This is a question concerning the *object* of experience. P2 says that 'whenever something perceptually *appears* to have a feature when it actually does not, we are aware of something that *does* actually possess that feature' (ibid., p. 25; my emphasis). And we introduce 'sense-datum' as a name for these perceived objects.[27] P3 is an application of Leibniz Law, saying that 'since the appearing physical object does not possess that feature which ... we are immediately aware of in the illusory situation, it is not the physical object of which we are aware in such a situation' (ibid., p. 25). Now one has established that sense-data are the *objects* of perception in the illusory cases. P4 is served to extend this conclusion to normal perceptions. A usual reason for this is that 'being aware of a sense-datum is *exactly like* perceiving a normal object' (ibid., p. 26). If we accept this, then the sense-datum theory follows. Here is not the place for me to peruse the details of this argument (Smith devotes more than two hundred and fifty pages for this), but I shall argue that Crane's way of conceiving extant theories of perception does *not* reflect the real structure of this argument. Furthermore, I will offer my alternative of conceiving those theories, arguing that with this apt framework we can see that there is *no* inner tension between McDowell's intentionalism and disjunctivism, and that we can have a better understanding of complicated issues concerning perception *only if* we respect the agenda set by the argument from illusion.

To repeat, Crane thinks that 'there is a large chasm in the philosophy of perception, [and] that is created by the dispute about whether experience is *relational*' (2006, p. 128). He then classifies the 'three dominant theories' as follows:

> [T]he sense-data theorist and the disjunctivist say that there is a perceptual relation, but while the sense-data theorist says that in cases of illusion and hallucination the relatum is not an ordinary mind-independent object, the disjunctivist says that genuine perception is a relation to ordinary mind-independent objects, but that there is *no common fundamental kind of state* – "perceptual experience" – present in cases of genuine perception, which is a relation to a mind-independent object, and illusion and hallucination, which are not. The intentionalist theory of perception in effect denies that perceptual experience is a relation at all.
>
> ibid., pp. 134–5; my emphasis

According to Crane, the sense-datum theory and disjunctivism belong to the relational view, and intentionalism belongs to the non-relational view. Notice that amongst the relational view, disjunctivism further objects to the 'common kind assumption'. This is true, to be sure, but one should wonder why this important thesis is relegated to a sub-category within the relational view. And it becomes fishier if we notice that often the sense-datum theory is a version of the common kind theory: it is *by virtue of this* thesis that the generalizing step can be accepted. Besides, intentionalism characterized by Crane is also a common kind theory, for what defines disjunctivism is its rejection of the common kind assumption (it wears this on its sleeve), and intentionalism in Crane's sense is outright incompatible with disjunctivism. Whether the common kind assumption is true is crucial for the argument from illusion, for it determines one's attitude towards the generalizing step. On the contrary, relationality seems to have no obvious place in the argument from illusion. As we have seen, Crane agrees with most others that the argument from illusion is our starting point, so he cannot propose a criterion that does *not* reflect the real structure of that argument.

The argument from illusion consists in four steps: the possibility of illusion, the sense-datum inference, Leibniz Law, and the generalizing step. No one disputes the possibility of illusion and the application of Leibniz Law, so virtually we have two ways to shape the battlefield. On the one hand, we can anchor the discussion with the sense-datum inference, saying that the crucial divide is between those who admit this inference, like the sense-datum theory, and those who refuse it, like intentionalism and the adverbial theory.[28] On the other hand, we can anchor the discussion with the generalizing step, saying that the crucial divide is between those who admit the step, like the sense-datum theory, and those who refuse it, like disjunctivism.[29] Neither corresponds to Crane's way of conceiving the debate. We can see this by noting that neither of them groups disjunctivism and the sense-datum theory together, *pace* the framework proposed by Crane.

Now I prefer the latter framework, though in fact they are equally legitimate. At the early stage of this debate, philosophers were divided into the sense-datum theorists and those who objected to it. Therefore the former way of shaping the battlefield – anchoring the debate through the sense-datum inference – may be preferable. But nowadays the core of the relevant debates has been shifted to whether any form of disjunctivism is true, and the defining feature of disjunctivism is the rejection of the generalizing step. In other words, now the central stage has been taken over by the debate between disjunctivism and the common kind theory. It is not that the older core issue has been solved; of course not: the question about whether we can introduce things like sense-data is still controversial. What I would like to stress is that the relative importance of the two crucial moves has been changed: at the early stage, most people focussed on the sense-datum inference (Austin seems to be an importance exception), but now more and more people are interested in whether there is a common kind – mental state, reason, phenomenology or content – shared by veridical experiences and their deceptive counterparts. Therefore it is preferable to invoke this latter framework. Besides, our present purposes are to understand McDowell's intentionalism(s) and whether it is (they are) compatible with his disjunctivism(s), so the former framework based on the sense-datum inference is in effect of no use for us.

Let me say something about the adverbial theory. It appeared in the mid-twentieth century, by C. J. Ducasse (1942) and Roderick Chisholm (1957). The adverbial theorists hold that 'we should think of [the experienced] qualities as modifications of the experience itself' (Crane and French, 2015, section 3.2). 'Experience' here is understood as an act, which is modified by an adverbial; 'perceiving brown*ly*' for example. One of its defining features is its rejection of the sense-datum inference. This theory does not occupy a central place in the present context, but we should remember that there is *nothing* about the generalizing step in the very idea of the adverbial theory.

We have reconceived the spirit of the argument from illusion, concentrating on the debate between disjunctivism and the common kind theory.[30] Now it should be clear that as far as the argument from illusion is concerned, there is *no* inconsistency between disjunctivism and intentionalism, and indeed, between disjunctivism and the sense-datum theory/the adverbial theory, for there is *nothing* about the generalizing step *in the very ideas* of the sense-datum theory, the adverbial theory, and crucially, intentionalism: the controversies between these three theories are located by the first framework, which concerns the sense-datum inference. Although those three theories are almost always associated with the common kind theory, conceptually they need not be. In particular, intentionalism can be a common kind theory if it holds that one and the same representation can occur in a veridical experience and its deceptive counterpart, but this is a further claim. As a disjunctivist, McDowell can subscribe to intentionalism by rejecting the sense-datum inference and explaining the good case and the bad case with different *intentional* nature, for instance the distinction between 'presentation' and 'representation', as Crane notices (2006, p. 140).[31]

Frank Jackson, who was converted into an intentionalist (2004; though see complications below), draws a relevant distinction between 'instantiated properties' and 'intensional properties'. This distinction seems to be incompatible with the common kind thesis, for if there is a single 'representation' shared by a veridical experience and its deceptive counterparts, how can it be that in one case it (re)presents instantiated properties and in the other it represents intensional properties? Notice that he uses 'intensionalism-with-a-s' instead of 'intentionalism-with-a-t' (2004, pp. 430–1). There is indeed something important in this, but we do not need to go into the details for current purposes. Also notice that in 'Intentionalism' (2009), Crane says that in illusion and hallucination what are represented are 'mere intentional objects', and he leaves open the question how this should be explained. However, it is quite reasonable to assume that he prefers a deflationary reading of this. If this is so, we can combine this with McDowell's 'mere appearance', also under a deflationary reading, suggested by Byrne and Logue (2008, p. 66). But again this is another story.

Crane plays down the importance of externalism in the disagreement between disjunctivism and intentionalism (2006, p. 135 and 137), but I disagree. According to my framework, if one wants a version of intentionalism incompatible with disjunctivism, she needs to supplement intentionalism with the common kind thesis. The outcome is to hold that there is a common 'representation' in the good case and in the bad case, regardless the presence of the worldly objects. But this is a version of internalism, which holds that the nature of representation is irrelevant to the directed external objects. By contrast, disjunctivism is a version of externalism, saying that the presence of the directed objects *changes* the nature of (re)presentation. This amounts to the broadness claim discussed in Chapter 3. A disjunctivist can further commit to the primeness claim, insisting that the way the directed objects change the nature of the mental states is *constitution*, as opposed to *causation*. McDowell holds this prime disjunctivism. This recognition of the relevance of the internalism/externalism debate helps us see that the framework provided by Tamar Szabó Gendler and John Hawthorne (2006) can be potentially misleading. They claim that there are two opposing 'analytical projects': '*factorizing accounts*' and '*disjunctive accounts*' (ibid., p. 21). This is a useful distinction, for the common kind theory does belong to the factorizing camp: it factorizes the good case into a representation shared by the bad case *and* the representation's directed objects. But it flies in the face of the fact that disjunctivism can be rendered compatible with the factoring approach, for it can claim that though the directed objects change the nature of the (re)presentation, the way they change it is one of causation, which means the directed objects themselves are not part of the mental states. The distinction between the factorizing/conjunctive view and the disjunctive view is useful but not without its potential problem.

Crane's insistence on the importance of relationality is not well-placed. He declares that his understanding of intentionalism is Brentano's one: intentionalism is 'the *non-relational*, representational conception of experience ...' (2006, p. 135; my emphasis). But this begs the question against another way of developing intentionalism, suggested by Terence Parsons (1980), that intentional objects are in a significant sense *real*. If this inflationary construal of intentionalism turns out to be true, then perceptions *are* relations even in the bad case. Crane (2009) says that he does 'not attempt to explain [the nature of intentional objects]' (p. 476), but he misses this claim of neutrality when he claims that intentionalism is by definition a non-relational view. Relationality *does* matter, but it does not create a large chasm in philosophy of perception, but rather figures in one of the family quarrels within intentionalism.[32] In fact, Brentano himself is not so determined about this:

> The terminus of the so-called relation does not need to exist in reality at all. For this reason, one could doubt whether we really are dealing with something relational here, and not, rather, with something somewhat similar to something relational in a certain respect, which might, therefore, better be called "quasi-relational."
>
> 1889/1973, Appendix

Here Brentano expresses scepticism about the prospect of developing intentionalism in the inflationary way, but he is extremely ambivalent. Relationality is not part of the definition of intentionalism, and even if it turns out that non-relational intentionalism is true, intentionalism is still compatible with disjunctivism, for a disjunctivist can hold that in the bad case there is *no* relation between representation and the relevant mere intentional objects, but in the good case there *is* a relation between the mental state and its directed external objects. Relationality does not seem to be one of the joints of the argument from illusion.[33]

4. To rehearse, disjunctivism and intentionalism are compatible because their defining characters lie at different levels: the former is at the level of the generalizing step, and the latter is at the sense-datum inference. This brings us to the further distinction between intentionalism in philosophy of mind and philosophy of perception. It is widely, if not universally, assumed that intentionalism in these two areas is one and the same theory. For example, Crane takes issue with Block's chasm-creating claim in the context of philosophy of perception, but the claim is made in the context of qualia. This is wrong, for the core tenet of intentionalism in philosophy of mind is that '*all* mental facts are representational facts' (Dretske, 1995, p. xiii); its opponent, the qualia theory, says that there are *some* mental facts that are non-representational, that is, intrinsic. So intentionalism in philosophy of mind is about the *scope* of the intentional. However, intentionalism in philosophy of perception is defined by the denial of the sense-datum inference, and offering its explanation with the notion of 'intentional object'. It does *not* make any claim about the scope of the intentional at all. I suggest that we reserve the term 'representationalism' for philosophy of mind, for as Block notices, the debate between it and the qualia theory can be nicely captured by asking 'is experiencing just *representing*' (1998/2007b; my emphasis)? And the term 'intentionalism' should be invoked in philosophy of perception, for the key claim of it is that in deceptive cases we perceive mere *intentional* objects, rather than sense-data. 'Representationalism' and 'intentionalism' are often interchangeable in the literatures.[34] This can be innocuous, but we need to remember that there is *no* single theory which is called 'intentionalism' or 'representationalism' that occur in philosophy of mind *and* philosophy of perception. Crane argues that the qualia theory is not central in philosophy of perception, and I agree with him (though I do not accept his argument for this based on relationality), but he should have noticed that if the qualia theory is *not* central for perception, *so* is its opponent representationalism (or intentionalism) in philosophy of mind. This view has a place in philosophy of perception only because of its claim about intentional objects, not because of its rejection of qualia.[35]

A few words about qualia. Crane tends to align the qualia theory with the adverbial theory, for the latter 'explains the phenomenal character of experience in terms of its *intrinsic* qualities' (2006, section 3.2.1; my emphasis). But this does not seem right, for while the adverbial theory conceives experiences as *acts*, the qualia theory tends to treat experiences as *things*: while the former uses adverbials to characterize experiences, the latter uses adjectives. Moreover, the qualia theory is not a response to the argument from illusion, so we are not obliged to give it a central place in philosophy of perception. It has some place, to be sure, like in the discussions concerning transparency of experience, which will be explained shortly, but this is far from central if we respect the thought that the central issues we are dealing with arise from the argument from illusion.

If I am right about the distinction between representationalism and intentionalism in my sense, the failure of distinguishing them is striking. What can possibly explain this? I propose two reasons. First, one line of argument for representationalism is the so-called 'transparency of experience'. Generally, it says that when we pay attention to our perceptual experiences, we are only aware of properties of external objects, as opposed to properties of experiences. If this is correct, the qualia theory seems to be falsified, for transparency shows that all properties present in perceptual experiences are not intrinsic to experiences. Philosophers like Tye use this to rebut the qualia theory. But notice that transparency (if any) is a phenomenon about *perceptual* experiences, not experience in general. Maybe transparency does show that in perceptual experiences, there is no intrinsic quality of experiences, but this is *not* the conclusion about the scope of the representational at the general level. In using transparency as an argument against the qualia theory, representationalists shift their topics to perception, a *particular kind* of experience. The second reason is that intentionalists like Crane read the argument from illusion as a *phenomenological* argument, for example he says that '[t]he adverbial theory explains the *phenomenal character* of experience in terms of its intrinsic qualities', as quoted above (I add emphasis this time), and that disjunctivism holds that 'the *phenomenal character* of a genuinely perceptual experience depends upon these [mind-independent] objects' (ibid., section 3.4; my emphasis). Phenomenology to an important extent underlies the sense-datum inference and the generalizing step, to be sure, but phenomenology itself is *not* the very thing for those theories to debate; rather, those theories disagree with one another mainly about the *object* of perception. They also disagree about phenomenology, but those are not *the* objective of responding to the argument from illusion. In reading the argument in the phenomenological sense, philosophers are led to think that intentionalism here is the same theory as the one in philosophy of mind. Martin also reads the argument in this way; that is why his disjunctivism is the phenomenal one. It is of course legitimate to urge phenomenal disjunctivism, but we should not, *pace* Martin, regard it as a direct response to the argument from illusion.

To sum up, McDowell is a *representationalist* in the sense that he rejects the existence of qualia, and he seems to be an *intentionalist* disjunctivist, for his talk about 'mere appearances' can be read as 'mere *intentional* objects', in the deflationary sense of course, and his commitment to the distinction between presentation and representation seems to allow him to say that perception is a form of *intentionality* without buying the common kind thesis. What is more, he seems to be a disjunctivist about *state, reason, content* and *phenomenal character* (at least the weak version), with the primeness reading. In this way, he can be an intentionalist without the narrow assumption that associated with the common kind version.[36]

I have argued that representationalism is a theory about philosophy of mind, not about perception. But I acknowledge that there are some relations between representationalism and disjunctivism. For example, above I mentioned Byrne's suggestion that content disjunctivism is consistent with weak representationalism, which explains qualia with the relation of supervenience. They are compatible because weak representationalism allows that different contents determine the same phenomenology; see also Tye (2007). The distinction between pure/impure representationalism may also be relevant: weak representationalism seems to encourage pureness, for it has allowed for different contents, and there seems to be no reason to complicate the issue by saying that the modes are also different. Besides, intentional modes may generate additional problems here, for perceiving and seeming to perceive are presumably different modes, but it seems clear that different phenomenal characters are not due to the difference between modes. But these issues deserve further considerations, for example, Crane (2009) identifies the impure version with the 'inter-modal' version, but this seems to be falsified by the fact that, say, seeing and seeming to see are different modes (I suspect that he thinks they are the same mode, given his common kind assumption). If we distinguish the impure from the inter-modal, maybe we can hold the latter without committing the former. I myself tentatively maintain inter-modal weak representationalism cum disjunctive intentionalism.

As I mentioned in the beginning of this section, McDowell does not say much about sentience *per se*. I attempt to say something about it for him by clarifying the issues about representationalism, the qualia theory, intentionalism and disjunctivism. Although this detour is far from satisfying, at least it fits well with the following remarks by McDowell:

> Not, of course, that we cannot distinguish sapience from sentience. But they are not two simply different problem areas: we get into trouble over sentience because we misconceive the role of sapience in constituting our sentient life.
>
> 1989c/1998a, p. 296

And explaining sentience is one of the most central projects for the followers of McDowell, or so I shall urge.[37]

7

Rational Animal and Conceptual Being

I feel kind of relief that you think my later self is more continuous with my earlier self. But I still disagree . . .

> John McDowell, commenting on a draft of this
> chapter at the AAP, 2010 (not verbatim)

Conceptuality

1. To remind ourselves, in the opening of *Mind and World*, McDowell swiftly relates his project to notable figures in philosophy:

> The overall topic I am going to consider in these lectures is the way *concepts* mediate the relation between mind and the world. I shall focus the discussion in terms of a familiar philosophical outlook, which Donald Davidson has described as a dualism of scheme and content. That will get us quickly to Kant.
>
> 1996a, p. 3; my emphasis

In this chapter, I am going to suggest that McDowell's focus on Davidson is not well chosen, and his turn to Kant might be too quick in a sense. The reason for these claims is that the notion of 'concept' should not, *pace* McDowell's own insistence, occupy the central place in McDowell's project. However, this chapter is *not* an argument against McDowell's conceptualism, but a reformation within the McDowellian camp. The positive aspect of my reason here is that what is vital for McDowell's project should be the notion of 'reason', not 'concept'. This amounts to a reservation to McDowell's claim that 'the domain of *rational* interrelatedness is coextensive with the domain of the *conceptual*' (McDowell 1999b/2008b, p. 121; my emphasis). Only a reservation, not a refutation, because what I am going to suggest is that McDowell's case for the co-extensiveness is not totally convincing. This is to echo the quote below: the best way to celebrate a philosopher's work is not to praise it, but to find it controversial:

> *I think the best way to celebrate [a philosopher's] work is not to praise it, but to find it controversial. Nobody gets everything exactly right, and what is most fruitful in philosophy is work that is worth taking issue with.*
>
> John McDowell, 'Subjective, Intersubjective, Objective'

What is the relation between McDowell's emphasis on 'concept' and his discussions of Davidson and Kant? The 'scheme' of the scheme-content dualism (hereafter SCD) is *conceptual* scheme, as Davidson himself identifies, and one of the famous Kantian contrasts figuring in McDowell's text is between intuition and *concept*. The reason McDowell takes the notion of concept so seriously is that he wants to preserve and develop insights from Kant and Davidson. My thesis here is that contrary to the appearance, the real Kantian and Davidsonian insights around this neighbourhood should be separated from their talks about *concept*. And what McDowell appropriates from them, by the same token, should be formulated in terms of the notion of 'reason', not 'concept'.

What is the point of this reformation? We can see this from two opposing angles. From McDowell's opponents' point of view, if we are not forced to accept the co-extensiveness of the rational and the conceptual, then even if McDowell is right in insisting that experiences are 'permeated with rationality' (McDowell, 2007c/2008b, p. 308), one is not thereby forced to accept that every bit of experiential content is conceptual. Again, this is not itself an argument against conceptualism or for non-conceptualism; rather, it is a plea for the *possibility* of non-conceptual elements in experiences. According to McDowell, non-conceptualism, as a version of the Myth of the Given, is incoherent, and therefore, impossible (I will say more about this later). If this is right, then most philosophers of perception are theorizing about impossible things. This situation is itself possible, to be sure, but I want to pursue another possibility, that is, though McDowell is right about his thesis that 'mind is pervasive' (ibid., p. 309), his insights can and should be separated from the notion of 'concept'. This sits better with the intuition that experience and judgement are very different.

The other angle, that is, McDowell's own point of view, is philosophically interesting as well. In relatively recent writings (2007c/2008b, 2008d/2008a), McDowell has modified his view of the content of experience. One change is that now he thinks that experiential contents, though conceptual, are nevertheless non-propositional. The other is that the content of experience does not need to include everything it inclines the subject to believe. In elaborating this new view, McDowell makes the notion of the conceptual rather tenuous,[1] and one wonders that why not just accept that there are non-conceptual elements in experiential contents. I will argue that the possibility of non-conceptualism is not ruled out by McDowell's argumentations, but not because of the 'quick argument' from the case of other animals McDowell rightly attributes to his opponents (McDowell, 2007c/2008b, p. 313).

In repudiating the old assumptions in earlier writings, McDowell seems to change his view in a drastic way, and it is natural to suspect that it is difficult for him to preserve many important points in *Mind and World*. However, if the notion of the conceptual is not as important as McDowell himself thinks, as I will urge here, then the suspicion will be dampened. In what follows, I will first compare McDowell's various introductions to *Mind and World* and the opening lecture, urging that McDowell himself was implicitly aware that the rational is *more fundamental* than the conceptual for his project, despite the fact that whenever he needs to write about the relevant issue explicitly, he always stresses that the rational and the conceptual weigh the same in his thinking. Then I will briefly discuss Kant and Davidson, attempting to show that though they did use the word of 'concept', when relating their thoughts to modern and contemporary discussions of concepts and experiential contents, we should read their use of concept in a deflationary way. Then I will focus on the key notion of McDowell's new view, the notion of 'intuitional content', and suggest the correct way to place McDowell's current view in the debate of the conceptuality of experiential content. Finally, I will consider how McDowell should perhaps modify the distinction between environment and world, and discuss its implications to the nature of language, experience and scientific practice.

2. I opened this section with a quotation from the opening of McDowell's Locke Lecture. In that passage, McDowell claims that what concerns him in this work is 'the way *concepts* mediate the relation between mind and the world'. He then carries the discussion through Davidson's attack on SCD and Kant's slogan on the relation between concepts and intuitions.[2] But here I will show that in various introductions to *Mind and World*, McDowell conducts his discussions in terms of the idea of the rational, as opposed to the conceptual, and this has philosophical consequences, *pace* McDowell's own take of the matter. In order to facilitate the following discussion, I shall introduce McDowell's four introductions now and give them abbreviations in terms of the years respectively:

'Précis of *Mind and World*' for the SOFIA conference[3]: 1995 Introduction (1995d)
'Introduction' in the new edition of *Mind and World*: 1996 Introduction (1996a)

'Précis of *Mind and World*' in the *PPR* book symposium: 1998 Introduction (1998k)

'Experiencing the World' for the MVP conference[4]: 1999 Introduction (2000c/2008b)

Readers do not need to memorize which abbreviation is for which, since I am going to urge that except for a few anomalies to be explained away, *all* the introductions point to my conclusion that what is crucial in McDowell's earlier picture is the idea of the rational, as opposed to the conceptual. The strand of the rational is from Sellars, so I shall call this strand 'SR'; the strand of the conceptual is from Kant and Davidson, so I shall call it 'KDC'. Now let me rehearse the main themes in the four introductions.

Since more people are familiar with the 1996 introduction contained in *Mind and World*, I shall focus on it here, with page references of other introductions in brackets. McDowell starts with the question that 'how can we understand the idea that our thinking is *answerable* to the empirical world, if not by way of the idea that our thinking is answerable to *experience*' (McDowell, 1996a, xii; my emphasis; see also McDowell, 1995d, p. 231; 2000c/2008b, p. 245)? McDowell thinks that we should respect the insight in Quine's 'tribunal of experience' metaphor (Quine, 1951/1961), and the position is named 'minimal empiricism' (McDowell, 1996a, p. xii; see also McDowell, 1995d, p. 231; 2000c/2008b, pp. 245–6, 'transcendental empiricism'). Then McDowell introduces Sellars's attack on 'the Myth of the Given', arguing that it commits to a version of the 'naturalistic fallacy', and how coherentists overreact by renouncing the very idea of the tribunal of experience, that is, minimal empiricism (McDowell, 1996a, pp. xiv–xvi; see also McDowell, 1995d, pp. 232–4; 1998k, pp. 365–6; 2000c/2008b, pp. 246–8). The shared assumption of the Myth of the Given and coherentism is that 'the space of reasons' and 'the realm of law' are different in kind (McDowell, 1996a, pp. xiv–xvi; see also McDowell, 1995d, pp. 233–4; 1998k, p. 367; 2000c/2008b, p. 247). A major way out of the dilemma constituted by the Myth of the Given and coherentism is named 'bald naturalism', denying the idea that the space of reasons is *sui generis* (McDowell, 1996a, p. xviii and pp. xx–xxiii; see also McDowell, 1995d, pp. 235–9). McDowell's own alternative is to preserve the idea that the space of reasons is *sui generis*, but insisting that nature can be 'second nature', and if we understand experiences as part of our second nature, we can respect the idea of the tribunal of experience without collapsing into the Myth of the Given (McDowell, 1996a, pp. xix–xx; see also McDowell, 1995d, pp. 236–7; 1998k, p. 367; 2000c/2008b, pp. 247–9).

Now, whether you are convinced by the argumentation or not, this is the general shape of the dialectic situation in *Mind and World*. The discussion is based on SR, for the argumentation is structured by the notion of the space of *reasons*, and it is not clear at which point KDC *has to be* introduced. Nevertheless, KDC *does* figure very often here and also in the four introductions and in the main text of *Mind and World*. What I am going to argue, then, is that none of the occurrences of KDC is indispensable.

McDowell's thoughts about concepts are abundant; I shall then divide my discussion into three parts: first, McDowell's appropriation of Kant's slogan, second, McDowell's adaptation of Davidson's attack on the dualism of scheme and content, and finally, McDowell's own reasons for the co-extensiveness of the rational and the conceptual. Let me start with Kant.

3. In the main text of *Mind and World*, McDowell mainly relies on Kant's famous slogan – 'Thoughts without content are empty, intuitions without concepts are blind' – when he brings out the supposed importance of the notion of concept in his own project. It is practically not possible to spell out Kant's conception of concept here, but fortunately it is not necessary either. What we need is to have some ideas about McDowell's conception of concept, and to see how different it is from Kant's one. McDowell argues that 'if we want to identify the conceptual realm with the realm of thought, the right gloss on "conceptual" is not "predicative" but "belonging to the realm of *Fregean* sense"' (McDowell, 1996a, p. 107; my emphasis). And we need to remember that McDowell is very careful in using the notion of concept; for example, he thinks it is *not* true that 'there is something wrong with just any notion of non-conceptual content' (McDowell, 1996a, p. 55). In later writings, he explicitly emphasizes that for him, 'the connection between conceptual capacities and rationality is a *stipulation*':

> It is not that there is a universally shared idea of conceptual capacities, which determines a subject matter about whose properties people disagree. The notion of the conceptual can be used in a variety of ways, for a variety of purposes.
> McDowell, 2005b/2008a, p. 132; my emphasis

I will come back to this stipulative relation between the rational and the conceptual when evaluating the co-extensiveness thesis. For now, we need to notice only that it is not clear that Kant's conception of concept fits McDowell's stipulation. McDowell warns us about the idea that the conceptual is predicative. This idea belongs to the classical Aristotelian logic before Frege's revolution, and Kant, in deducing the categories from the Aristotelian table of judgement, belongs to this pre-Fregean tradition. If we take Kant's talk about concept literally, it would be unreasonable to combine his slogan to what McDowell wants to say about concepts; to read Frege into Kant seems to be a case of 'historical monstrosity' (McDowell 1996a, p. 79), to use McDowell's own term.[5]

So we should not take the relevant remarks from Kant literally. However, the Kantian spirit can nonetheless be retained. What I am suggesting is that the contrast between intuition and concept is *not* suitable for us to develop the Kantian insight. As McDowell reminds, we need to be clear about the sense in which we use the word 'concept'. Given McDowell's own stipulation, we should not use 'concept' when appropriating Kant's thinking. Then how about the contrast between sensibility and understanding? I think it is also unsuitable, for both terms are used too often in ordinary English. Of course we can give them specific technical meanings by stipulation, but it is still easy to lump ordinary and technical meanings together. I think the most useful contrast for us is between *receptivity* and *spontaneity*. Granted, they are sometimes used in ordinary English, but arguably, not as much as sensibility and understanding. Therefore it is safer to conduct our discussions of Kant in terms of receptivity and spontaneity. Kant struggled to combine what he thought were right in empiricism and rationalism respectively: the former is right in stressing that our mental states and episodes can bear on the reality at all only because subjects can *receive* materials from the reality, and the latter is right in insisting that subjects' *spontaneous* capacities are also essential. It is dangerous for us (probably not for Kant) to capture this insight in terms of intuition and concept, since they are so often used in daily life and cognitive sciences, and in particular 'concept' is widely used in philosophy and related branches of psychology. McDowell says that in his context '"spontaneity" can be simply a label for the involvement of conceptual capacities' (McDowell, 1996a, p. 9), but this is tendentious. Maybe Kant can do that, but that is not so for us, since in our era the notion of 'concept' can mean various things, and to stipulate all of our spontaneous capacities are conceptual is not helpful for discussions. As Christopher Peacocke noticed some time ago, '[t]he term "concept" has by now come to be something of a term of art' (Peacocke, 1992, p. 1). Again, McDowell would presumably insist that he could settle this by the fact that in order to take issue with him, we need to agree with his stipulation first, and empirical psychology apparently does not. When evaluating the co-extensiveness thesis, I will argue that this move is not legitimate in the context of the non-conceptual content debate. Before that, let me turn to Davidson for a moment. For now I shall conclude that Kant's slogan does not successfully motivate KDC.

4. Davidson's case is more complicated. As our contemporary, Davidson's use of 'concept' is supposed to be closer to McDowell's. It is at least obvious that Davidson does *not* accept the Aristotelian conception of logic.[6] But there are other troubles in adapting Davidson's case against SCD to motivate KDC.

> First, that the linkages between concepts that constitute the shape, so to speak, of a conceptual scheme are linkages that pertain to what is a *reason* for what. Second, that if matter, in this application of the form-matter contrast, is supplied by the deliverances of the senses, then the structure of *reason* must lie on the other side of the matter-form contrast, and hence must be *formal*; reason is set over against the senses.
>
> McDowell, 1999b/2008b, p. 116

I agree with McDowell about the reasons why the SCD picture looks attractive: the deliverances of the senses supply the matter, and the structure of reason provides the form. Notice, however, that it is not at all clear that at which point the idea of the conceptual *has to be* involved. I use a modal notion, since McDowell also uses one in attacking non-conceptualism: he urges that non-conceptualism, as a version of the Myth of the Given, in incoherent, hence *impossible*. Maybe non-conceptualism will turn out to be false at the end of the day, but I am suggesting that McDowell, though supporting his claim with various grounds, has *not* established that non-conceptualism is an impossible position. A concept has its form and matter; it is not, as McDowell tries to conceive, that conceptual scheme is only formal.

This partly explains a crucial difference between McDowell's formulation of SCD and Davidson's one. McDowell notices that 'where [he has identified] a scheme as one of two putative determinants of, say, a world view, Davidson ... equates world view and scheme' (McDowell, 1999b/2008b, p. 119). For Davidson, 'the scheme may be thought as an ideology, a set of concepts ... or ... a language' (Davidson, 1988/2001c, p. 41). And later he adds 'world view' and 'theory' (ibid., p. 42). All these items are, as McDowell rightly says, contentful. The contentfulness here is why Davidson can classify those items as *conceptual* schemes; a theory, for example, is a set of propositions constituted by concepts, which is contentful. The form-matter analogy makes the idea of the conceptual unavailable to McDowell: a set of concept is not a *formal* system.

Nevertheless, I agree with McDowell that Davidson's 'diagnosis of the dualism's hold on modern thinking does not quite go to the roots' (McDowell, 1999b/2008b, p. 115). As McDowell often emphasizes, intentionality is presupposed by knowledge, and Davidson's understanding of SCD is epistemological. When talking about 'theory and cues', what Davidson has in mind is more like the so-called 'under-determination of theory by data' in philosophy of science. So even if the SCD Davidson identifies is not the most fundamental one, it is still very important. I think the moral here is this: McDowell's discussion of SCD is indeed more fundamental than Davidson's, since SCD under McDowell's construal threatens the very idea of world-directness, which is presupposed by knowledge. However, only the scheme of SCD under Davidson's construal can be identified as *conceptual* scheme, since it is already contentful. And notice that even for Davidson, the word 'concept' is not very important: he tends to avoid any term that leads to reification of meaning. What McDowell characterizes in the relevant passages should be identified as the dualism between *reason* and Given[7]; the idea of the conceptual does *not* have to figure in here. What McDowell argues for is SR, not KDC. I conclude that though plausible, McDowell's general position should be formulated not in terms of concept.

5. The last part of my argument against McDowell's motivations for KDC is to cast doubt on his conviction that the rational and the conceptual are co-extensive. Again, I am *not* here trying to refute it; I just want to suggest that McDowell's case for the co-extensiveness thesis is *not* as convincing as it might appear.

I take the co-extensiveness as a bi-conditional claim: something is conceptual if and only if it is rational, in the sense that it 'make[s] a special place in the animal kingdom for rational animals' (McDowell, 2005b/2008a, p. 128). McDowell is very careful in using these theory-laden terms; he does not and need not deny that other animals are rational in other senses, as José Luis Bermúdez (2003) and many others try to cash out.[8] I shall discuss the 'conceptuality → rationality' claim first.

As mentioned above, this direction of implication is a *stipulation*: the notion of the conceptual, for McDowell, implies rationality in the demanding sense. As a result, if one wants to attribute 'concept' to other animals or even to sophisticated machines, that will *not* be contradicted to McDowell's view. Actually, McDowell's stipulation here is to respect other disciplines' uses of the term. A trouble with this, however, is that this is at odds with many philosophers' hope that talks about concepts in philosophy can make contact with theories of concept in empirical sciences. There is indeed a big issue about the relation between science and philosophy, and many have taken issue with McDowell around this area.[9] But for our purposes, we do not need to take sides in this debate here, for if one insists that science and philosophy should use the word 'concept' in the same way, McDowell could just choose another word for his purposes. It seems to me that the 'conceptuality → rationality' claim is not troublesome, given that it is a stipulation.

By contrast, the 'rationality → conceptuality' claim is far more controversial. To my knowledge, McDowell nowhere says that this direction is also a stipulation, so presumably it is a substantial claim.[10] There are two further reasons for this reading: first, if this direction were a stipulation as well, the co-extensiveness thesis will be nearly empty, since it would be true by stipulation. Secondly, non-conceptualists want to dispute this claim; in McDowell's wording, they argue that 'the space of reasons ... extend more widely than the space of concepts' (McDowell, 1996a, p. 5). If this were a stipulation, then there would be nothing for McDowell and non-conceptualists to debate about, and this hypothesis is refuted by the fact that McDowell considers various arguments from non-conceptualists in the third lecture of *Mind and World*. So 'rationality → conceptuality' is a substantial claim on McDowell's part. But what are the grounds for it?

One possible ground derives from the relation between the Myth of the Given and SCD. As coherentism, the Myth of the Given also relies on the thought that the space of reasons is *sui generis*. However, the proponents of the Given also insist that experiences, as natural occurrences, belong to the realm of law. Furthermore, they want experiences to play rational roles in grounding beliefs. The three thoughts, taken together, yield a contradiction: experiences are part of the realm of law, which is different in kind from the space of reasons, but experiences also play rational roles, which only exist in the space of reasons. McDowell thinks that 'Sellars's attack on the Given *corresponds* ... to Davidson's attack on what he calls "the third dogma of empiricism"' (McDowell, 1996a, p. xvi; my emphasis. See also McDowell, 1995d, p. 234). It is not clear what 'correspondence' amounts to, but in the co-extensiveness context, we can say that here McDowell wants to say that the space of reasons and conceptual scheme are co-extensive. But again, McDowell's ground for this 'correspondence' is not clear. And recall that in McDowell's understanding of SCD, as I have tried to argue, the 'scheme' does not deserve the name 'conceptual'. In discussing the Myth of the Given and SCD, Anil Gupta says that '[p]hilosophers who would use ... the Dualism of Scheme and Content or the Myth of the Given ... will do well not only to sharpen their weapons but to aim more carefully at their target ... Otherwise, they merely swing blunt metal in a fog of their own creation' (Gupta, 2006, p. 197). I do not agree with his positive proposal, but he is surely right to remind us that we should be more precise when using those 'weapons'. I also agree with Peacocke that 'all representational content is *conceptual* content' is an 'additional thesis', independent of the Myth of the Given (Peacocke, 2008, p. 191, my emphasis). This additional thesis might be true to be sure, but what is important here is that it is *additional*.[11]

McDowell regards the transcendental anxiety exemplified by the Myth of the Given as a typical symptom in modern philosophy. Davidson argues that SCD sets the agenda of modern philosophy. Maybe this partly explains why McDowell thinks that there is a correspondence between the Myth of the Given and SCD. But as argued above, what Davidson has in mind is Quine's (and Kuhn's) picture, so the 'agenda' he is identifying is pretty different from McDowell's target. Therefore, the 'agenda-setting' role cannot be a good reason for thinking that there is a correspondence between the Myth of the Given and SCD.

In the opening lecture of *Mind and World*, McDowell considers the picture in which 'the space of reasons is made out to be more extensive than the space of concepts' (McDowell, 1996a, p. 6). He thinks the picture has the following implication:

> The idea is that when we have exhausted all the available moves within the space of concepts, all the available moves from one conceptually organized item to another, there is still one more step we can take: namely, pointing to something that is simply received in experience. It can only be pointing, because *ex hypothesi* this last move in a justification comes after we have exhausted the possibilities of tracing grounds from one conceptually organized, and so articulable, item to another.
>
> McDowell, 1996a, p. 6

A relevant distinction here, as McDowell reminds after two pages, is the one between 'justification' and 'exculpation' (McDowell, 1996a, p. 8). Why *pointing* to something can only be *exculpation*? At this point McDowell connects the discussion to his interpretation of Wittgenstein's Private Language Argument: the 'something' to be pointed is *bare presence*, since it is outside of the space of *concepts*, as the above quotation says (McDowell, 1996a, p. 19). 'Bare presence' is used by philosophers to mean, for example, *unstructured* things; the only thing we can say about them is that they are present. But why should we accept that the *conceptual* things are the only *structural* stuffs? To be sure, non-conceptualists need to spell out what kinds of structure are possessed by various non-conceptual contents, and why those structures can provide justification as opposed to exculpation, but this project seems initially feasible, in the sense that it is *not impossible in principle*. McDowell often rightly reminds us, in the context of the Myth of the Given, that people usually mistake impossibility with difficulty (e.g. McDowell, 1999b/2008b, p. 245), but this reminder does not automatically transit to non-conceptualism, since the putative co-extensiveness has not been established. It is not clear that the structural *has to be* the conceptual.[12]

McDowell appeals to Davidson not only in the context of SCD, but also in that of justification. The position here can be encapsulated in the slogan that 'nothing can count as a reason for holding a belief except another belief' (Davidson, 1983/2001c, p. 141). McDowell suggests the following emendation: 'nothing can count as a reason for holding a belief except something else that is also in the space of *concepts*' (McDowell, 1996a, p. 143; my emphasis). Now I would like to highlight the point that Davidson does not accept even the *minimal* version of empiricism, as McDowell characterizes. So for Davidson, there is no such thing as *non-inferential* justification between experiences and beliefs. I take this as the spirit of Davidson's slogan. McDowell, although disagreeing with Davidson about the slogan, nonetheless accept the spirit in insisting that only the conceptual can be reasons for other conceptual stuffs. But the spirit behind Davidson's slogan is the *inferential* model of justification; McDowell, as a minimal empiricist, should not accept that. Indeed McDowell explicitly says that he thinks the relations between experiences and beliefs are non-inferential (e.g. McDowell, 2008d/2008a, p. 258). In this aspect, Brandom's inferentialist picture is more in line with Davidson's slogan, and this is surely incompatible with what McDowell wants to say.

Or perhaps the argument is from the idea of 'second nature'? In many places, McDowell argues that our second nature needs to be initiated by language, and language is conceptual if anything is (e.g. McDowell, 1996a, pp. 115–19, 124–6). However, even if we agree with McDowell at this point, as I do, it is a different thesis that the structure of second nature is *thoroughly* conceptual: from the fact that S needs to be triggered by L, and L has the property C, it does *not* follow that S also has C.

At the end of the 1996 introduction, McDowell identifies his aim as making sense of 'how *freedom*, in that sense [i.e. responsiveness to *reasons*], fits into the natural world' (McDowell, 1996a, p. xxiii; my emphasis). 'Underlying the dualism of scheme and content', he says, 'is the dualism of freedom – the freedom of reason – and nature' (McDowell, 1999b/2008b, p. 132). I concur with McDowell here, and I think these remarks show, together with the grounds offered above, that conceptuality is *not* essential to what McDowell really wants and needs to say. The conceptuality of experience is an additional claim; it might be true, but its denial – non-conceptualism – has not been shown as impossible.

So far I have been urging that in *Mind and World* and other early writings, what is really important for McDowell is SR, not KDC, *pace* McDowell's conviction that they are of the same importance. In the next section, I am going to argue that in his later writings, McDowell's modification of his view comes close to a version of non-conceptualism, but this is not a disaster for him. Since SR is where McDowell's real insight resides, KDC/conceptuality is not as crucial as McDowell he himself thought. Despite giving up the two old assumptions, McDowell's later view preserves what is deeply right in his earlier picture, and he implicitly recognizes that KDC is too strong in many respects.

Intuitionality

1. McDowell explicitly proposes his modified view of experience in 'Avoiding the myth of the given' (2008d/2008a). However, in his 2007 response to Hubert Dreyfus's objections from phenomenology (2007c/2008b), he already stepped toward the new view. I shall discuss both papers here, with an emphasis on conceptuality, rationality and propositionality.

In his new picture, McDowell does not think that 'any aspect of that content is already, just as such, the content of a conceptual capacity possessed by the subject of the experience'. He thinks that in this kind of case,

> If it is to become the content of a conceptual capacity of hers, she needs to *determine* it to be the content of a conceptual capacity of hers. That requires her to carve it out from the categorially unified but as yet, in this respect, unarticulated experiential content of which it is an aspect, so that thought can focus on it by itself.
>
> McDowell, 2007c/2008b, p. 318

In this passage, McDowell seems to acknowledge that not every aspect of experiential content is already conceptual. As he makes clear later, he is 'acknowledging that at least some of the content of a typical world-disclosing experience is not conceptual in that sense' (McDowell, 2007c/2008b, p. 319). The sense in which McDowell is using is Brandom's sense that 'grasping a concept is mastering the use of *a word*' (Brandom, 2000, p. 6, 'Sellars's principle'; my emphasis). This seems to make McDowell's remark here innocent, for Brandom's stipulation of the word 'concept' is even stronger than McDowell's, and McDowell does not need to insist that every bit of experiential content already has its linguistic counterpart. It appears that so far McDowell has not weakened his conceptualist view.

However, when responding to the question 'what is the point of insisting that the content of a world-disclosing experience is conceptual' (McDowell, 2007c/2008b, p. 319), he also says that 'if an experience is world-disclosing ... *all* its content is present in a *form* in which ... it is suitable to constitute contents of conceptual capacities' (ibid., p. 319; notice that McDowell does not use emphasis very often). The crux here is the notion of 'form', as appeared in the form/matter metaphor earlier. Some bits of experiential content are *not already* conceptual, but they are in a form in which it can *become* conceptual later. The sense in which they are not conceptual is Brandom's sense, and this is plain: no sensible person would insist that every bit of experiential content always has its linguistic counterpart. However, McDowell holds that according to his own use of the term 'concept', we can and should say that experiential contents are conceptual through and through, since they are *in a form* to constitute conceptual contents. Does his insistence here make good sense?

To answer this question, we need to go back to McDowell's stipulation of his notion of the conceptual. He says that for him, the idea of the conceptual implies the idea of the rational. So when he says that experiential contents are 'conceptual in form' (McDowell, 2007c/2008b, p. 320), we can reasonably interpret him as rehearsing the point that experiences are within the space of *reasons*. His 'in a form' talk echoes his point in *Mind and World* that *bare presence* cannot have rational significance. But as I have suggested, to insist the good point concerning the space of reasons, we need to insist only that experiential contents are *structural*, or in a suitable *form*; the thought that they are *conceptual* is an additional thesis. What do we need if we want to maintain this additional thesis? We need the 'rationality → conceptuality' claim, but what McDowell stipulates is the opposite direction, and as argued above, the conditional from rationality to conceptuality cannot be a stipulation as well, because it would trivialize the co-extensiveness thesis, and it would make the debate between conceptualism and non-conceptualism unintelligible.

If I am right so far, McDowell's new picture admits non-conceptual content, even if we are not using Brandom's strong sense of the notion. What is essential to the McDowellian picture is that experiential episodes are in the space of reasons, so they are structural, or in a special form, but to say that they are conceptual requires further arguments. The essence of McDowell's view is SR, not KDC. However, the version of non-conceptualism is very special, because it does not gain its plausibility from what McDowell calls the 'quick argument', which starts with the fact that 'we share basic perceptual capacities and embodied coping skills with other animal', and infers that 'those capacities and skills, as we have them, cannot be permeated with rationality, since other animals are not rational' (McDowell, 2007c/2008b, p. 313). Most versions of non-conceptualism accept one form or another of this argument. McDowell's version (of course he would not accept this label), however, is unmoved by this kind of consideration. He argues that though 'there are descriptions of things we can do that apply also to things other animals can do', those descriptions 'need not *exhausted* by the match with what can be said about, say, a cat's correspondingly describable response to a corresponding affordance (ibid., pp. 313–4). To accommodate other animals' responsiveness to reasons, we need only a further notion of 'responsiveness to reasons *as such*' (McDowell, 2005b/2008a, p. 128). In my words, as human beings, we can *reflect on* our own reasons, and this distinguishes us from other animals; besides, this facts does *not* imply, *contra* Dreyfus's reading (2006, 2007a, 2007b), that we are *always monitoring* our own actions and other intentional episodes. Now, what is distinctive in McDowell's view is that some bits of experiential content, though non-conceptual according to me, nevertheless have a distinctive form, and this enables rational animals like us to reflect on them when needed. Some bits of world-disclosing experiential content, though non-conceptual now, *has the potential to be conceptualized*, and this would not fall prey to Peter Geach's argument against abstractionism (Geach, 1957, mentioned in McDowell 1996a, p. 7), since what is to be conceptualized is not *bare presence*, which do not have any structure in the relevant sense.

2. McDowell has been hostile to the notion of 'conceptualization' (e.g. his objections to Evans' view in the third lecture of *Mind and World*), but I think it is because he holds that to conceptualize bare presence commits to the Myth of the Given. What I have been urging is that conceptualization, *just as such*, is innocent; what is problematic is the notion of bare presence: since it has no structure in the relevant sense, it cannot be a part of the space of reasons. But we need not conceive bits of experiential contents as bare presences; as McDowell now holds, they have a distinctive form, and it is not a myth to say that we can conceptualize those structural experiential contents. What I am resisting is the idea that those bits of experiential content are *conceptual in form*, since they need to be 'carved out', in McDowell's own term, or 'conceptualized', in my term; the notion of carving things out in this context is very metaphorical, and I see no difference between it and conceptualizing. And the notion of conceptualization as such is not problematic anyway. I will propose a way to cash out the 'carving-out' metaphor later in this chapter.

McDowell agrees that it is likely that some bits of experiential content are not already conceptual, but since they have a distinctive form, they have the *potential* to be conceptualized. I think this talk of potentiality is significant. I shall name this claim from McDowell the 'potentiality thesis': we can say that experiential contents are conceptual through and through, in a derivative sense, because they have the *potential* to be conceptualized, and this potential comes from the distinctive form. This thesis is important to distinguish McDowell's view from those who accept the quick argument characterized above. I think the main reason why McDowell insists that every bit of experiential content is *conceptual in form* is that though he now admits that not every bit of content is already conceptual, they nevertheless are very different from other animals' mental episodes. I think he is quite right at this point, but the label 'conceptual in form' is not well chosen, since some bits of the content are just *non-conceptual* at a given time. Consider the case from tadpoles and frogs. We can say that tadpoles have the potential to become frogs, but we do not want to say that tadpoles are 'froggy in form'. To insist the good point that rational animals' mental episodes are distinctive, we do not need to say that they are conceptual in form, since some bits of them are, as McDowell rightly acknowledges, not already conceptual. Again, what is essential for McDowell is SR; KDC, though might be correct at the end of the day, is nevertheless an additional claim.

This leads us to 'Avoiding the myth of the given' (2008d/2008a). In this piece, McDowell explicitly abandons two assumptions:

> I used to assume that to conceive experiences as actualizations of conceptual capacities, we would need to credit experiences with *propositional* content, the sort of content judgments have. And I used to assume that the content of an experience would need to include *everything* the experience enables its subject to know non-inferentially. But these assumptions now strike me as wrong.
> McDowell, 2008d/2008a, p. 258

I shall name the first assumption the 'propositionality thesis', and the second the 'comprehensiveness thesis'. Let me start with the second, since it is more relevant to the potentiality thesis I just introduced. McDowell uses the concept of 'cardinal' to explain why he now thinks comprehensiveness is wrong. He invites us to imagine that in matching circumstances, two subjects perceptually confront a cardinal, but while one can rightly identify that the animal in front of one is a cardinal, the other cannot, perhaps because this second subject has no concept of cardinal. McDowell thinks that the matching experiences incline the first subject to say that it is a cardinal, but this is not true of the second subject, and '[t]here is no ground here for insisting that the concept of a cardinal must figure in the content of [the] experience itself' (ibid., p. 259). To use the terminology introduced earlier, the second subject lacks the capacity to *carve out* the part of the experiential content we can attribute as 'cardinal'. The comprehensiveness assumption has been given up in responding to Dreyfus, though McDowell did not make this explicit. I think part of the reason is that in answering Dreyfus's objection, McDowell did not need to revise his picture; all he needs is to point out that conceptuality and mindedness are more to attention, as we have seen in Chapter 5. In what follows, though, I will explain in what way attention comes in for McDowell, though it is not one of his terms.

3. McDowell's new notion – 'intuitional content' – is introduced in the context of abandoning the propositionality assumption. 'What we need,' he says, 'is an idea of content that is not *propositional* but *intuitional*, in what I take to be a Kantian sense' (McDowell, 2008d/2008a, p. 260; my emphasis). For example, 'this is a cube' is propositional, and its corresponding intuitional content, McDowell cites Sellars, is 'this cube' (ibid., p. 260). While propositional content is 'putting significances together', the unity of intuitional content is *'given'* (McDowell, 2008d/2008a, p. 263). Now why does intuitional content still deserve the name of the *conceptual*? Again it is because 'every aspect of the content of an intuition is present in a form in which it is already suitable to be the content associated with a discursive capacity, if it is not – at least not yet – actually so associated' (ibid., p. 264). As I suggested above, the potential to be conceptualized signifies that those bits of experiential content are *non-conceptual* at some points, and this will not cause problems for McDowell, since they are not bare presences. To say they are conceptual in form is misleading; we do not need this even if we want to insist on the good point that the 'quick argument' does not work.

I have some doubts about McDowell's use of Sellars here. As McDowell already endorsed in *Mind and World* and other earlier writings (e.g. McDowell, 2000c/2008b, p. 253), Sellars thinks that experiences 'contain claims'. In earlier writings, McDowell took this as urging that experiences are propositional. Now he changes the view and thinks that the corresponding intuitional content of 'this is a cube' is 'this cube'. I think this is unsatisfying. To say that experiences contain claims is metaphorical, so we need to figure out the spirit behind it. I take Sellars to mean that experiences, like judgements in this respect, have *assertoric force*; experiences are not neutral passing shows, just standing there like signposts that wait to be interpreted (to echo McDowell's criticism to Kripke's Wittgenstein). Rather, experiences reveal, or at least purport to reveal how things are in the world. If 'this cube' can be an example of intuitional content of experience, it is not clear where assertoric force resides in. After all, 'this cube' is at best a demonstrative concept. It is indeed difficult to preserve the idea of assertoric force while abandoning propositionality, but anyway phrases like 'this cube' does not serve for our purposes.

Many things remain to be said about this. However, I want to go back to my main line, which is this: for McDowell, what is essential is SR, not KDC, and this is true of both the earlier and the later picture. In abandoning the two old assumptions, McDowell is able to accommodate the notion of non-conceptual content, with the proviso that those non-conceptual bits of content have suitable structures. McDowell has not said much about what *forms* he has in mind, but it can be a research project for many philosophers, contrary to McDowell's own view that since non-conceptual content is an incoherent notion, to theorize about the details of the structures of those contents is doomed to fail.

In this context, it is appropriate to ask this question: how to carve out conceptual contents without falling prey to the Myth of the Given? When responding to Dreyfus, I mentioned that mindedness should not be equated with *attention*. Here I shall suggest that attention *does* have a role in McDowell's picture: it helps us cash out what he should mean by 'caring out'.

It should be recognized that at least in one sense, givenness in experience is innocuous; this is McDowell's emphasis that experiences are *passive*: it is not up to you what you will experience given specific perceptual conditions (McDowell, 1996a, p 29; *pace* Tim Crane in his 2013 paper on the Given: 'it is clear that in recent work McDowell does accept something like a distinction between what is given to us, and what we bring to experience' [p. 230], which falsely implies that in earlier works McDowell did not acknowledge this passivity). Then in what sense is givenness a myth? As discussed in Chapter 3, the Myth of the Given was first introduced and criticized by Sellars (1956) in his celebrated 'Empiricism and the Philosophy of Mind'. As explained in Chapter 5, many contemporary philosophers identify the myth with indubitability, but that was not Sellars's original formulation.[13] Again let's focus on McDowell's formulation. McDowell first introduces the idea of the *sui generis* character of *the space of reasons*, compared with *the realm of law*. The former is in the 'normative contexts', whereas the latter is exhausted by the 'empirical descriptions':

> Sellars separates concepts that are intelligible only in terms of how they serve to place things in the logical space of reasons, such as the concept of knowledge, from concepts that can be employed in 'empirical description' …whatever the relations are that constitute the logical space of nature [i.e., the realm of law], they are *different in kind* from the normative relations that constitutes the logical space of reasons.
>
> McDowell, 1996a, pp. xiv–xv

And if we place something in the realm of law, but demand it to do something only an inhabitant of the space of reasons can do, then we commit something like the 'naturalistic fallacy':

> The idea of a tribunal belongs ... in what Sellars calls 'the logical space of reason' ... But the idea of experience, at least construed in terms of impressions, evidently belongs in a logical space of natural connections. That can easily make it seem that if we try to conceive experience as a tribunal, we must be falling into the naturalistic fallacy ...
>
> McDowell, 1996a, p. xvi

The key premise here is that rational relations are not law-like relations. This is, of course, philosophically controversial, and has been firmly denied by many philosophers, for example Jerry Fodor (2007, p. 114). One worry is that in formulating the Myth of the Given, McDowell presupposes his naturalism of second nature, i.e. the space of reasons and the realm of law are not only different aspects; they are different in a more radical way, and this is way too much. Most contemporary analytic philosophers are naturalists in a more restricted way; they are physicalists. I believe, however, we can still formulate the Myth of the Given in a McDowellian line without presupposing his radical version of naturalism. Consider Davidson's anomalous monism again (e.g. 1970/2001a): certain physical tokens have both physical and mental aspects, and they can be satisfactorily described only with very different terms, e.g. normative or not. To formulate the Myth of the Given, we need only this much. Now consider Quine. As McDowell reminds, Quine intends experiences to serve as 'tribunals', but at the same time conceives them as neural firings. Neural talks are of course realm-of-law talks. Now, if one intends neural firings to serve as tribunals, i.e. to exert *rational* constraint to thoughts, then one commits the Myth of the Given: the givenness in this context is a member of the realm of law, but we demand it to do something only members of the space of reasons can do. This is a myth because we start by acknowledging that laws and reasons are different in kind. To formulate the Myth of the Given, then, McDowellian naturalism of second nature is not required.

Now let's come back to the question: 'why doesn't McDowell's new view commit him to the Myth of the Given?' After all, Kantian intuitions are not conceptual, and this seems to be the main reason why Evans' view does not work according to McDowell. Recall that the key passage is this: 'if an experience is world-disclosing ... *all* its content is present in a *form* in which ... it is suitable to constitute contents of conceptual capacities' (McDowell, 2007c/2008b, p. 319;

original emphasis). To avoid the Myth of the Given, this *form* has to be something in the space of reasons, as opposed to the realm of law. In both his 2007 and 2008 papers, McDowell attempts to cash this out by elaborating his reading of Kant. I will not go into this here; rather, I will develop an account with more scientifically acceptable terms. I do *not*, however, intend this to be an objection to McDowell's project: I intend my account to be compatible with McDowell's Kantian characterization of the 'carving-out' story and his naturalism of second nature. To see how this is possible (i.e. cashing it out with more scientific terms without rejecting second nature), we need to develop the account first.

To develop my positive account, some digression is necessary. The account is derived from a response to Ned Block's contention (2007a, c, 2008, 2015) that phenomenology overflows cognitive accessibility (identification, demonstration, etc.; differences between these accessibilities are crucial to Block's position, but not relevant for the present context).

The key cases for Block are Sperling (1960) and Landman et al. (2003). For simplicity, let's focus on the former, since the latter is a combination of the Sperling paradigm and the change blindness paradigm. In a standard Sperling experiment, participants are shown three rows of four alphanumeric letters briefly. Sometime after the stimuli, participants will be cued by a specific tone as to which row they should report. Although they have a clear feeling that they see most letters, they can only report with accuracy about the cued row. The crucial point is that the cue appears *after* the stimuli disappear. Block argues that 'there *have to be* such specific representations *given* that any location can be cued with high accuracy of response' (Block 2007c, p. 531, my emphasis). More specifically,

> For the Sperling experiment, the relevant generic/specific difference would be that between a phenomenal presentation *that there is* an array of alphanumeric characters and a phenomenal presentation of specific shapes of all or most items in the array ... My argument was that before the cue, there is specific phenomenology for all or almost all items.
>
> Block, 2007c, p. 531; original emphasis

I believe something along this line is correct, since there is a similar distinction in psychology, and many commentators of Block draw similar distinctions too. However, I do not agree with Block's specific way of conceiving this distinction and relevant disagreements, which are crucial to his view. He argues that 'the objectors *have to agree* that before the cue, there are specific ... visual representations of all or almost all...items' (ibid., p. 531, my emphasis). I demur. Here I quote James Stazicker's recent response:

> Suppose that you're first conscious of a letter-like shape in the bottom corner of the grid, and that when you shift your attention to that shape, you become conscious of the shape as an "F" [*contra* Block]. How could you distinguish this from a case in which you were conscious of the shape as an "F" all along, though you weren't attending to this aspect of it [Block's view]? Attention to what you see is required if you're to report on changes in the determinacy of your visual consciousness. But if attention to what you see *effects* changes in the determinacy of your visual consciousness, keeping track of the changes will be difficult at best.
>
> Stazicker, 2011, p. 176; original emphasis

I believe the reason why Block cannot accept the hypothesis that there is a transition from generic to specific phenomenology without participants' notification is that he has a wrong view of generic phenomenology, which is *propositional* seeing ('that there is...'), and therefore very different from specific phenomenology. However, It is not at all clear how seeing can be *propositional* and at the same time *phenomenal*. Of course my contention here is controversial too, and I cannot refute his view by a simple denial like this. But without the prior commitment to propositional seeing, the possibility of transitions from generic to specific phenomenology should be left open, *contra* Block.

Now why are all these relevant to McDowell's new view and its relation to the Myth of the Given? First of all, his abandoning of the assumption of propositional seeing is in line with my suggestion above. Secondly, generic phenomenology, say visual impressions of various letters in the Sperling paradigm, is McDowellian intuitional contents: they are contents, since they are *about* things on the screen, and they are intuitional, as opposed to conceptual, since participants *cannot report* most of them before the cue (they can report few of them, which means those parts are conceptual; this will be accommodated in a few sentences). After being cued to a specific row, subjects can generally report those cued letters, since their *attentions* are drawn to a given row, and those specific phenomenologies are thereby *carved out as conceptual contents*. They are conceptual now, since they are available for reporting as specific letters that are conceptual. If there is no cue at all, subjects will still be able to report some letters, since their attentions will flow around randomly. Attention *carves out* conceptual contents.[14]

Why doesn't this commit the Myth of the Given? Recall that the key of the myth is to demand something characterized with realm-of-*law* terms to exert *rational* powers. Now, generic phenomenology is *not* something outside the space of reasons: subjects have clear feelings that they have those phenomenologies, and can thereby cite them to tell experimenters that generic phenomenologies contain letter-like items. They, intuitional contents, are in the space of reasons, though they need to wait to be carved out as conceptual contents for further deployments.

This is compatible with McDowellian naturalism of second nature, since it leaves open whether the space of reasons is *sui generis* in the way McDowell demands. But it does *not* entail that radical naturalism, so the burden of the present account is quite light. This is certainly a possible line for McDowellians to take. The present account is an attempt to connect more empirically oriented works to McDowell's thinking in a positive way; although more details are needed, I believe what has been done here is sufficient to open the possibility that the McDowellian view can be supplemented by naturalistic philosophy of mind.[15]

4. I now want to draw some implications from the discussions so far. McDowell's notion of the conceptuality of second nature has been closely related to the distinction between environment and world he descends from Hans-Georg Gadamer (1960/2004). If I am right in arguing that McDowell's picture should have been liberated from the notion of the conceptual to some extent, the details of his view on the environment and the world might need to be revised as well. I will try to say something about this before closing, together with its implications to his views of language, experience and science.

It is unfortunate that McDowell's distinction between environment and world is often ignored by philosophers in the Anglo-Saxon tradition.[16] This is also, I suspect, to do with SR and KDC. The first three lectures of *Mind and World* are more about the conceptual, while the other three are more about the rational. Many 'analytic' philosophers are not responsive to important points from the later lectures. A crucial point relevant to the present discussion is that McDowell's notion of 'experience' is inextricably connected to the environment/world distinction, so it is impossible to have a satisfactory understanding of that notion without paying enough attention to the distinction. Let me briefly explain why.

Many people find it difficult to accept the consequence of McDowell's picture that other animals do not have 'experiences' strictly speaking. 'Granted,' they might say, 'you can again *stipulate* that for you the word "experience" is applicable only to human beings, but it is not as if philosophy can be settled by stipulation alone. Without a satisfying account of other animals' perception, to stipulate words in idiosyncratic ways debars real communications, and there is no reason why other philosophers should listen to you.' This complaint is quite to the point, but I want to argue that McDowell does have an account of that, reasonable to some extent, and the impression that he just stipulates words in weird ways might derive from the ignorance of his distinction between environment and world. Let me start with 'environment'. This notion occupies the place normally occupied by 'world'; we can understand the notion of environment here as 'physical world' as philosophers normally understand. Since for many philosophers, physicalism in one form or another is true, or *must* be true, there is no need to distinguish between environment and world. But we should not read this conviction to physicalism into McDowell. The heart of the McDowellian picture is the idea of 'second nature', as we have seen along the way, so we need another notion for that. Although McDowell does not put things this way, we can say that 'first nature', the physical nature, refers to environment, and 'second nature' refers to world. Now, only animals with second nature, namely us, can 'experience' the *world*, while other animals, if you like, 'experience' the *environment* only. This is how McDowell dodges the stigmatism that his picture implies 'Cartesian automatism' (McDowell, 1996a, p. 116). In his recent writings, McDowell uses '*world*-disclosing experience' to emphasize human animal's case, and presumably this is to allude to the other notion of experience, which is *not* world-disclosing, because its object is environment instead. However, I think we need to consciously bear the environment/world distinction in mind when reading McDowell, or the message alluded in the adjective 'world-disclosing' cannot be heard.

How is this related to SR and KDC? I said that analytic philosophers generally pay more attention to the first three lectures, and the single-most point remembered is McDowell's claim that experiences are conceptual through and through. As a result, SR is often downplayed, since it becomes important only after the third lecture. But we need to remember that in his 1996 introduction, McDowell reminds that his 'reflection about perceptual experience ... is just one example of a type' (McDowell, 1996a, p. xxiii). What is more important is SR, mainly presented in the last three lectures, and as I have argued, even in the case of perceptual experience, KDC is not necessary for McDowell's purposes. In any case, the environment/world distinction is crucial to McDowell's picture, *pace* many readers' understanding.

Having established the close relation between the environment/world divide and McDowell's notion of experience, we can go back to our main line. Since McDowell has changed his view of experience, it seems that he needs to adjust his view of world accordingly. McDowell's notion of world is from Wittgenstein's *Tractatus Logico-Philosophicus* (1921/1922): the world is the totality of facts. McDowell appropriates this for its own purposes:

> [T]here is no ontological gap between the sort of thing one can mean, or generally the sort of thing one can think, and the sort of thing that can be the case. When one thinks truly, what one thinks *is* what is the case. So since the world is everything that is the case ... there is no gap between thought, as such, and the world.
>
> McDowell, 1996a, p. 27

McDowell thinks that the structure of the world and the structure of thought are the same, and so is for experience, though he was not explicit about this here. As we have seen, however, now he thinks that experiences are non-propositional, so his account of the structure of thought, experience and world cannot be so neat. What would he say about this?

5. McDowell has not been explicit about this yet, but let me try to elaborate a bit along his line. He would want to say that we both think and perceive the world directly, but since the former is propositional, the latter not, it seems that we need to say that the world is both propositional and non-propositional, and this sounds paradoxical, or worse, contradictory. I would like to suggest that it is not as bad as it appears. With language, we can think and talk about the world in ways not available to those who cannot speak or think linguistically. And though we have language, we can still perceive the world, and it is a plain fact that thinking about the world and perceiving it are very different. We can describe the world to someone who cannot perceive, and we can perceive situations that are difficult to put with words. Does this prevent us from saying that what we think about and what we perceive is the same world? It seems that the answer is 'no'. We have different ways to explore the world, and the ways the world disclosed for us correspond to the ways we explore it. It does not follow that there are more than one world. Seeing and touching are very different, but it does not follow that we are in touch with different worlds, literally speaking.

Granted we can both think about and perceive the world, but how about environment? Environment is the physical world, and it seems to be a disaster if a picture implies that human beings can be in touch only with the world, but not with the environment. In *Mind and World*, McDowell insists that human beings both '[live] in the world' and '[cope] with an environment', and to deny this is 'absurd' (McDowell, 1996a, p. 118). It is indeed absurd to hold that we lose our touch to the physical world after being mature, but given that our thinking and experiencing are parts of our second nature, there seems to be a tension within the idea of thinking about/perceiving (second nature) the environment (first nature).

To resolve the tension, one hypothesis is that the distinction between environment and world comes into degrees. If the distinction were sharp, it seems to be mandatory to hold that as mature human beings, the world replaces the environment for us. The environment/world distinction looks like a version of the things in themselves/appearances distinction on this picture, and this is unbearable.

The idea that the distinction comes into degrees matches another idea that both perception and language have degrees of abstraction. After being initiated into second nature, we can talk about and perceive the world. This does not mean that we are no longer in touch with the environment. The world is disclosed to us gradually, so the environment also becomes alien to us gradually. In the case of perception, it is relatively difficult to have higher level of abstraction, but with language we can do more. For example, when we are doing sciences, we try our best to abstract out all the meaningful elements in view; we try to describe the environment/physical world. But as the general lesson from the hermeneutic tradition, there is no such thing as *pure* descriptions. Interpretations are always with us; the idea of absolute objectivity is only an ideal. Although in language we can reach higher levels of abstraction, we cannot reach one hundred percent. As we abstract more, we are closer to environment, but in a different way from other animals and human infants. Animals' and infants' relations to the environment are *coping*, whereas in doing sciences, mature human beings are *describing* the environment, the *physical* world (as mature human beings, we cope with the *world* as well). With different levels of abstraction, we are in touch with both the environment and the world, with different degrees. It is like a spectrum, but we can never reach the two poles of it, since human beings are mixed beings. To use an Aristotelian metaphor, there is no pure form or pure matter in reality. Human beings are not purely rational, and not purely biological either.

But there is a potential objection. The distinction between environment and world seems to correspond to the one between the realm of law and the space of reasons, but if as I argued, environment and world are different only in degrees, shouldn't we say the same thing with the realm of law and the space of reasons? But if so, the proposal I just outlined above is not acceptable by McDowellians.

The realm of law and the space of reasons are *ontological* realms. They are not different *ways* of seeing things. If they were only different ways, then we should have said, for example, that experiences viewed from the reason's point of view can justify beliefs, while when viewed from the law's point of view, they are just neural firings. But this is not what McDowell has in mind; it is the Davidsonian view. McDowell urges that experiences *belong* to the space of reasons, which is to say that it is not part of the realm of law. World and environment, one might think, are *epistemic* notions instead. They are different aspects of the same reality; mature human beings, human infants, other animals, plants, inanimate objects, are within the same reality, as a matter of course. But there are different modes of being. Inanimate things are not 'in touch' with reality in significant ways; plants are sensitive to environmental changes, and so are other animals and human infants, in more complex manners; mature human beings can cope with the world and the environment,[17] and they can talk about and perceive both, with different degrees. Different aspects of reality can be revealed to us if we change our stances, and I think this is part of the meaning of human freedom. However, a difficulty is that now we cannot say that the distinction between environment and world corresponds to the distinction between first nature and second nature, as the former is epistemic and the latter is ontological. I must admit that I have not reached a stable view here, and the difficulty seems to correspond to the choice between the two-aspect vs two-world readings of Kant's distinction between phenomena and noumena.

Another, perhaps simpler hypothesis is that the distinction between environment and world is sharp, corresponding to the sharp distinction between first nature and second nature. Now, other animals have only environment, while mature human beings have only world in daily life, as we cannot *unlearn* our upbringings, so we cannot *unseen* our world. However, we are able to have our environment as well from a theoretical point of view: when we theorize about it in sciences and philosophy, we think of the physical world, environment or first nature as the subject matter of our studies. This is also different from McDowell's original thinking, and again I have not decided which view to take.[18]

The ideas I covered in this chapter – conceptuality, rationality, propositionality, experience, language, environment, world and so on – are all difficult and elusive, and of course there is still much left out. Still, I hope my re-understanding and reformation of McDowell's earlier and later thoughts are both interpretatively and philosophically interesting. I hope to pursue issues scratched here on future occasions.

Epilogue

Self-Determining Subjectivity

When I say: I think, I act, etc., then either the word "I" is used falsely or I am free. Were I not free, I could not say: I do it, but rather I would have to say: I feel a desire in me to do, which someone has aroused in me. But when I say: I do it, that means spontaneity in the transcendental sense.

Immanuel Kant, Metaphysics, L₁

The I shall be a self-determined I.

J. G. Fichte, Fichtes Werke, IV

Freedom

1. When McDowell introduces the notion of 'the space of reasons', he identifies it with 'the realm of freedom'. His project is to show how human beings' standings in the space of reasons can be natural, and how this second nature endows each of us a *Cogito*, being a perceiver, knower, thinker, speaker, agent, person and conscious/self-conscious subject. In earlier chapters, I have tried to describe and evaluate this project of McDowell. Since 'the space of reasons' and 'the realm of freedom' are virtually the same, we need to understand how McDowell understands the very notion of 'freedom' and how this understanding fits his thinking about the space of reasons as described above. The situation, however, is rather dim.

To be free, a subject must initiate its thinking and actions by itself; the *causes* of its thinking and actions must be part of the very idea of that subject. And by hypothesis, human freedom is located in the space of reasons. It follows that to understand human freedom, human 'self-determining subjectivity', we need to have an intelligible notion of 'causation in the space of reasons'

(Gaskin, 2006, p. 28). As I mentioned in Chapter 2, the notion of 'cause' can present in both the space of reasons and the realm of law. The reason for this, to rehearse, is that reasons can be causes, and to say we are free agencies is *not* to say that we live in a causeless world. Freedom is not random. As inhabitants in the space of reasons, we enjoy 'space of reason causations'. This is at odds with the scientific understanding of the world, but as we have seen, McDowell objects to this:

> [S]cientific hijacking of the concept of causality, according to which the concept is taken to have its primary role in articulating the partial world-view that is characteristic of the physical sciences, so that all other causal thinking needs to be based on causal relations characterizable in physical terms.
>
> 2002b/2008b, p. 139[1]

But as Gaskin notices, 'this merely negative elucidation of the notion of space of reason causation cannot be regarded as satisfactory' (2006, p. 31). We learn that causality should *not* be restricted in the realm of law, and that the space of reasons is constitutively *sui generis*, i.e. *not* a special case of the realm of law. But one wishes to know more about its positive features. To be sure, McDowell does say a lot about the space of reasons, and I myself think most of the relevant remarks make good sense. The trouble is that there seems to be something still being left out after McDowell's efforts. As discussed in Chapter 2, Paul Bartha and Steven Savitt mistakenly think McDowell is willing to let the same kind of causality occupy both the space of reasons and the realm of law, but their misunderstanding is reasonable to some extent, because McDowell does says less than he needs to say about causality in the space of reasons. In particular, philosophers of science try hard to understand causality and related notions in the realm of law, and for most of them that kind of causality is the only kind. To rebut this, McDowell and his followers need to at least say more about extant understandings of causality and in which respects they need to be improved.

We can say something on McDowell's behalf. For him, the urgent task is to find a way of thinking that exempts us from the anxiety characteristic of our modern conception of the world. In doing this, one only needs to undermine the assumptions that generate the anxiety in question. And McDowell does exactly this. Nonetheless, one might still want to know more about the nature of self-determining subjectivity and causality in the space of reasons, for philosophy is not restricted to diagnoses. McDowell is quite right that we should stop and reflect our seemingly unproblematic assumptions, but it should not prevent us from trying to understand the nature of things. To understand more does not amount to engage in constructive philosophy in any negative sense.[2]

2. In recent years, McDowell spends more time writing about self-determining subjectivity, especially in the context of German Idealism. As he says, '[a] stress on self-determining subjectivity is characteristic of German Idealism in general' (2005e/2008a, p. 90)[3]. This descends the main theme of *Mind and World*: to have an appropriate understanding of subjectivity, we need a satisfying conception of *external* and *rational* constraint. In his various papers on Hegel (2003a/2008a, 2003b, 2009a, 2009b, 2010a/2008a, 2018a, 2018b), McDowell further elaborates his thoughts about the shape of this crucial external constraint. In particular, in a piece on apperception in Kant and Hegel, McDowell talks about constraint from otherness.[4] None of these, however, says directly about how self-determining subjectivity *per se* is to be understood. We hear the familiar McDowellian voice in the following:

> One is *responsible* for how one's mind is made up. To *judge* is to engage in *free* cognitive activity, as contrasted with having something merely happen in one's life, outside one's *control*. So *freedom* is central to Kant's picture of *conceptual* capacities.
>
> 2003a/2008a, p. 79; my emphasis

My emphasis points to many interrelated notions that need to be understood together, and indeed McDowell has done a lot to shed light on those relations. But we hope to know more about *exactly how* reasons can be causes, i.e. what causality in the space of reasons looks like. To this McDowell might reply that we demand too much here, for maybe there are some 'reductive' impulses lurking in this kind of query. I am not sure.

Self-determining subjectivity defines 'I', and as discussed in Chapter 5, McDowell thinks that 'there is no commitment to some peculiar extra ingredient, which would ensure determinateness of identity, in a person's make-up' (1997c/1998a, pp. 378–9). I said that I am hesitant to think with McDowell that 'there is no further fact'. Although I have not come up with any satisfying answer to this, I venture to put my very tentative thought in the following: there are further facts about the 'I' and its self-determining subjectivity, that is, they are *socially, as opposed to physically*, real. Even if they are social *constructs*, they are as real as any physical phenomenon. It is just that their realities are constituted by social interactions, or in McDowell's term from Wittgenstein, by *forms of life*. Our task is to understand how those social institutions enable us to be 'us', to be equipped self-determining subjectivity, through the space of reasons causations.[5] I think this is central for any development in McDowell's vein, for what makes us distinctively human is the fact that we live in *the realm of freedom*. Furthermore, this chimes well with the 'idea that we sometimes exercise freedom without being *aware* of it is at best awkward' (2005e/2008a, p. 96).

The greatest difficulty in McDowell's philosophy seems to concern with the relation between the realm of law and the space of reasons, and as a quietist McDowell refuses to say more about it. In contemporary terms, the realm of law and the space of reasons can be understood in terms of *ontological levels of existence*: the realm of law covers physics, chemistry, and perhaps biology and empirical psychology (scientific image), while the space of reasons covers folk psychology (manifest image). How can folk psychology be naturalized without being reduced? One intuitive way of developing this line is to hold that the space of reasons *exist as a higher-level phenomenon*, which enjoys a unique ontological status. In the context of free will, Christian List (2019) has argued that free will is such a higher-level existence. However, he holds that both *supervenience* and *emergence* hold for free will, which results in an unstable position (Cheng, in preparation): supervenience as he understands it implies necessitation, which is not compatible with a robust notion of emergence. McDowell, I believe, needs to insist that the space of reasons as a whole is an *emergent* phenomena, because this is the only way any dualism can hold in this area. Other relations, such as supervenience, necessitation, metaphysical explanation, realization, grounding, ontological dependence and constitution, all make the space of reasons too close to the realm of law, and therefore does not fit McDowell's purposes. How this emergence can be cashed out is of course a daunting task, and in this respect, McDowell's view concerning reasons and mentality as a whole is very similar to Chalmers' view concerning consciousness (1996). McDowell's own statement on the personal and subpersonal levels (1994/1998a) cannot be satisfactory without a positive account of emergence.[6]

Wisdom

1. To reflect on our self-determining subjectivity is to touch on the root of McDowell's overall project, and we shall remember that the root of the project is his use of the Aristotelian notion 'second nature'. It should be clear that the notion is essentially *ethical* and *practical*, though I do not pursue this line in the present essay. Consider this passage:

Epilogue: Self-Determining Subjectivity

> The practical intellect's coming to be as it ought to be is the acquisition of a second nature, involving the moulding of motivational and evaluative propensities: a process that takes place in nature. The practical intellect does not dictate to one's formed character – one's nature as it has become – from outside. One's formed practical intellect – which is operative in one's character-revealing behavior – just is an aspect of one's nature as it has become.
>
> 1996b/1998a, p. 185

In this final section, I do not intend to reopen the discussion about second nature. All I would like to do here is to remind that perhaps we can find some resources in this practical notion, since *wisdom* and *freedom* constitute the dual cores of McDowell's naturalism. In understanding and evaluating McDowell's thoughts in this practical domain, we shall bear the concerns and perhaps misgivings discussed in my previous section in mind: we know that he thinks our second nature endows us with the ability to exercise the space of reasons causations, in both practical and theoretical domains; the concern is that how that is supposed to get a foothold in our animal nature, given that before gaining abilities to be responsive to reasons as such, we are *mere* animals. It seems that in this practical domain the same challenge arises for McDowell and his followers.

This needs collaborations. As mentioned above, causality or causation is a big topic in philosophy of science and metaphysics, but most of the people in those disciplines, I presume, advocate bald naturalism. Bald naturalism may turn out to be true, but before that can be demonstrated, we need to leave room for the possibility of naturalism of second nature. Experts in philosophy of science need to have that possibility in view; otherwise, we cannot have the best players in the relevant field to work out the details about how reasons can be causes. Davidson offers a possible, and to some extent plausible, way for us to think about, but as evaluated towards the end of Chapter 5, that proposal tends to result in epiphenomenalism, to put it mildly. Most of McDowell's arguments for causality in the space of reasons are *transcendental*, but even for those who have accepted its ontology, *how* that is supposed to work is an independently interesting and important question. One of the merits of McDowell's works is that it arouses more attentions to an important theoretical option: instead of simply pointing to a conceptual possibility, he offers a strong case for this alternative. But we need more attentions, especially from those who specialize in the problem of causality and that of freedom of the will. Younger generations should take more responsibilities, for they (we) grew up in a century that has been heavily under McDowell's influence, in a very positive way, or so I shall urge.

2. The Western tradition has it that the hierarchy of understanding starts from data, information, knowledge and finally to wisdom. This reflects an atomist intuition, and even nowadays the intuition is still widespread and deep-rooted. If data means sub-sentential contents, the data-information order has been confirmed by Frege's context principle (Frege, 1884/1950). The order between information and knowledge is fine and natural; as McDowell notices, the problem (if any) about intentionality is always conceptually prior to that about knowledge. But McDowell also reverses the knowledge-wisdom order: by his light, we need to be *initiated into a tradition* first, understood in terms of 'practical wisdom', in order to have thoughts and knowledge. This is compatible with the commonsense that we can learn most wisdom only after we are equipped with plenty of information and knowledge; McDowell's revolutionary move is that information and knowledge are constitutively dependent on wisdom, in the sense we have discussed throughout the essay: practical wisdom is what brings us from mere animals to mature human beings or rational animals, from proto-subjectivity to self-determining subjectivity, manifesting ourselves as genuine perceivers, knowers, thinkers, speakers, agents, persons and (self-) conscious beings in the world. If Tyler Burge's primary concern is the origins of *objectivity* (2010), it might be fair to say that McDowell's primary concern is the origins of *subjectivity*.[7] I hope the plausibility of this general picture has been raised by this essay to some extent, and I hope the remaining questions I tried to point out in this epilogue are sensible and positive. Subjectivity in a broad sense has always been a central concern in Western philosophy, and the key to having a satisfying understanding of it is to investigate the way self-determining subjectivity, which is able to exert causality in the space of reasons, relates to causality in the realm of law. I commit myself to this challenging task.

It might be helpful if a summary or analytical content is included at this point, so I end this essay with the following.

Prologue. Oxford Kantianism and Pittsburgh Hegelianism

Background

1. I propose to use two labels to situate McDowell's philosophy into wider contexts, with some caveats, for example McDowell himself would not approve this approach.

2. I explain what 'Oxford Kantianism' roughly means, and introduce a basic distinction between two strands in this tradition: 'left-wing Oxford Kantians', includes Gareth Evans, Naomi Eilan, John Campbell, José Luis Bermúdez and myself, who seek to accommodate empirical considerations, and 'right-wing Oxford Kantians', includes John McDowell, Quassim Cassam and Anil Gomes, who refrain themselves from doing so.
3. I explain what 'Pittsburgh Hegelianism' roughly means, and state that it will mostly stay in the background compared to the Kantianism introduced above, as we have seen more recent works on this theme, notably Chauncey Maher's book-length treatment on the Pittsburgh School of Philosophy.
4. I consider criticisms to Oxford Kantianism from Andrew Brook and David Papineau, and propose how to think of them for the present purposes. The distinction between naturalism and physicalism is made relevant here: one can be a non-physicalist naturalist.

Foreground

1. I briefly explain how phenomenology and cognitive sciences will figure in this project. Basically, they are largely embedded in the flow of the discussions, as opposed to being singled out in certain chapters. McDowell's exchanges with Dreyfus might be an exception, as that is where he explicitly addresses phenomenological objections.
2. I introduce my own perspective 'Naturalised Strawsonianism', and explain how descriptive metaphysics can potentially chime well with transcendental phenomenology. Basically, describing connections in conceptual schemes can involves necessary connections that might merit the label of 'transcendental'.

Chapter 1. The Many Faces of Human Subject

World

1. I introduce the main theme of this essay, distinguishing my leading concern – human subject(ivity) and its place in the world – from the one in philosophy of mind in the narrow sense, i.e. about the mind or mentality and its place in nature. The notion of 'nature' will be pivotal throughout the essay, so I intend to have a more careful treatment of it.

2. The central thesis of the essay – the world and minded human subject are constitutively interdependent – is explained. A neutral attitude towards the notion of 'world' is recommended through considering the traditional way of conceiving the problem of perception: metaphysics first (realism or not), and then epistemology (directness or not). A. D. Smith, who exemplifies this way of thinking, assumes that we have the world at the beginning. I argue that the methodology behind this way of thinking is metaphysically biased. A similar failure, though with the opposite direction, is attributed to René Descartes, in particular his 'method of doubt'. In Descartes' case, the world is 'bracketed' at the starting point.

Subject

1. Here I mainly argue for two points. First, the problems about mentality and those about human subject should be tackled together, for to think otherwise is to separate 'mind' and 'self'. Second, to understand human subject is to understand various aspects of it, for a self is always a *functioning* self. I also distinguish 'subject' from 'self' in the course of discussion, arguing that only the former is broad enough for my purposes.
2. John McDowell, my main figure, is introduced at this point. I note that his style of philosophizing creates difficulties for his commentators. In particular, we need to balance between the question-oriented and the figure-centred styles. I emphasize more on the latter because I hope to provide a more systematic investigation of McDowell's philosophy as an integrated whole and its place in the philosophical map.
3. I identify two strands of my project. The first one is about the tension between the rational and the natural; the second one is about how the biological-rooted rational capacities enable us to be perceivers, knowers, thinkers, speakers, agents, persons and (self-) conscious subjects. I emphasize the latter strand, and summarize McDowell's engagements with other philosophers, including Aristotle, Robert Brandom, Hans-Georg Gadamer, Crispin Wright, Saul Kripke, Michael Dummett, Donald Davidson, Hubert Dreyfus, Maurice Merleau-Ponty, Derek Parfit and Immanuel Kant, amongst others. I also say why I need an epilogue on self-determining subjectivity.

Chapter 2. *Cogito* and *Homo sapiens*

Nature

1. I characterize the tension between reason and nature (conceived with scientific terms), and the fact that to have a satisfying self-image is to relieve this putative tension.
2. Wilfrid Sellars' remark is quoted here to pave the way for distinguishing 'the space of reasons' and 'the realm of law', corresponding to Sellars' 'manifest image' and 'scientific image'. I introduce two ways of confronting this distinction – bald naturalism and rampant platonism – and discuss why McDowell thinks both of them are unsatisfying.

Nurture

1. McDowell's alternative picture – a naturalism of second nature, or naturalized platonism – is described as a middle course between bald naturalism and rampant platonism. I then briefly discuss the notion of 'second nature' in Aristotle. The naturalistic credential of 'phronesis' is urged by relating it to the notion of *Bildung* in German philosophy. And then I discuss how McDowell invokes these resources to argue against a *factorizing* understanding of Aristotle's thought that humans are rational animals.
2. Two lines of objection are described and answered. They concern the contrast between the space of reasons and the realm of law, and the differences between naturalized and rampant platonism. Two key points are argued; first, there are two kinds of causality according to McDowell, and second, McDowell never attempts to knock rampant platonism down.
3. McDowell's view on mere animals is illustrated by the distinction between world and environment from Hans-Georg Gadamer. The notion of 'world' is connected to language, freedom and openness. I explain how this distinction helps us avoid two strands in the Cartesian thinking: that mere animals are automata, and that humans are immaterial souls.
4. Brandom's accusation of residual individualism is partially answered by considering McDowell's criticism to Davidson's 'triangulation', and a reservation of McDowell's presentation of Davidson – that is, triangulation is between 'self-standing subjects' – is made.

Chapter 3. Perceiver and Knower

Primeness

1. I invoke Timothy Williamson's two notions 'broadness' and 'primeness' to illustrate the differences between internalism and weak/strong externalism: internalism rejects both, weak externalism accepts broadness but rejects primeness, and strong externalism accepts both.
2. How Cartesian 'method of doubt' results in the 'inner space model' is discussed. McDowell's objection to scepticism is distinguished from others' ones, for example Barry Stroud's objection to the KK principle. The case of perception is identified as a prominent example of the inner space model. I discuss the debate between the common kind theory and disjunctivism, and relate this to the traditional debate about the analysis of knowledge raised by Edmund Gettier. Later an objection from Simon Blackburn is discussed and answered.
3. McDowell argues that the inner space model makes intentionality unavailable to us, because on that model we are never in touch with the world. Two motivations of the inner space model – from modern science and first-person authority – are dampened: the former unjustly eliminates the space of reasons, and the latter renders our authority excessive. A stronger argument from the Fregean sense is answered by introducing the correct understanding of the notion of 'the cognitive realm'.
4. I go back to the parallel story in epistemology. The relation between justification and epistemic luck is strengthened in McDowell's picture. And then I discuss how McDowell's argument against the 'interiorization of the space of reasons' works against the traditional hybrid view of knowledge. According to him, the traditional view cannot make sense of our critical reasons and epistemic lucks, and it is *ad hoc* as far as scepticism is concerned. Traditionalist' argument from BIV is also answered by noting the distinction between justification and exculpation.

Openness

1. Primeness naturally leads to openness. I discuss how McDowell combines Kant's discursivity thesis and Davidson's objection with the dualism of scheme and content. The dialectic between coherentism and the Myth of the Given is characterized, with McDowell's 'see-saw' metaphor: we need *external* as well as *rational* constraint, but the see-saw seems to show that we

cannot have it both ways. Bald naturalism appears here as a possible way of dismounting the see-saw through repudiating the *sui generis* character of the space of reasons. And then I introduce McDowell's central claim in his Locke Lecture that experiences are passively conceptual all the way out.
2. McDowell's central transcendental argument concerning how intentionality is possible is discussed. And his denial of 'the ontological gap' is explained. I then turn to the charge of idealism against the 'unboundedness of the conceptual' and how McDowell uses the act/content distinction to reply.
3. Brandom argues against McDowell's emphasis on 'experience', and thinks that the emphasis betrays a 'residual individualism'. I reply to this by clarifying the notion of 'experience' adopted by McDowell; the significance of this is reflected by the fact that the same misreading seems to occur in other philosophers' thinking, notably Michael Ayers. This leads to the question about how McDowell conceives the social elements of intentionality.

Chapter 4. Thinker and Speaker

Custom

1. I investigate McDowell's conception of the social elements of intentionality by considering his criticisms to Kripke's Wittgensteinian sceptical paradox. Kripke's sceptical doubt from 'the infinite regress of interpretation' and his corresponding sceptical solution are characterized.
2. Wittgenstein's remarks in *PI* §201 are referred to indicate a way to say 'no' to the sceptic. I then explain why we should see Wittgenstein as distancing himself from reductionism about meaning. McDowell's various citations from Wittgenstein are interpreted, and Kripke's ways of pressing the sceptical challenge are discussed. In answering the challenge, I introduce Wittgenstein's notion of 'bedrock'.
3. I contrast McDowell's way of understanding 'communal' practices with Kripke's and Wright's ones; the former respects Wittgenstein's notion of 'custom', while the latter renders a group of people 'a wooden community'. It turns out that Brandom's picture has a similar problem. I connect the wooden picture to the inner space model introduced before.
4. Kripke's objections to McDowell's so-called 'primitivism' are discussed. I put the emphasis on objections raised by Martin Kusch. Kusch argues that

dispositionalism does not rely on the infinite regress of interpretation, and McDowell's view is similar to dispositionalism. I dispute both of these. In addition, I rebut Kusch's insistence that Kripke's picture is essentially social. I also disagree with his way of connecting the indeterminacy of meaning to reductionism. Finally, I briefly argue that McDowell advocates a delicate version of realism about meaning.

5. I trace the source of Kripke's and Wright's conviction in reductionism to the traditional dichotomy between the Cartesian and the Rylean, between psychologism and behaviourism. Quine is also responsible for this dichotomy. I discuss Dummett's effort to avoid the problem and McDowell's criticisms to it. Dummett distinguishes between 'full-blooded' and 'modest' theory of meaning, and thinks the latter unavoidably collapses into psychologism. I explain how McDowell invokes his conception of 'membership' to sustain the claim that in conversations we 'hear someone else's meaning in his words'. I then shift from McDowell's emphasis on custom and in turn on language to Davidson's claim that 'there is no such a thing as a language'.

Bildung

1. I introduce Davidson's target – the conventional view of communication – and his putative counterexamples from malapropism. Although McDowell agrees on this, he nevertheless dissents to Davidson's 'leap', that a public language plays no role in the constitution of subjectivity. This reflects their different conceptions of 'language games'.
2. I argue that McDowell sides with Davidson that we should not participate the rule-following discussions generated by Kripke's celebrated work on Wittgenstein. This involves giving up the conviction that communication is constituted by shared rules or conventions. The relevance of *Bildung* is also indicated.

Chapter 5. Agent and Person

Embodiment

1. I start the argumentation by deepening my characterization of conceptualism, which has been introduced in the context of 'openness'. I

emphasize McDowell's distinction between 'responsiveness to reasons' and 'responsiveness to reasons *as such*'. This concerns the relation he draws between conceptuality and rationality. Another crucial distinction about the way conceptual capacities enters the picture – between 'exercise' and 'operative' – is also explained. I then consider Ayers' objection that the picture recommended by McDowell makes our experiences 'quasi-linguistic'. This is a misunderstanding based on the dualism of the sensory and the intellectual. I then show that McDowell has a parallel story for 'action', indicating that the locus of the disagreement between him and Dreyfus is the very idea of 'passivity' in perceptions and actions.

2. I note that Dreyfus launches his objections by contrasting McDowell with Samuel Todes's *Body and World*. Dreyfus first introduces his general framework between 'detached rule-following' and 'situation-specific way of coping'. I argue that actually McDowell regards conceptual capacities as situation-specific, and we can see this in his objections to Kripke's 'infinite regress of interpretation'.

3. Dreyfus improves his framework by replacing the original distinction with the one between 'subjectivity' and 'absorption'. However, I argue that his example from the baseball player Chuck Knoblauch betrays his confusion of 'conceptual mindedness' and 'attention'. I then argue that McDowell never regards attention as central in his picture, though he probably should. And I explain why Dreyfus's conception of self-awareness is problematic and how McDowell argues that Dreyfus and sometimes Maurice Merleau-Ponty lapse into 'the Myth of the Disembodied Intellect'.

4. I argue that Dreyfus conflates the Myth of the Given and foundationalism, and thereby unwittingly falls into the former: his notion of 'solicitation' belongs to the realm of law, but it is used by him to do the 'base-providing' work. I then note that Dreyfus is ambivalent about the status of human body: sometimes it is distinctively human-like, but sometimes it is like an automaton.

5. I remind my readers that the Myth of the Disembodied Intellect is in effect a version of the inner space model. And I connect McDowell's talks about 'I' to his conception of 'personhood'.

Embedment

1. Derek Parfit's reductive approach to develop John Locke's general picture about self-consciousness is introduced. Against this, McDowell elaborates

Gareth Evans' argument based on 'identification-freedom'. Parfit's thinking is faulty because in responding to the identification-freedom in the first-person case, he implicitly holds the so-called 'narrow assumption'.

2. Since the trouble is due to the narrow assumption, McDowell's argument against it is from the notion of 'broadness'; in this context, this amounts to the emphasis on the third-person perspective. McDowell's diagnosis of Parfit is that the latter, as well as many others, mistakenly think the root of the Cartesian is immaterialism. I then explain how McDowell reconciles Locke's insight with 'animalism'. Later I discuss McDowell's argument that any account based on the notion of 'quasi-memory' – first introduced by Sydney Shoemaker and endorsed by Parfit – nevertheless commits the factorizing way of conceiving memory.

3. In talking about personhood, McDowell seems to oblige himself to take a stance towards the mind-body problem. I envisage what McDowell would say by discussing his criticisms against Davidson's anomalous monism. Two motivations – the unity of science and avoidance of Cartesian dualism – are dislodged. I explain why McDowell thinks that the premise to be renounced is 'the Principle of the Nomological Character of Causality'. Furthermore, McDowell argues that Davidson's position leads to epiphenomenalism. Finally, McDowell's own position 'event dualism' is sketched but without enough elaborations.

Chapter 6. *Apperceiver* and *Homo sentiens*

Objectivity

1. The Evans-Strawson argument based on 'identification-freedom' is applied to Kant's thinking about 'apperception'. McDowell argues that the interdependence of self-consciousness and consciousness of the world argued by Kant in Transcendental Deduction would be more satisfying if it can accommodate the fact that humans are 'bodily presences in the world'. Unlike Parfit, Kant is not attracted by reductionism; instead he argues that the 'I think' must be a merely formal condition. Nevertheless, McDowell's argument against Parfit works in Kant's case as well.

2. Here I consider Maximilian de Gaynesford's objections that McDowell's Kant is not Kant. His reconstruction of McDowell's argument, however, is problematic at various points. For example, he thinks that McDowell's

argument relies crucially on the notion of 'reference', and that McDowell mistakenly attributes the anti-immaterialism premise and the narrow assumption to Kant, and so on. I dispute all of these.

3. I argue that McDowell's argument against Kant's formal 'I think' is an example of his general denial of 'scheme-content dualism'. Davidson's initial introduction to this dualism is discussed. I concentrate on McDowell's construal of it, discussing several applications of his criticisms, including anti-interiorization of the space of reasons, the conceptuality of experience, a novel reading of the private language argument, and his repudiation of 'Nomological Character of Causality', the fourth dogma of empiricism. McDowell's thought is that we can retain real objectivity only if we firmly reject forms of scheme-content dualism.

Subjectivity

1. The narrow sense of 'subjectivity' – the 'what-it-is-like' respect – is the main theme here. I start with Ned Block's claim that the great chasm in philosophy of mind is between the qualia theory and representationalism. The essential features of 'qualia' are identified as 'non-cognitive' and 'intrinsic'. I argue that McDowell's case against them can be found in his holism of the mental and his objections to scheme-content dualism. As a result, McDowell is a representationalist in philosophy of mind.

2. 'Representationalism' and 'intentionalism' are often interchangeable terms, so I need to address Tim Crane's claim that intentionalism and disjunctivism are incompatible. In order to engage with this point, I investigate versions of McDowell's disjunctivism. According to my interpretation, McDowell commits state, reason, content and (weak) phenomenal disjunctivism (the 'state' and 'reason' ones are my own terminology). I take issue with Alex Byrne and Heather Logue concerning McDowell's commitment to metaphysical (in my term, 'state') disjunctivism.

3. Since the issues between disjunctivism and intentionalism originally arise from the argument from illusion/hallucination, I introduce a version of the argument and identify two crucial features of it, arguing that we can anchor the debate with either of them, but Crane's framework corresponds to neither. I prefer one of the frameworks since it reflects nowadays' heated debate between disjunctivism and the 'common kind theory'. This framework helps us see the essential claim of intentionalism. And I further relate the present discussion to the internalism/externalism debate. I thereby

argue that the 'disjunctive versus factorizing framework' proposed by Tamar Szabó Gendler and John Hawthorne is not fine-grained enough for certain purposes.
4. I suggest that we should not use 'representationalism' and 'intentionalism' interchangeably. The former is a theory in philosophy of mind in general, claiming that *all* mental facts are representational facts; the latter is a theory in philosophy of perception in particular, claiming that 'intentional object/content' is a better explanation than sense-datum. I also find fault in Crane's assimilation of the adverbial theory and the qualia theory. The failure to distinguish representationalism from intentionalism is due to a misunderstanding of the transparency (if any) of experience and a misreading of the main aim of the argument from illusion, I submit. I tentatively conclude that in philosophy of mind McDowell is an inter-model weak representationalist, and in philosophy of perception he is a disjunctive intentionalist.

Chapter 7. Rational Animal and Conceptual Being

Conceptuality

1. I explain how McDowell repudiated two views concerning experiential content, and propose that we should downplay the importance of conceptuality throughout his writings, contrary to what he has been intending. The basic idea is that his later picture is actually more continuous with his earlier picture, *pace* his own judgement.
2. I single out two strands in McDowell's thinking: Sellars on rationality (SR) and Kant and Davidson on conceptuality (KDC), and show that four of his introductions of *Mind and World* primarily rely on SR only. These textual analyses help us see that McDowell's insistence on conceptuality is not well motivated.
3. I argue that relying on Kant on concepts is a red herring for McDowell's purposes, for while Kant was operating with the Aristotelian model, McDowell himself is operating with the Fregean model. The relevant Kantian insights concerning spontaneity should be preserved, but only in spirit.
4. I compare McDowell's and Davidson's understandings of scheme-content dualism, and explain their crucial difference here debars McDowell from invoking the Davidsonian resources in concepts. Perhaps McDowell's

diagnosis of the problem does go deeper in that it aims at intentionality, but under his construal the 'scheme' cannot be conceptual scheme.
5. I argue that McDowell has not made a convincing case for the co-extensiveness between the rational and the conceptual. On the one hand, the 'conceptuality → rationality' claim is relatively plain, as McDowell emphasizes that this is a stipulation. On the other hand, the 'rationality → conceptuality' claim seems to be a substantive one, and I argue that rationality only imposes a certain structure of the justifiers, and that structure does not have to be conceptual.

Intuitionality

1. I explain how McDowell softens his views on experiential contents in response to Dreyfus's objections, and why he still insists on conceptuality in his later views. His later emphasis on 'world-disclosing' experience is significant, and this is crucial to his distinction between 'responsiveness to reasons' and 'responsiveness to reasons *as such*'.
2. I discuss why McDowell's remarks on 'conceptual in form' are no good, and why 'conceptualization' is not a harmful notion. I also explain how he gave up 'propositionality thesis' and 'comprehensiveness thesis' concerning experiential contents, though in response to Dreyfus, these adjustments are not required.
3. McDowell's new notion of 'intuitional content' is introduced, and whether it should be understood as conceptual content is considered. I also question McDowell's interpretation of Sellars on the assertoric force of experiences. The fact that McDowell's core thinking concerns SR but not KDC is emphasized again. I also explain how McDowell's updated view can avoid collapsing into a version of the Myth of the Given. This is where *attention* should come into McDowell's overall picture, and also where cognitive sciences can be relevant to his thinking.
4. I connect the above discussion to the distinction between environment and world from Gadamer. Basically, if McDowell wants to hold that the structure of thought, experience and world coincide, then the repudiation of propositional contents in experience has to have some impacts to the overall picture. It is curious that McDowell himself does not seem to be sensitive to the issues here.
5. I suggest that there is no easy way out here, and put two proposals on the table. The first states that the distinction between environment and world comes into degrees, and this fits the idea that both perception and language have degrees of abstraction. This is problematic, however, as environment

and world correspond to the realm of law and the space of reasons, and they are different in kind. The other proposal states that mature humans cannot be in touch with environment directly, but they can study it *via* theoretical perspectives such as in sciences and philosophy.

Epilogue. Self-Determining Subjectivity

Freedom

1. McDowell identifies 'the space of reasons' with 'the realm of freedom', which is closely related to our 'self-determining subjectivity'. To understand this, we need to have an intelligible notion of 'the space of reasons causation'. I agree with Richard Gaskin that McDowell has not provided a fully satisfying conception of it. However, I think McDowell's transcendental argument for the *existence* of that kind of causality is convincing. Besides, I suggest that though providing a satisfying explanation of this kind of causality does not lie in the heart of McDowell's philosophical outlook, still it would be better if we have a deeper understanding of it.
2. I note the fact that McDowell says a lot about self-determining subjectivity in the context of German Idealism, but those efforts do not directly improve the situation. My own suggestion is that self-determining subjectivity is socially real, but the details of this sketchy picture have not been worked out.

Wisdom

1. I remind that the same considerations about self-determining subjectivity apply to McDowell's thinking about practical wisdom. I suggest that philosophers of science should leave open the possibility of the naturalism of second nature, so that they can help us understand more about causality in the space of reasons, if any.
2. I close the essay by relating McDowell's emphasis on wisdom to the familiar hierarchy of understanding from data, information, knowledge, to wisdom. McDowell provides a fruitful way for us to reconsider the importance of wisdom. I then rehearse my main theme that practical wisdom initiates us into the space of reasons, and this second nature endows each of us a *Cogito*, which can be a perceiver, knower, thinker, speaker, agent, person and (self-)conscious being in the world.

Notes

Prologue

1. McDowell has four paper collections so far. When referring to papers included in those volumes, the original and reprinted years will both appear. For the four volumes, they will be referred as: *Mind, Value, and Reality* (1998a); *Meaning, Knowledge, and Reality* (1998b); *Having the World in View: Essays on Kant, Hegel, and Sellars* (2008a); *The Engaged Intellect: Philosophical Essays* (2008b).
2. This is not to deny that McDowell's Kant is also heavily influenced by Sellars; for example see McDowell (1998c/2008a, 1998d/2008a, 1998e/2008a). It is just that McDowell himself has expatiated this aspect in various places, so here I emphasize the Strawsonian rather than the Sellarsian lineage. Sellars will be situated in the Pittsburgh Hegelian camp.
3. Issues concerning Kant and Hegel cannot be entirely separated; see for example McDowell (1999a, 2007a/2008a, 2007b/2008a). Relevant discussions, also in relation to phenomenology, see McDowell (2000a).
4. For an early work comparing Husserl and Strawson, see Gorner (1971). Also see Christensen (2008) for interplays between McDowell and phenomenology.

Chapter 1

1. Chalmers (1996) regards supervenience as necessary though not sufficient for reductive physicalism. It is possible to accept supervenience and opt for non-reductive physicalism (e.g. Davidson, 1970/2001a).
2. Compare the 'placement problem' defined by Huw Price (2011).
3. One notable exception can be found in *The Embodied Mind: Cognitive Science and Human Experience* (2017), by Varela, Thompson, and Rosch. It is interesting to observe that Smith himself (2003) warns us about this pitfall in the context of understanding Husserl's later philosophy (pp. viii–ix).
4. And of course also in Husserl's appropriation of this method (1931/2013).
5. This echoes what McDowell identifies as the 'inner space' model, which will be discussed especially in Chapter 3.

6 Some use it to capture the crucial difference between oneself and others, for example Thomas Nagel asks, 'how can it be the case that one of the people in the world is *me*?' (2007, p. 36).
7 For McDowell's own exposition of this view, see for example McDowell (2009c) and (2015).

Chapter 2

1 Chalmers (1996) elaborates a parallel dialectic for the case of consciousness.
2 Notice that the realm of law should not be understood as the space of 'causal relations to objects', as Rorty does in *Philosophy and the Mirror of Nature* (1979, p. 157). McDowell offers two reasons for this. First, following Russell's 'On the Notion of Cause' (1917), McDowell thinks that 'the idea of causation should be replaced, in the role of basic organizing principle for the world as viewed by natural science, with something like the idea of law-governed processes' (1996a, p. 71, n. 2). This is controversial, to be sure. Second, 'it is also disputable in its implication that the idea of causal connections is restricted to thinking that is *not* framed by the space of reasons' (ibid., same footnote). Reasons can be causes; causations that figure in the space of reasons are called the 'space of reason causations' by Richard Gaskin (2006). This qualification will become important when we later consider some objections against McDowell's position. For issues on Rorty and objectivity, see McDowell (2000b/2008b).
3 The metaphor is based on Sellars' classic paper 'Philosophy and the Scientific Image of Man' (1962).
4 I will say more about this later in this chapter when I discuss Crispin Wright's objection.
5 Correspondingly, McDowell calls his own position 'a partial reenchantment of nature' (1996a, p. 97). For the relation between this issue and the objectivity of aesthetic values, see his (1983/1998a).
6 See McDowell (1985a/1998a, 2004b) for his discussions of this in relation to colours and subjectivism. For more on Aristotle's ethics, see McDowell (1980a/1998a, 1995a/2008b, 1996b/1998a, 1996c/2008b, 1996d/2008b, 1998f/1998a). For his early discussion of virtue and reason, see McDowell (1979/1998a); of hypothetical imperatives, see McDowell (1978a/1998a); of projection and truth in ethics, see McDowell (1987a/1998a). McDowell's views here are strikingly similar to Iris Murdoch (1970).
7 The insistence that the meaningfulness of the world is different from that of the text will be important in Ch. 5, when I consider how McDowell replies to objections from Michael Ayers and Arthur Collins.
8 The notion of 'factorization' is supposed to be contrasted with 'integration'. To say that AB can be factorized into A and B is to say that the individuation conditions of

them respectively are mutually independent. Similar ideas can be found in Husserlian phenomenology, e.g. 'The distinction between pieces and moments is very important in philosophical analysis. What often happens in philosophy is that something that is a moment is taken to be a piece, *taken to be separable* from its wider whole and other parts; then an artificial philosophical "problem" arises about how the original whole can be reconstituted' (Sokolowski, 2000, pp. 24–5; my emphasis).

9 B&S quotes John Passmore's *Philosophical Reasoning* (1961, p. 44) at this point, but I think this is redundant given that we are so familiar with the trouble instantiated by Cartesian dualism.

10 B&S also cites the above paper from McDowell, but for another purpose. It is puzzling that they did not notice the enabling/constitutive distinction in the very same paper. It is possible to argue, though, that the realm of law has to be an enabling condition for the space of reasons as well.

11 To my knowledge, Wright never explicitly identifies himself as a bald naturalist, but his identity is clear in the context of the theory of meaning: he sides with his teacher Dummett in holding that a theory of meaning should be 'full-blooded'. I will say more about this in my Chapter 4.

12 I will say more about this in Chapter 4, where I evaluate the debate between McDowell and Donald Davidson whether a public language plays any significant role in constituting the human intellect; also see Chapter 7 for different interpretations of this distinction.

13 Here I do not refer to Descartes in particular. Indeed, terms like 'platonism' and 'Cartesian' figured in McDowell's texts only serve to illustrate different ways of thinking vividly here. On the contrary, he does refer to particular philosophers when he elaborates the relation between concept and intuition, the role of second nature, and the distinction between world and environment. He also specifically discusses Plato in McDowell (1969–70/1998b, 1973, 1982a/2008b).

14 The distinction between responsiveness to reasons and responsiveness to reasons *as such* will be important when it comes to the disagreements between McDowell and Hubert Dreyfus, but I shall leave the nuance in Chapter 5; for now I just want to stress that we are subjects who are in the games of giving and asking for reasons.

15 McDowell's presupposition about freedom will be briefly discussed in my Epilogue. For his view concerning animal ethics, see McDowell (2008c).

Chapter 3

1 These notions are from Timothy Williamson's *Knowledge and Its Limits* (2000). I do not make explicit reference in the main text because his context is slightly different

from mine, and it takes unnecessary effort to appropriate his wordings. I discuss the relation between his invocation of the notions of broadness/primeness and his anti-scepticism in my 'Evaluating Williamson's Anti-Scepticism' (2008). Perception and knowledge are different topics, but they are closely connected in various ways (McDowell, 2011a).

2. Here I bypass the distinction between state and content, for it does not make significant difference in the present discussion.

3. In a different context, Chalmers (1996) similarly distinguishes primary and secondary intensions and this forms the basis of his two-dimensional semantics.

4. As before, the term 'Cartesian' is not invoked to make explicit reference to the philosopher Descartes (McDowell might disagrees with this). 'The inner space model' may be a more neutral label. In this context we do not discuss reason and rationality explicitly, but McDowell (1986b, 1995c/1998a) has discussed this aspect. For discussions concerning Wright (1989) in this regard, see McDowell (1991a/1998a). This is also related to epistemology of other minds and communications in his (1993a/1998b).

5. In these paragraphs McDowell, following M. F. Burnyeat, ventures an interpretation concerning the crucial difference between ancient scepticism and Descartes' more radical version. Since I have distanced myself from exegesis here, in what follows I will characterize McDowell's understanding of the Cartesian inner space without worrying about its historical accuracy. What interests me here is how the inner space model renders the idea of direct contact with the world unintelligible, and how we manage to avoid this unpalatable result. I am interested in the real history too, but that will take us too far. From now on I will simply call the target 'the inner space model'. I am indebted to Christian Wenzel about this. This model is similar to the 'Cartesian theatre' metaphor (Dennett, 1991), and elsewhere I have explained how this can be harmful in the context of Kripkenstein's sceptical paradox (Cheng, 2016).

6. This is similar to Williamson's target, the 'luminosity view' (2000). This issue has generated a huge literature; for a recent example, see Smithies (2019), ch.11. That entire book can be seen as a defence of the luminosity view. Smithies' main opponent there is Williamson, but actually McDowell is also an implicit target. See for example when Smithies discusses 'factivism' and 'factive mentalism' (p. 98, p. 99, p. 205, p. 223). In a way, Smithies' own 'phenomenal accessibilism' is a rival of McDowell's 'epistemological disjunctivism' (p. 226).

7. I have more to say about the relevant matters in Chapter 6.

8. In Chapter 6, I shall argue that we should not use 'intentionalism' and 'representationalism' interchangeably, and the former should be used in the context of perception; besides, the common kind assumption introduced here is *not* built in the very idea of intentionalism. But we do not need all these qualifications now.

9 The terminology here is suggested by the introduction of Gendler and Hawthorne (2006). In Chapter 6 I will argue that this way of carving the ballpark is non-ideal because it might (though does not have to) leave out weak externalism, which accepts broadness but rejects primeness. This does not matter in the present theme.
10 One version of the inner space model might be the causal theory of perception (Grice, 1961; Lewis, 1980).
11 The good/bad case talk is appropriated from Williamson's *Knowledge and Its Limits* (2000).
12 I will say more about this 'disjunctivism' in Chapter 6, when I discuss how McDowell conceives the conscious aspect of our human lives.
13 M. G. F. Martin seems to develop this line of thought in a more detailed way (2004).
14 The topic of the epistemology of other mind is the main theme of his (1982b/1998b).
15 McDowell discusses self-knowledge and related issues in his diagnosis of Cartesian immaterialism. He attempts to argue that immaterialism is *not* the deepest problem with the Cartesian way of thinking. I appropriate his remarks there for my own purposes, namely to show the weakness of the inner space model.
16 The vague term 'something' is supposed to leave open various questions concerning the notion of 'knowledge'.
17 For a book length treatment of this notion, see Pritchard (2005). Issues concerning the value of knowledge is also relevant (Kvanvig, 2003).
18 McDowell (2014) discusses one version of such scepticism.
19 The distinction between exculpation and justification is used by McDowell to criticize the Myth of the Given (1996a, p. 8), which will be discussed presently. Although the context is different right now, the distinction nicely uncovers the central motivation of the interiorisation of the space of reasons. Duncan Pritchard's notion of 'blameless' is similar to McDowell's exculpation (2012, p. 42).
20 I shall not go into the details of Davidson's criticisms and his disagreements with Davidson in the present context. The details and disagreements are important, but for my purposes all these issues will be postponed towards the end (Chapter 7) of the whole project.
21 Although from the start McDowell makes use of the term 'concept' in almost all the contexts, he mainly relies on insights from Frege and Evans, such as the distinction between sense and reference (Frege, 1892/1930), and the generality constraint (Evans, 1982). See for example McDowell (2005a/2008b). It would be helpful if we can draw connections between empirical works on concepts in the relevant branches of psychology, for example Susan Carey (2009) on both the empiricist and the rationalist theories of concept and how developmental psychology can help us think through debates in philosophy concerning concepts. Carey's view is explicitly conceptualist: 'core cognition has rich integrated conceptual content. By this I mean that the representations in core cognition cannot be reduced to perceptual or

sensori-motor primitives, that the representations are accessible and drive voluntary action, and that representations from distinct core cognition systems interact in central inferential processes' (p. 67). For a contrasting case, see Prinz (2002). How to connect these literatures will be an important task for those who are interested in concepts.

22 This will prove to be important when we consider Dreyfus's objections in Chapter 5. Note that in current epistemology, the divide is still between foundationalism and coherentism. McDowell's dialectic is slightly different from the standard one (Hasan, 2017).

23 For more on this, see his 'Conceptual capacities in perception' (2005b/2008a). McDowell also uses 'actualization' in his Woodbridge Lecture. Dreyfus disagrees with McDowell at this point; I shall come back to this in Chapter 5. In explicating Husserl's philosophy, R. A. Mall says: 'In the reduced realm of "constituting intentionality," the distinction between reason and experience seems to *vanish*, and these two concepts become *interchangeable* terms' (1973, p. vii). How this can be properly done remains to be seen, but I must say this sounds all too optimistic.

24 I say more about the relations between Kant, Husserl, and McDowell in Cheng (forthcoming, a). McDowell (2012) comments more on Travis in relation to Putnam. McDowell (1992/1998b) also comments on Putnam's view on intentionality. For his more recent view on the given, see McDowell (2008d/2008a).

25 Note that fineness-of-grain and richness should be distinguished (Tye, 2006). In addition to this on-going debate, there are empirical parallels that illuminate the discussion. Ned Block has argued that experiences are imprecise (2015) and they overflow, i.e. have higher capacities than, cognitive access and working memory (2007a, 2008). Although people have not made the connections between these works and McDowell's, they are actually closely connected and therefore considerations from cognitive sciences can potentially shed lights on the original debate that concerns McDowell and his interlocutors such as Evans (1982) and Peacocke (1998). Roughly, imprecision corresponds to fineness-of-grain, and overflow corresponds to richness. My take on the relevant issue is in Cheng (2017). For a recent development, see Quilty-Dunn (forthcoming). I will briefly come back to this in Chapter 7.

26 Recall my quotation of A. D. Smith at the early stage of Chapter 1. He thinks 'Realism' and 'Idealism' constitutes a dichotomy, and notices that in formulating this he uses terms like 'cognized' and 'states', which belong to the 'act' side in the act/content distinction. Smith's formulation leaves open the possibility that we can have a reasonable idealism formulated in terms of 'content.'

27 And both of them express their faithfulness to Wittgenstein's remark: '[w]hen we say, and *mean*, that such-and-such is the case, we – and our meaning – do not stop anywhere short of the facts; but we mean: this-is-so' (1953/2001, §195). See Brandom (1994), p. 333 and McDowell (1996a), p. 27.

28 The quotation is appropriated for encompassing both Davidson and McDowell. According to Ginsborg, this debate between the two is in some sense only a family quarrel, for there is a more fundamental issue concerning the status of psychological states as reasons in general. Michael Ayers raises a similar consideration in his (2004). Vernazzani (forthcoming) argues against the idea that facts themselves are visually perceptible from empirical evidence concerning object detection and tracking.

29 McDowell further argues that Brandom commits to the composite picture in his account of knowledge (2002a/2008b); I bypass this for that will take us too far. See also McDowell (1997a, 2005d/2008b) for his comment on Brandom's *Making It Explicit* (1994). McDowell (2008e/2008a) also tackles relevant issues in the context of Sellars' 'Empiricism and the philosophy of mind'. I was lucky enough to be there when McDowell and others presented these papers to celebrate the 50th anniversary of EPM at Institute of Philosophy, London.

Chapter 4

1 Part of the ideas here are drawn from my 'The Sceptical Paradox and the Nature of the Self' (2016). McDowell also discusses relevant issues independent of Kripke's context, for example in McDowell (2008f/2008b).
2 Actually, infinity as such is not always a problem, especially when we notice examples from mathematics. I think the infinity in the present context is indeed a problem because it violates the normativity of meaning; it prevents us from deciding non-arbitrarily which interpretation is correct. I am indebted to David McCarty on this point.
3 Some readers might have noticed that I do not have any special interpretation of Kripke. One thing to be noted, however, is that I do not accept George Wilson's *reductio* interpretation of the paradox (1994/2002), which is supposed to cast doubt on the standard interpretation I adopt. I side with Alexander Miller (2002) in thinking that Wilson's interpretation violates Kripke's distinction between the straight solution and the sceptical solution, which seems to me perfectly legitimate. See his introduction in the volume, pp. 1–15. Obviously, this should not be regarded as a sweeping objection to Wilson, whose discussions are abundant and delicate. I temporarily ignore his interpretation because that will lead me too far away from my central concern. This remark applies to all other different interpretations to Kripke.
4 Kripke (1982) quotes this in p. 7; my emphasis.
5 Here I am indebted to Scott Soames.
6 McDowell goes on to cite many other passages from *PI*; I am not going to repeat all of them here.

7 Wittgenstein and McDowell never make this qualification, but I think we should take them as saying that *in general cases*, understanding is not interpretation. To read them as holding the universal claim is uncharitable.
8 Also, 'no matter what is in my mind at a given time, I am free in the future to interpret it in different ways', p. 107.
9 This line of thinking is pursued by Simon Blackburn (1984).
10 McDowell says more in McDowell (1981a/1998b; 1982b/1998b). Concerning understanding meanings in speech, Barry Smith (2009) draws empirical considerations to argue that our auditory awareness of voices can account for this phenomenon; hearing meaning directly might be too strong a view. There is a rich tradition connecting *touch* and other minds in French phenomenology, e.g. Henry (2000/2015) and Merleau-Ponty (1960/1964).
11 Readers who are new to McDowell's philosophy might want to start with this later paper; it is much more user-friendly than the dense 'Wittgenstein on Following a Rule'. In what follows I will not say much about this later paper, for most of the contents relevant to my purposes have been discussed when I concentrated on the earlier, denser paper. For the relation between rule-following and ethics, see McDowell (1981b/1998a).
12 In 'The Sceptical Paradox and the Nature of the Self' (2016), I further connect the inner space model to the homunculus fallacy in philosophy of mind. This will burden Kripke's sceptic as well.
13 Barry Stroud in conversation suggested this way of putting the matter. I talk about 'ownership' here; what I mean is the asymmetry between first-person and third-person knowledge. To invoke the asymmetry is sometimes thought to be a Cartesian move, but I do not think there is anything Cartesian in the present case. See 'The Sceptical Paradox and the Nature of the Self' (2016) where I evaluate the relevant debate between Colin McGinn and Crispin Wright.
14 Crispin Wright (1989) also notices and criticizes the Cartesian 'walled garden'. Although this sounds congenial to McDowell's attack on the inner space, actually their views are quite different. Wright finds fault in the notion of 'inner observation', but McDowell insists that what is at fault should be the 'sign-post' conception of mental items, not 'observation' *per se*. McDowell is 'not defending the model of inner observation', but only 'insist[ing] that the observational model of self-knowledge is not in play here'. We should recognize that '[observational] model is merely a natural form for the epistemology of self-knowledge to take if the [inner space] framework is in place': if mental items are self-standing, normatively inert *objects before the mind*, we do need to observe and interpret them. See McDowell's (1991a/1998a, at p. 315, 319, 321, respectively). Also see his 'Response to Crispin Wright' (1998h) and (2011b).
15 I do not refer to specific passages of it, for I do not want to get into the details of the distinction *per se*. McDowell offers an interesting example to illustrate the point; see

his (1991a/1998a). It is instructive to compare Kripke's position with Quine's. Quine (1960) presses his indeterminacy of translation even to the first-person case, and I suspect that the inner space model is also in play in his thinking.

16. For discussions of the so-called 'cognitive phenomenology', see Chudnoff (2015) and Bayne and Montague (2011).

17. Quine elaborates his indeterminacy thesis in various places, but see his *Word and Object* (1960) for a classic presentation. There are issues about whether Quine is a reductionist, as opposed to an eliminativist, but I need to bypass it in order to stay on my main line.

18. As usual, I am not using these adjectives of philosophers' names in a very strict way. For comments on Brandom's Wittgenstein, see McDowell (2002b/2008b).

19. Daniel Dennett follows him in *The Intentional Stance* (1987).

20. See Kripke's attitude toward Quine in his 1982 book, pp. 14–5, 55–8.

21. The reason I bring this debate in is that it is about what a theory of meaning should be like, e.g. should we accept reductionism? McDowell's thought is that the puzzle about meaning that makes philosophers oscillate back and forth between psychologism and behaviourism, and Kripke does not succeed in developing a stable position. In his objections to Dummett, McDowell explicitly discusses this oscillation, so I think it is helpful to relate it to the rule-following issue. For this reason, I will only discuss Dummett's oscillation and McDowell's way out. I will say more about Davidson towards the end of this chapter.

22. For an example, see McDowell (1980b/1998b). For issues concerning Tarski, see McDowell (1978c/1998b).

23. For the relations between Frege and Davidson in this regard, see McDowell (1976/1998b, 1977/1998b).

24. See the quotation from *Word and Object* above.

25. I leave open whether McDowell's interpretation of Dummett is entirely fair. For more on the relevant theme, see McDowell (1982c/1998b, 1989b/1998b, 2007e).

26. In a footnote in the next page Davidson reminds his readers that his point there is related to the point he argues in 'A Nice Derangement of Epitaphs' that 'communication does not demand that language be shared'.

27. Here Davidson invokes the notion of 'convention', but it is interchangeable with 'rule' and 'regularities' in his context.

28. The other principal function is 'vehicle of thought'.

29. To be sure, Davidson's claim here is supported by his view about linguistic meaning as a whole. By 'the main argument' I mean the *most direct* argument. To investigate Davidson's entire argumentations will obviously take us too far.

30. McDowell invokes Brandom's distinction between '*I-thou* sociality' and '*I-we* sociality' to conduct further discussions. See *Making It Explicit* (1994), p. 659, for citing Davidson with approval. Through this, we can see that McDowell's requirement of publicity is more demanding than Davidson and Brandom.

Chapter 5

1. I start my exposition of this chapter from this piece because it is also what Dreyfus had in mind when he gave his presidential address and later responses. To my knowledge Dreyfus never cites this paper from McDowell explicitly.
2. I think the distinction here can be understood together with McDowell's invocation of Gadamer's distinction between 'world' and 'environment', discussed in Chapter 2. With this new distinction, McDowell reinforces the point that the discriminatory capacities do *not* qualifiy as conceptual capacities in his sense. This point is very important when he debates with varieties of non-conceptualism.
3. I say 'normally', because we do sometimes conduct top-down inferences in perceiving things. Consider the case in which an expert is in a better position to see something almost invisible from a vulgar point of view. The same consideration applies to action. Such discussions are sometimes under the label of 'cognitive penetration' or 'cognitive penetrability' (Raftopoulos, 2019).
4. Hyman (2015) urges that *voluntary* actions and *intentional* actions should be separated under certain circumstances.
5. Searle says something similar when he declares that what he is doing is 'logical analyses' (1983, p. 5). Also see Anil Gupta's 'logical inquiry' (2019).
6. I will say more about this in my Epilogue.
7. The former concept is introduced by J. J. Gibson: '"affordance": all action possibilities latent in the environment, objectively measurable, and independent of the individual's ability to recognize these possibilities' (1979). The latter concept will be characterized and discussed when I introduce Dreyfus's thoughts later.
8. McDowell's own term for this is 'dualism of embodiment and mindedness' in 'Response to Dreyfus' (2007d/2008b).
9. Some of the following materials are drawn from my 'Self, Action, and Passivity' (2015). I take issue with Dreyfus in great detail because his debate with McDowell also touches on the issue of conceptuality and the Myth of the Given, two of the main themes in this essay.
10. In more recent writings, McDowell has further developed his picture of actions and intentions, mostly in the Anscombian context (2010b, 2011c, d, e). For his early discussion of reason and action, see McDowell (1982d).
11. Dreyfus has a series of objections and modifications, so I will refer to specific pieces in due course.
12. However, McDowell opposes to his colleague Brandom's interpretations of those big names (e.g. 2002d).
13. Husserl might be an exception. Dreyfus is also hostile to Husserl's thoughts, so he regards his objections to McDowell as both Heideggerian and Merleau-Pontyan. Indeed, McDowell's notion of 'passive actualization of conceptual capacities in

experiences' is very congenial to Husserl's notion of 'passive synthesis', as pointed out by Lilian Alweiss in 'The Myth of the Given' (2005). See also Husserl's *Analyses Concerning Passive and Active Synthesis: Lectures on Transcendental Logic* (1920–1926/2001), and also his *Experience and Judgment* (1939/1975).

14 The familiar voice of this passage confirms that in this debate what Dreyfus and McDowell have in mind is McDowell's earlier paper 'Conceptual Capacities in Perception' (2005b/2008a) This is important, because for some reasons unbeknownst to me, neither of them refers to that piece explicitly, but this is not good for readers.

15 McDowell himself, in his replies to Dreyfus, has attempted to clarify his relevant notions, and Dreyfus concedes that he misunderstood McDowell at some points. But his concessions are *piecemeal*, and there are still some significant misunderstandings lurking in Dreyfus's final response. What I will do here is to correct the misunderstandings in a *systematic* way, and through this I hope the lurking misunderstandings will thereby be dislodged.

16 For a detailed discussion concerning the relations between Todes, Dreyfus and McDowell, see Joseph Rouse, 'Mind, Body, and World: Todes and McDowell on Bodies and Language' (2005). To be fair to Dreyfus, the distinction between perception and conception is quite standard not only in philosophy but also in psychology.

17 An earlier version of it is 'Detachment, Involvement, and Rationality: are We Essentially Rational Animals?' given at Harvard. We can clearly see the disagreement between McDowell and Dreyfus in this title. Dreyfus mentions Aristotle because he and McDowell conduct the discussion by focussing on Aristotle's notion of 'phronesis', which has been discussed in Chapter 2. Since they have reached agreement at this point, I shall not talk more about it here. I relate the discussion to Kripke and Wittgenstein instead, for the connection is relevant but missed in their exchanges. As to the relation between phronesis to demonstrative thoughts, see McDowell (2007c/2008b). On demonstrative thought in relation to Evans and Peacocke, see McDowell (1990).

18 This remark suggests that what Dreyfus is describing here is a distinction, not a dichotomy: the differences between attentive, involved and absorbed actions are a matter of degree. This will become important later in my discussion.

19 I did not quote this example when I characterized McDowell's position, for I want to leave it here to compare with the Knoblauch example from Dreyfus.

20 And McDowell never uses the notion of 'mindful'. Although 'mindful' and 'minded' are almost interchangeable according to many dictionaries, 'mind*ed*' is supposed to capture the *passivity* of the mind. This thought is not available to Dreyfus for he always identifies mind with attention etc.

21 It may be more plausible to view attention as the mark of the conscious, but even this is not settled. One needs to first decide whether that means attention is

necessary to/sufficient for consciousness, and many difficult issues ensue. For relevant empirical considerations, see Cheng (2017).

22. He mentions Homer at this point; see ibid., p. 374.
23. Here he recognizes that the stepping back at issue is retrospective, but he lapsed earlier in discussing Knoblauch's case.
24. Recall the dualism of intellect and sensory/bodily criticized at the earlier stage of this chapter.
25. If McDowell is right here, affordances can be 'data for [one's] rationality' (Ibid., p. 315). Also see p. 321 for the example of going through a hole.
26. In the context of the difference between human being and mere animals, McDowell invokes the distinction between 'being open to the world' and 'merely inhabiting an environment' (2007c/2008b, p. 315). What McDowell insists is that our coping with the environment and animals' case are different in kind. After entering the space of reasons, we cannot 'unlearn'. I will come back to this point at the end of Chapter 7. For more on skillful coping and related issues, see for example Stanley (2011), Montero (2016, 2019), Fridland (2015, 2017, 2019). Montero argues that McDowell is also wrong in thinking that lightning chess does not involve conscious reasoning. I believe McDowell can allow that the chess master can be conscious in reasoning during the process; it is just that she or he cannot *overthink*, otherwise the flow will be violated.
27. Willem deVries and Timm Triplett make an admirable effort to gloss this formidable piece. In pages xxii and xxiii, they point out that Sellars did *not* identify the myth with incorrigibility (indubitability). See Willem deVries and Timm Triplett (2000).
28. For a theory of intentionality that seeks to avoid the Myth of the Given and absorb phenomenological insights, see Sachs (2017).
29. For more on Merleau-Ponty in this regard, with a comparison to Wittgenstein, see Romdenh-Romluc (2016). Cassam's *Self and World* (1997) is a much-neglected work on spatial self-awareness. In the special issue celebrating the 20th anniversary of this book, Cassam himself, Béatrice Longuenesse, Anil Gomes, Dan Zahavi and myself have discussed this and related issues (forthcoming, b 2020).
30. From the context we can see that by 'consciousness' Locke means 'self-consciousness'.
31. McDowell refers to Evans' *The Varieties of Reference* (1982), in particular p. 326–7.
32. As usual, the term 'Cartesian' only signifies a way of thinking, but later I will justify of my (and McDowell's) usage of this label to some extent.
33. The term 'narrow assumption' is from Maximilian de Gaynesford's paper 'Kant and Strawson on the Firs Person' (2003), at p. 157. The notion of 'narrow' comes presumably from the notion of 'narrow content', and is contrasted with Williamson's 'broadness'. In this context, 'narrow' means 'irrelevant to external, wider conditions'. De Gaynesford criticizes McDowell's argument against Kant's thesis that the transcendental apperception is only a 'formal' condition; I will say something on

McDowell's behalf in Chapter 6. McDowell (1998j/2008b) discusses Strawson on referring to oneself.
34 This will be clearer when we see that McDowell applies the same argument to Kant; see Chapter 6.
35 We can see this in *Reasons and Persons* (1984), pp. 204–5. My emphasis is on the Evans-McDowell line of thought, however.
36 McDowell does not proceed with these terms, but I think this is a good way to understand the issue. The exact formulation of the ego/bundle theory distinction is a big topic on its own, but I think the characterization provided by McDowell is sufficient for our purposes.
37 McDowell mentions G. E. M. Anscombe in this context, but this applies to everyone who rejects Cartesian immaterialism but nevertheless commit to the inner space model. I will say more about this later.
38 In McDowell's own word, 'to maintain a firm and integrated conception of ourselves as rational animals' (1997c/1998a, p. 382).
39 This characterization should be qualified, as McDowell says, memory 'of the appropriate sort'.
40 This is first devised by Sydney Shoemaker, in 'Persons and Their Past' (1970). Also see Parfit's *Reasons and Persons* (1984), pp. 220–2.
41 After recognizing this, we can compare situations here with earlier discussions in Chapter 3. Parfit's commitment to the narrow assumption brings in the inner space model, and thereby brings in the trouble discussed earlier. McDowell says more about this in p. 381.
42 I will say more about this in the Epilogue, with a rather strong notion of 'emergence'.
43 See *Mind and World* (1996a), pp. 74–6, and also 'Functionalism and anomalous monism' (1985b/1998a). I believe that ultimately McDowell commits himself to certain kind of emergentism, or at least some version of 'naturalistic dualism' (Chalmers, 1996).
44 McDowell acknowledges his indebtedness to Jennifer Hornsby's 'Which Physical Events are Mental Events?' (1980–1), reprinted in her *Simple Mindedness: in Defense of Naïve Naturalism in the Philosophy of Mind* (1997).
45 Although I do not go into the details of Davidson's argument, the basic shape is as follows: any causal relation is under a strict law, but given the anomalism of the mental, there is no psycho-physical strict law. It seems to follow that the mind-body interaction is impossible. To avoid this, Davidson says that physical events can sustain mental properties, and strict laws in the physical realm are not problematic. Hence his event monism cum property dualism.
46 Also see the first chapter of Hornsby's book (1997). McDowell's further reason to repudiate this conception of causality is that it commits a form of scheme-content

dualism, which is under forceful attacks by Davidson himself. I shall postpone this to Chapter 6.

47 My inability to dig deeper here is due to the fact that the issues here seem to involve revisionary metaphysics and philosophy of science, which will take much more time on my part to research in the future. It seems to me that Paul Pietroski defends a version of this view. See his *Causing Actions* (2000), especially chapter 5, 'Personal Dualism'. Again please see my Epilogue for some speculations.

Chapter 6

1. This is the main theme of Cassam (1997) and Cheng (2018).
2. There have been many objections against McDowell at this point, but de Gaynesford's objections are based on a thorough reconstruction and evaluations. For other dissent voices, see for example Graham Bird, 'McDowell's Kant: *Mind and World*' (1996); Truls Wyller, 'Kant on *I*, Apperception, and Imagination' (2000). De Gaynesford has a paper exclusively on the plausibility of the 'identification-freedom' itself: 'On Referring to Oneself' (2004b).
3. I omit de Gaynesford's point that 'Strawson's argument for it seems to be indebted not to Kant but to Wittgenstein', especially his *Blue Book* (1958), for here our main concern is not the latter. Notice that though de Gaynesford refers only to Strawson here, his arguments can be generated to McDowell also.
4. According to McDowell, though Davidson is definitely hostile to this dualism, he nevertheless falls into coherentism, for his formulation of the dualism does not quite go to the root.
5. Also see McDowell's discussions in 'Meaning and Intentionality in Wittgenstein's Later Philosophy' (1993b/1998a).
6. Recall the discussions of 'Singular Thought and the Extent of Inner Space' (1986a/1998b) in Chapter 3. For interesting connections between scheme-content dualism, conceptual relativism, Davidson, and Gadamer, see 'Gadamer and Davidson on understanding and Relativism' (2002c/2008b).
7. Tim Crane disputes this observation in 'Is There a Perceptual Relation?' (2006). I will discuss this later, and that will bring us back to McDowell's disjunctive conception of appearance.
8. All examples here are controversial, but for our purposes we do not need to go into them.
9. Again, details are pretty complicated. The relation between intentionalism and functionalism is itself a big issue, but for our purposes, we only need to remember that the contrast between them and the qualia theory is that the later commits to *intrinsic* qualities of experience. Block's version is a rather special case, for he thinks qualia are physically reducible, therefore might not count as intrinsic.

10 Dennett identifies four characteristics of qualia; they are 'ineffability', 'intrinsicality', 'privacy' and 'immediate apprehensibility'; see his 'Quining Qualia' (1988); most philosophers agree that 'intrinsicality' is essential to the notion of qualia. Although other properties are often regarded as characteristics of qualia as well, I will focus on only 'intrinsicality'.
11 The situation here is parallel to that of the qualia theory. Here I will keep complications to a minimum.
12 Later I will argue that we should use the term 'representationalism' in the present context.
13 They also discuss disjunctivism about action, but we do not need to enter that in the present context.
14 See Snowdon, 'Perception, Vision, and Causation' (1980–1).
15 In his paper, Byrne does not explicitly commit to this disjunctivism, but since here what I am doing is classification, I shall leave open whether he subscribes to content disjunctivism.
16 To rehearse, the 'inextricability' stands for 'primeness', which implies 'broadness', signified by 'externality'.
17 Also consider McDowell's criticisms against Kripke's 'master thesis'. Kripke's 'common kind assumption' is definitely *not* about reason and justification.
18 Their terminologies are 'metaphysical/epistemological disjunctivism', and I have said why I prefer my own way of labelling.
19 The potential problem here may also be reflected in the fact that they lump Martin with Hinton together under the label 'metaphysical disjunctivism'.
20 In personal conversations McDowell also said perceivings and seemings can share the same content.
21 M. G. F. Martin, 'The Transparency of Experience' (2002).
22 M. G. F. Martin, 'On Being Alienated' (2006).
23 In recent terminology, McDowell holds 'weak intentionalism', which claims that the phenomenal *supervenes* on the intentional, for the same phenomenology in different cases is explained by different contents. By contrast, 'strong intentionalism' holds that the relation between the phenomenal and the intentional is *identity*. I use 'intentional part' to stay neutral between so-called 'pure' and 'impure' versions of intentionalism. For details of these matters, see Crane's 'Intentionalism' (2009). Also see David Chalmers, 'The Representational Character of Experience' (2004).
24 Gregory McCulloch takes a similar line in his 'Phenomenological Externalism' (2002). In his reply in the same volume (2002d), McDowell says nothing against this.
25 For a comprehensive and profound discussion of these matters, see A. D. Smith, *The Problem of Perception* (2002).
26 For our purposes, we do not need to note the differences between this argument and the one from hallucination.

27 As an intentionalist, Smith thinks that P2 'is the heart of' the argument from illusion, and he devotes 'all of the Part I' of his book to 'consideration of this claim and to attempting to see a way around it' (ibid., p. 25). This will prove to be important in my objections to Crane.

28 I will say more about the adverbial theory presently. I do not mention disjunctivism here because it is not necessary to reject the sense-datum inference for being a disjunctivist. For example, Austinian disjunctivism accepts the inference but rejects the generalizing step. See Byrne and Logue (2008), pp. 63–5.

29 I do not mention intentionalism and the adverbial theory here because the defining feature of them is the rejection of the sense-datum inference. They often do not object to the generalizing step, but we need to keep clear about what is essential for being a certain theory. Actually we should not mention the sense-datum theory either, for though it almost always accepts the generalizing step, this step is not part of its definition. Again, consider Austinian disjunctivism.

30 In 'On Being Alienated' (2006) Martin also proposes this framework (p. 357), but he does not find fault in Crane's chasm-creating claim. In addition, he places the sense-datum theory into the common kind theory, but in effect the existence of sense-datum is compatible with disjunctivism, as Austinian disjunctivism shows.

31 There he mentions Searle's *Intentionality* (1983), pp. 45–6, and McDowell's comments on this in 'The Content of Perceptual Experience' (1994/1998a). For more on presentation, see Brentano (1889/1973), Russell (1910–11/1986), Kalderon (2015, 2017), for example.

32 If one holds non-relational intentionalism, relationality becomes a family quarrel within the common kind theory, for the sense-datum theory holds that perceptions are relations between a subject and her sense-data. See Martin (2006, p. 357). McDowell (2013b) has argued that perceptual experience is both relational and contentful.

33 A further trouble with relationality is that it is not clear whether it is compatible with prime disjunctivism, for the notion of relation seems to imply that two relata are distinct. Fortunately, the framework constituted by disjunctivism and the common kind theory does not make use of the notion of relationality.

34 Philosophers have their own idiosyncratic preference, for example Michael Tye prefers 'representationalism', Crane prefers 'intentionalism', and Block uses 'representationism'.

35 Crane insists that the qualia theory 'is not simply the denial of representationalism . . .' (2006, p. 131). His reason for this is that there is room for the view that uses 'intentional *mode*' and other intentional factors to explain phenomenal characters (ibid., p. 143); this is his 'impure intentionalism' (2009). But this is of no use in the present context, for impure intentionalism is representationalism after all; it holds that experiencing is just representing.

36 McDowell himself does not approach these matters in this way. Rather, he focusses on Tyler Burge's criticism of him (McDowell, 2010c, 2013c; Burge, 2005, 2011).
37 He does say more about it in a historical context in McDowell (2006d/2008a).

Chapter 7

1 He will not accept this description, but again I need to deal with this later.
2 'Thoughts without content are empty, intuitions without concepts are blind' (1787/1998, A51/B75).
3 The Eighth Annual Philosophy Conference of Sociedad Filosofica Ibero Americana, 1995.
4 The third Münsteraner Vorlesungen zur Philosophie, 1999.
5 When using this phrase, McDowell is talking about reading modern science's conception of nature into Aristotle's thinking.
6 This should be clear evidence for thinking that Kant's use of 'concept' and Davidson's use of 'concept' are pretty different. However, when McDowell discusses Davidson's attack on SCD in detail, he says that '[t]he picture can be encapsulated in the familiar Kantian tag: "Thoughts without content are empty, intuitions without concepts are blind"'. I think we should be suspicious about this kind of suggestion. The same is true of the opening of *Mind and World*, as I quoted above.
7 In *Mind and World*, McDowell suggests that 'dualism of scheme and Given' is a better label than 'dualism of scheme and content' (McDowell, 1996a, p. 4), since the idea of content seems to presuppose that it is conceptual, and this does not fit his construal of SCD. Here I further suggest that 'reason' is more suitable than 'scheme', since the latter implies the idea of the conceptual, and as I have argued, this idea is not available to McDowell's understanding of SCD.
8 McDowell (2005b/2008a) also tries to say more about rationality in our case and in other animals' cases by the distinction between 'responsiveness to reasons *as such*' and 'responsiveness to reasons' (*passim*). Although significant, this distinction is not directly relevant to my discussion here, so I shall not go into the intricacies now. However they will become important presently, so I shall discuss it only in that context.
9 For McDowell's insistence on the different level of explanation, see McDowell (1994/1998a). For a recent criticism of his view, see Burge (2005, 2011).
10 The only place he comes close to say that 'rationality → conceptuality' is a stipulation is this remark: 'its sensory presence to her is an operation of a capacity that belongs to her responsiveness to reasons as such, and *hence* is conceptual in the sense of my stipulation' (McDowell, 2005b/2008a, p. 136; my emphasis). But elsewhere the stipulative relation is always from the conceptual to the rational; I therefore

disregard the remark quoted here. Besides, if 'rationality → conceptuality' is really a stipulation as well, it will face two problems I propose in the main text immediately.

11 Gupta's conversations with McDowell since that time has been ongoing; from McDowell's side, see his (2009d, 2018c, 2019a, 2019b).

12 A similar line of McDowell's argument uses the notion of 'brute impact' (McDowell, 1996a, p. 8), but again it is not clear why non-conceptual stuffs can only provide *brute* impacts. In the Woodbridge Lecture, McDowell says that Sellars commits another version of the Myth of the Given, which is not based on the idea of bare presence, but on 'sheer receptivity'. Although sheer receptivity is not bare presence, their structures are not the right kind we need. In this sense, we can still say that sheer receptivity provides only brute impact.

13 Again, in deVries and Tiplett (2000), they point out that Sellars did not identify the myth with incorrigibility/indubitability (xxii and xxiii).

14 How attention figures in the entire mental economy is an issue worthy of further explorations. The predictive processing framework, for example, has interesting things to say about attention and the mind-world relation: 'the prediction error account of *attention* helps us understand the perceptual fluctuations that we experience *as our minds take possession of the world, and as the world takes possession of the mind*' (Hohwy, 2013, p. 205; my emphasis). For more on this, see Cheng, Sato, and Hohwy (forthcoming, c).

15 The empirical issues here are very complicated. I develop positive views concerning these matters in Cheng (2017, forthcoming b).

16 From now on I will not signify the fact that the distinction is drawn from the phenomenological and hermeneutical traditions.

17 For different ways of coping and their relations to the environment and the world, see McDowell's responses to Dreyfus (McDowell, 2007c/2008b).

18 This view is inspired by, though not identical to, the one proposed in Lin (2008).

Epilogue

1 For similar lines of thought, see his "Naturalism in the Philosophy of Mind" (2004a/2008b).

2 McDowell (2000d) explicitly refuses to offer positive accounts of causation in the space of reasons. For an example of causation as philosophers of science conceive it, see Anjum and Mumford (2018).

3 Compare my opening quotation from Fichte.

4 Notice that McDowell insists that 'Hegel is not here talking about multiple human beings' (p. 160), so 'otherness' has a rather special meaning in McDowell's context.

5 Here I am inspired by Robert Brandom. During the conference in Taipei in 2008 I asked a question about the self, and he says something along this line. Of course he holds no responsibility of my thoughts here.
6 Sometimes McDowell deals with the issues concerning freedom and autonomy in the contexts of ethics and political philosophy (2010d). This is perfectly legitimate, but ultimately ethical and political dimensions presuppose a satisfactory metaphysical account. I side with Chalmers (1996) that such a strong notion of emergence is incompatible with logical supervenience.
7 This is not to deny that Burge also concerns with subjectivity, while McDowell also concerns with objectivity.

Bibliography

Works by John McDowell

McDowell, J. (1969–70/1998b). Identity mistakes: Plato and the logical atomists. *Proceedings of the Aristotelian Society*, 70, pp. 181–95. Reprinted in his *Meaning, knowledge, and reality*, pp. 157–70. Cambridge, MA: Harvard University Press.

McDowell, J. (Ed.) (1973). *Theaetetus*. Oxford: Oxford University Press.

McDowell, J. (1976/1998b). Truth-conditions, bivalence, and verification. In G. Evans and J. McDowell (Eds), *Truth and meaning: Essays in semantics*. Oxford: Oxford University Press. Reprinted in his *Meaning, knowledge, and reality*, pp. 3–28. Cambridge, MA: Harvard University Press.

McDowell, J. (1977/1998b). On the sense and reference of a proper name. *Mind*, 86(342), pp. 159–185. Reprinted in his *Meaning, knowledge, and reality*, pp. 171–98. Cambridge, MA: Harvard University Press.

McDowell, J. (1978a/1998a). Are moral requirements hypothetical imperatives? *Proceedings of the Aristotelian Society, supplementary volumes*, 52(1), pp. 13–42. Reprinted in his *Mind, value, and reality*, pp. 77–94. Cambridge, MA: Harvard University Press.

McDowell, J. (1978b/1998b). On "The reality of the past." In C. Hookway and p. Pettit (Eds), *Action and interpretation: Studies in the philosophy of the social sciences*, Cambridge: Cambridge University Press, pp. 127–44; reprinted in his *Meaning, Knowledge, and Reality* (1998b), pp. 295–313, Cambridge, MA: Harvard University Press.

McDowell, J. (1978c/1998b). Physicalism and primitive denotation: Field and Tarski. *Erkenntnis*, 13, pp. 131–52. Reprinted in his *Meaning, knowledge, and reality* (1998b), pp. 132–54. Cambridge, MA: Harvard University Press.

McDowell, J. (1979/1998a). Virtue and reason. *The Monist*, 62(3), pp. 331–50. Reprinted in his *Mind, value, and reality* (1998a), pp. 50–73. Cambridge, MA: Harvard University Press.

McDowell, J. (1980a/1998a). The role of Eudaimonia in Aristotle's ethics. In A. O. Rorty (Ed.), *Essays on Aristotle's ethics*. Berkeley, CA: University of California Press. Reprinted in his *Mind, value, and reality* (1998a), pp. 3–22. Cambridge, MA: Harvard University Press.

McDowell, J. (1980b/1998b). Quotation and saying that. In M. Platts (Ed.), *Reference, truth, and reality*. London: Routledge and Kegan Paul. Reprinted in his *Meaning, knowledge, and reality* (1998b), pp. 51–86. Cambridge, MA: Harvard University Press.

McDowell, J. (1980c/1998b). Meaning, communication, and knowledge. In Z. V. Straaten (Ed.), *Philosophical subjects: Essays presented to p. F. Strawson*. Oxford: Clarendon Press. Reprinted in his *Meaning, knowledge, and reality* (1998b), pp. 29–50. Cambridge, MA: Harvard University Press.

McDowell, J. (1981a/1998b). Anti-realism and the epistemology of understanding. In H. Parret and J. Bouveresse (Eds), *Meaning and understanding*, Berlin: Walter de Gruyter, pp. 225–48; reprinted in his *Meaning, Knowledge, and Reality* (1998b), pp. 314–43. Cambridge, MA: Harvard University Press.

McDowell, J. (1981b/1998a). Non-cognitivism and rule-following. In S. Holtzman and C. M. Leich (Eds), *Wittgenstein: To follow a rule*. Oxford: Routledge. Reprinted in his *Mind, value, and reality* (1998a), pp. 198–218. Cambridge, MA: Harvard University Press.

McDowell, J. (1982a/2008b). Falsehood and not-being in Plato's Sophist. In M. Schofield and M. C. Nussbaum (Eds), *Language and Logos*, pp. 115–34. Cambridge: Cambridge University Press. In his *The engaged intellect: Philosophical essays* (2008b), pp. 3–22. Cambridge, MA: Harvard University Press.

McDowell, J. (1982b/1998b). Criteria, defeasibility, and knowledge. *Proceedings of British Academy*, 68, pp. 455–79; reprinted in his *Meaning, Knowledge, and Reality* (1998b), pp. 369–94. Cambridge, MA: Harvard University Press.

McDowell, J. (1982c/1998b). Truth-value gaps. In L. J. Cohen (Ed.), *Logic, methodology and philosophy of science VI: Proceedings of the six international congress of logic, methodology, and philosophy of science*, p. 299–314. Amsterdam: North Holland Publishing Co. Reprinted in his *Meaning, knowledge, and reality* (1998b), pp. 199–213. Cambridge, MA: Harvard University Press.

McDowell, J. (1982d). Reason and action. *Philosophical Investigations*, 5(4), pp. 301–5.

McDowell, J. (1983/1998a). Aesthetic value, objectivity, and the fabric of the world. In E. Schaper (Ed.), *Pleasure, preference, and value*, pp. 1–16. Cambridge: Cambridge University Press. Reprinted in his *Mind, value, and reality* (1998a), pp. 112–30. Cambridge, MA: Harvard University Press.

McDowell, J. (1984a/1998b). *De re* senses. *Philosophical Quarterly*, 34(136), pp. 283–94. Reprinted in his *Meaning, knowledge, and reality* (1998b), pp. 214–27. Cambridge, MA: Harvard University Press.

McDowell, J. (1984b/1998a). Wittgenstein on following a rule. *Synthesis*, 58, pp. 325–64; reprinted in his *Mind, value, and reality* (1998a), pp. 221–62. Cambridge, MA: Harvard University Press.

McDowell, J. (1985a/1998a). Values and secondary qualities. In T. Honderich (Ed.), *Morality and objectivity*, pp. 110–29. *London*: Routledge. Reprinted in his *Mind, value, and reality*, pp. 131–50. Cambridge, MA: Harvard University Press.

McDowell, J. (1985b/1998a). Functionalism and anomalous monism. In E. LePore and B. McLaughlin (Eds) *Actions and events: Perspectives on the philosophy of Donald*

Davidson. Oxford: Blackwell, pp. 387–98; reprinted in his *Mind, value, and reality*, pp. 325–40. Cambridge, MA: Harvard University Press.

McDowell, J. (1986a/1998b). Singular thought and the extent of inner space. In p. Pettit and J. McDowell (Eds), *Subject, thought, and context*, pp. 137–68. Oxford: Clarendon Press; reprinted in his *Meaning, knowledge, and reality*, pp. 228–59, Cambridge, MA: Harvard University Press.

McDowell, J. (1986b). Critical notice. *Mind*, 95(379), pp. 377–86.

McDowell, J. (1987a/1998a). *Projection and truth in ethics*. Lawrence, KS: University Press of Kansas. Reprinted in his *Mind, value, and reality*, pp. 151–66. Cambridge, MA: Harvard University Press.

McDowell, J. (1987b/1998b). In defense of modesty. In B. Taylor (Ed.), *Michael Dummett: Contributions to philosophy*, Dordrecht: Martinus Nijhoff, pp. 59–80; reprinted in his *Meaning, knowledge, and reality*, pp. 87–107. Cambridge, MA: Harvard University Press.

McDowell, J. (1989a). Wittgenstein and the inner world. *Journal of Philosophy*, 86(11), pp. 643–4.

McDowell, J. (1989b/1998b). Mathematical platonism and Dummettian anti-realism. *Dialectica*, (1–2), pp. 173–92. reprinted in his *Meaning, knowledge, and reality*, pp. 344–65. Cambridge, MA: Harvard University Press.

McDowell, J. (1989c/1998a). One strand in the private language argument. *Grazer Philosophische Studien*, 33/34, pp. 285–303; reprinted in his *Mind, value, and reality*, pp. 279–96. Cambridge, MA: Harvard University Press.

McDowell, J. (1990). Peacocke and Evans on demonstrative content. *Mind*, 99(394), pp. 255–66.

McDowell, J. (1991a/1998a). Intentionality and interiority in Wittgenstein. Klaus Puhl (ed.) *Meaning Scepticism*, De Gruyter, Berlin and New York, pp. 148–69; reprinted in his *Mind, Value, and Reality*, pp. 297–321. Cambridge, MA: Harvard University Press.

McDowell, J. (1991b/1998b). Intentionality *de re*. In E. LePore and R. V. Gulick (Eds), *John Searle and his critics*. Cambridge: Blackwell. Reprinted in his *Meaning, knowledge, and reality*, pp. 260–74. Cambridge, MA: Harvard University Press.

McDowell, J. (1992/1998b). Putnam on mind and meaning. *Philosophical Topics*, 20(1), pp. 35–48. Reprinted in his *Meaning, knowledge, and reality*, pp. 275–91. Cambridge, MA: Harvard University Press.

McDowell, J. (1993a/1998b). Knowledge by hearsay. In A. Chakrabarti and B. K. Matilal (Eds), *Knowing from words*. Dordrecht: Kluwer Academic Publishers. Reprinted in his *Meaning, knowledge, and reality*, pp. 414–44. Cambridge, MA: Harvard University Press.

McDowell, J. (1993b/1998a). Meaning and intentionality in Wittgenstein's later philosophy. In p. A. French, Theodore E. Uehling, Jr., and Howard K. Wettstein (Eds) *Midwest Studies in Philosophy, vol. 17: The Wittgenstein Legacy*, University of Notre Dame Press, Notre Dame, pp. 40–52; reprinted in his *Mind, Value, and Reality*, pp. 263–78. Cambridge, MA: Harvard University Press.

McDowell, J. (1994/1998a). The content of perceptual experience. *The Philosophical Quarterly*, 44, pp. 190–205; reprinted in his *Mind, Value, and Reality*, pp. 341–58. Cambridge, MA: Harvard University Press.

McDowell, J. (1995a/2008b). Eudaimonism and realism in Aristotle's ethics. In R. Heinaman (Ed.), *Aristotle and moral realism*. Boulder, CO: Westview Press; reprinted in his *The Engaged Intellect: Philosophical Essays*, pp. 23–40. Cambridge, MA: Harvard University Press.

McDowell, J. (1995b/1998b). Knowledge and the internal. In *Philosophy and Phenomenological Research*, 55, pp. 877–93; reprinted in his *Meaning, Knowledge, and Reality*, pp. 395–413. Cambridge, MA: Harvard University Press.

McDowell, J. (1995c/1998a). Might there be external reasons? In J. E. J. Altham and R. Harrison (Eds). *World, mind and ethics: Essays on the ethical philosophy of Bernard Williams*. Cambridge: Cambridge University Press; reprinted in his *Mind, Value, and Reality*, pp. 95–111. Cambridge, MA: Harvard University Press.

McDowell, J. (1995d). Précis of *Mind and world*. *Philosophical Issues*, 7, pp. 231–9.

McDowell, J. (1996a) *Mind and World*, 2nd edition. Cambridge, MA: Harvard University Press.

McDowell, J. (1996b/1998a). Two sorts of naturalism. In R. Hursthouse, G. Lawrence, and W. Quinn (Eds), *Virtues and reasons: Philippa Foot and moral theory*, Clarendon Press, Oxford, pp. 149–79; reprinted in his *Mind, Value, and Reality*, pp. 167–97. Cambridge, MA: Harvard University Press.

McDowell, J. (1996c/2008b). Deliberation and moral development in Aristotle's ethics. In S. Engstrom and J. Whiting (Eds), *Aristotle, Kant, and the Stoics*. Cambridge: Cambridge University Press. Reprinted in his *The Engaged Intellect: Philosophical Essays*, pp. 41–58. Cambridge, MA: Harvard University Press.

McDowell, J. (1996d/2008b). Incontinence and practical wisdom in Aristotle. In S. Lovibond and S. Williams (Eds), *Identity, truth, and value: Essays for David Wiggins*. Oxford: Blackwell; reprinted in his *The Engaged Intellect: Philosophical Essays*, pp. 59–76. Cambridge, MA: Harvard University Press.

McDowell, J. (1997a). Brandom on inference and representation. *Philosophy and Phenomenological Research*, 57(1), pp. 157–62.

McDowell, J. (1997b/1998b). Another plea for modesty. In R. G. Heck (Ed.), *Language, thought, and logic: Essays in honour of Michael Dummett*. Oxford: Oxford University Press; reprinted in his *Meaning, knowledge, and reality*, pp. 108–31. Cambridge, MA: Harvard University Press.

McDowell, J. (1997c/1998a). Reductionism and the first person. In J. Dancy (Ed.), *Reading Parfit*, Blackwell, Oxford, pp. 230–50; reprinted in his *Mind, Value, and Reality*, pp. 359–82. Cambridge, MA: Harvard University Press.

McDowell, J. (1998a). *Mind, value, and reality*. Cambridge, MA: Harvard University Press.

McDowell, J. (1998b). *Meaning, knowledge, and reality*. Cambridge, MA: Harvard University Press.

McDowell, J. (1998c/2008a). Sellars on perceptual experience. *Journal of Philosophy*, 95(9), pp. 431–50; reprinted in his *Having the world in view: Essays on Kant, Hegel, and Sellars*, pp. 3–22. Cambridge, MA: Harvard University Press.

McDowell, J. (1998d/2008a). The logical form of an intuition. *Journal of Philosophy*, 95(9), pp. 451–70; reprinted in his *Having the world in view: Essays on Kant, Hegel, and Sellars*, pp. 23–43. Cambridge, MA: Harvard University Press.

McDowell, J. (1998e/2008a). Intentionality as a relation. *Journal of Philosophy*, 95(9), pp. 471–91; reprinted in his *Having the world in view: Essays on Kant, Hegel, and Sellars*, pp. 44–65. Cambridge, MA: Harvard University Press.

McDowell, J. (1998f/1998a). Some issues in Aristotle's moral psychology. In S. Everson (Ed.), *Ethics*. Cambridge: Cambridge University Press; reprinted in his *Mind, value, and reality*, pp. 23–49. Cambridge, MA: Harvard University Press.

McDowell, J. (1998g/2008a). The constitutive ideal of rationality: Davidson and Sellars. *Critica*, 30(88), pp. 29–48; reprinted in his *Having the world in view: Essays on Kant, Hegel, and Sellars*, pp. 207–20. Cambridge, MA: Harvard University Press.

McDowell, J. (1998h). Response to Crispin Wright. In C. Wright, B. C. Smith, and C. Macdonald (Eds), *Knowing our own minds*. Clarendon Press, Oxford, pp. 47–62.

McDowell, J. (1998i). Reply to commentators. *Philosophy and Phenomenological Research*, 58, pp. 403–31.

McDowell, J. (1998j/2008b). Referring to oneself. In L. E. Hahn (Ed.), *The philosophy of P. F. Strawson*, pp. 129–45. Chicago: Open Court; reprinted in his *The engaged intellect: Philosophical essays*, pp. 186–203. Cambridge, MA: Harvard University Press.

McDowell, J. (1998k). Précis of *Mind and world*. *Philosophy and Phenomenological Research*, 58(2), pp. 365–8.

McDowell, J. (1999a). Comment on Robert Brandom's "Some pragmatists themes in Hegel's idealism." *European Journal of Philosophy*, 7(2), pp. 190–3.

McDowell, J. (1999b/2008b). Scheme-content dualism and empiricism. In *Philosophy of Donald Davidson*, pp. 87–104. Chicago, IL: Open Court; reprinted in his *The engaged intellect: Philosophical essays*, pp. 115–33. Cambridge, MA: Harvard University Press.

McDowell, J. (2000a). Comments. *Journal of the British Society for Phenomenology*, 31(3), pp. 330–43.

McDowell, J. (2000b/2008b). Towards rehabilitating objectivity. In R. B. Brandom (Ed.), *Rorty and his critics*, pp. 109–21. Malden, Mass: Blackwell; reprinted in his *The engaged intellect: Philosophical essays*, pp. 204–24. Cambridge, MA: Harvard University Press.

McDowell, J. (2000c/2008b). Experiencing the world. In M. Willaschek (Ed.), *John McDowell, reason and nature*, pp. 3–18. Münster: LIT Verlag; reprinted in his *The engaged intellect: Philosophical essays*, pp. 243–56. Cambridge, MA: Harvard University Press.

McDowell, J. (2000d). Responses. In M. Willaschek (Ed.), *John McDowell, reason and nature*, pp. 91–114. Münster: LIT Verlag.

McDowell, J. (2002a/2008b). Knowledge and the internal revisited. *Philosophy and Phenomenological Research*, 64, pp. 97–105; reprinted in his *The engaged intellect: Philosophical essays*, pp. 279–87. Cambridge, MA: Harvard University Press.

McDowell, J. (2002b/2008b). How not to read *Philosophical Investigations*: Brandom's Wittgenstein. In R. Haller and K. Puhl (Eds), *Wittgenstein and the future of philosophy: A reassessment after fifty years*. Vienna: Obvhpt; reprinted in his *The engaged intellect: Philosophical Essays*, pp. 96–111. Cambridge, MA: Harvard University Press.

McDowell, J. (2002c/2008b). Gadamer and Davidson on understanding and relativism. In J. Malpas, U. Arnswald, and J. Kertscher (Eds), *Gadamer's century: Essays in honor of Hans-Georg Gadamer*, pp. 173–93. Cambridge, MA: MIT Press; reprinted in his *The engaged intellect: Philosophical essays*, pp. 134–51. Cambridge, MA: Harvard University Press.

McDowell, J. (2002d). Responses. In *Reading McDowell: on Mind and World*, pp. 269–305. New York: Routledge.

McDowell, J. (2003a/2008a). The apperceptive I and the empirical self: Towards a heterodox reading of "lordship and bondage" in Hegel's *Phenomenology*. *Bulletin of the Hegel Society of Great Britain*, 47/48, pp. 1–16; reprinted in his *Having the world in view: Essays on Kant, Hegel, and Sellars*, pp. 147–65. Cambridge, MA: Harvard University Press.

McDowell, J. (2003b). Hegel and the myth of the given. In W. Welsch and K. Vieweg (Eds), *Das Interesse des Denkens: Hegel aus heutiger Sicht*, pp. 75–88. München: Wilhelm Fink Verlag.

McDowell, J. (2003c/2008b). Subjective, intersubjective, objective. *Philosophy and Phenomenological Research*, 67(3), pp. 675–81; reprinted in his *The engaged intellect: Philosophical essays*, pp. 152–9. Cambridge, MA: Harvard University Press.

McDowell, J. (2004a/2008b). Naturalism in the philosophy of mind. In M. de. Caro and D. Macarthur (Eds), *Naturalism in question*, pp. 91–105, Cambridge, MA: Harvard University Press; reprinted in his *The engaged intellect: Philosophical essays*, pp. 257–75. Cambridge, MA: Harvard University Press.

McDowell, J. (2004b). Reality and colours: Comment on Stroud. *Philosophy and Phenomenological Research*, 68(2), pp. 395–400.

McDowell, J. (2005a/2008b). Evans's Frege. In J. L. Bermúdez (Ed.), *Thought, reference, and experience: Themes from the philosophy of Gareth Evans*, pp. 42–65. Oxford: Oxford University Press; reprinted in his *The engaged intellect: Philosophical essays*, pp. 163–85. Cambridge, MA: Harvard University Press.

McDowell, J. (2005b/2008a). Conceptual capacities in perception. In G. Abel (Ed.), *Kreativität: 2005 Congress of the Deutsche Gesellschaft für Philosophie*, pp. 1065–79; reprinted in his *Having the world in view: Essays on Kant, Hegel, and Sellars*, pp. 127–44. *Cambridge*, MA: Harvard University Press.

McDowell, J. (2005c). The true modesty of an identity conception of truth: A note in response to Pascal Engel. *International Journal of Philosophical Studies*, 13(1), pp. 83–8.

McDowell, J. (2005d/2008b). Motivating inferentialism: Comments on *Making it explicit*. *Pragmatics and Cognition*, 13(1), pp. 121–40; reprinted in his *The engaged intellect: Philosophical essays*, pp. 288–307. Cambridge, MA: Harvard University Press.

McDowell, J. (2005e/2008a). Self-determining subjectivity and external constraint. In K. Ameriks and J. Stolzenberg (Eds), *International yearbook of German idealism 2005: German idealism and contemporary analytic philosophy*, pp. 21–37, Walter De Gruyter Inc; reprinted in his *Having the world in view: Essays on Kant, Hegel, and Sellars*, pp. 90–107. Cambridge, MA: Harvard University Press.

McDowell, J. (2006a). Response to Dancy. In *McDowell and his critics*, pp. 134–41. Oxford: Blackwell Publishing.

McDowell, J. (2006b). Response to Rovane. In *McDowell and his critics*, pp. 114–20. Oxford: Blackwell Publishing.

McDowell, J. (2006c/2008b). The disjunctive conception of experience as material for a transcendental argument. *Theorema*, 25(1), pp. 19–33. Reprinted in his *The engaged intellect: Philosophical essays*, pp. 225–40. Cambridge, MA: Harvard University Press.

McDowell, J. (2006d/2008a). Sensory consciousness in Kant and Sellars. *Philosophical Topics*, 34(1/2), pp. 311–26; reprinted in his *Having the world in view: Essays on Kant, Hegel, and Sellars*, pp. 108–26. Cambridge, MA: Harvard University Press.

McDowell, J. (2007a/2008a). Hegel's idealism as radicalization of Kant. In J. Stolzenberg and K. p. Ameriks (Eds), *Metaphysics*. Berlin: Walter de Gruyter. Reprinted in his *Having the world in view: Essays on Kant, Hegel, and Sellars*, pp. 69–89. Cambridge, MA: Harvard University Press.

McDowell, J. (2007b/2008a). On Pippin's postscript. *European Journal of Philosophy*, 15(3), pp. 395–410; reprinted in his *Having the world in view: Essays on Kant, Hegel, and Sellars*, pp. 185–203. Cambridge, MA: Harvard University Press.

McDowell, J. (2007c/2008b). What myth? *Inquiry*, 50, pp. 338–51; reprinted in his *The engaged intellect: Philosophical essays*, pp. 308–23. Cambridge, MA: Harvard University Press.

McDowell, J. (2007d/2008b). Response to Dreyfus. *Inquiry*, 50, pp. 366–70; reprinted in his *The engaged intellect: Philosophical essays*, pp. 324–8. Cambridge, MA: Harvard University Press.

McDowell, J. (2007e). Dummett on truth conditions and meaning. In R. E. Auxier and L. E. Hahn (Eds), *The philosophy of Michael Dummett*, pp. 351–66. Chicago, IL: Open Court.

McDowell, J. (2008a). *Having the world in view: Essays on Kant, Hegel, and Sellars*. Cambridge, MA: Harvard University Press.

McDowell, J. (2008b). *The engaged intellect: Philosophical essays*. Cambridge, MA: Harvard University Press.

McDowell, J. (2008c). Comment on Stanley Cavell's "companionable thinking." In *Philosophy of animal life*, S. Cavell, C. Diamond, J. McDowell, I. Hacking, and C. Wolfe, pp. 127–38. New York: Columbia University Press.

McDowell, J. (2008d/2008a). Avoiding the myth of the given. In J. Lindgaard (Ed.), *John McDowell: Experience, norm, and nature*, pp. 1–14. Oxford: Blackwell; reprinted in his *Having the world in view: Essays on Kant, Hegel, and Sellars*, pp. 256–71. Cambridge, MA: Harvard University Press.

McDowell, J. (2008e/2008a). Why is Sellars's essay called "empiricism and the philosophy of mind?" In his *Having the world in view: Essays on Kant, Hegel, and Sellars*, pp. 221–38. Cambridge, MA: Harvard University Press.

McDowell, J. (2008f/2008b). Are meaning, understanding, etc. definite states? In A. Ahmed (Ed.), *Wittgenstein's* Philosophical investigations: *A critical guide*, pp. 162–77. Cambridge: Cambridge University Press; reprinted in his *The engaged intellect: Philosophical Essays*, pp. 79–95. Cambridge, MA: Harvard University Press.

McDowell, J. (2009a). Response to Stephen Houlgate. *The owl of Minerva*, 41(1/2), pp. 27–38.

McDowell, J. (2009b). Response to Stephen Houlgate's response. *The owl of Minerva*, 41(1/2), pp. 53–60.

McDowell, J. (2009c). Wittgensteinian "Quietism." *Common Knowledge*, 15(3), pp. 365–72.

McDowell, J. (2009d). The given in experience: Comment on Gupta. *Philosophy and Phenomenological Research*, 79(2), pp. 468–74.

McDowell, J. (2010a/2008a). Towards a reading of Hegel on action in the "reason" chapter of the *Phenomenology*. In his *Having the world in view: Essays on Kant, Hegel, and Sellars*, pp. 166–84. Cambridge, MA: Harvard University Press; reprinted in A. Laitinen and C. Sandis (Eds), *Hegel on action*. London: Palgrave-Macmmilan.

McDowell, J. (2010b). What is the content of an intention in action? *Ratio*, 23(4), pp. 415–32.

McDowell, J. (2010c). Tyler Burge on disjunctivism. *Philosophical Explorations*, 13(3), pp. 243–55.

McDowell, J. (2010d). Autonomy and its burdens. *The Harvard Review of Philosophy*, 17(1), pp. 4–15.

McDowell, J. (2011a). *Perception as a capacity for knowing*. Milwaukee, WI: Marquette University Press.

McDowell, J. (2011b). David Finkelstein on the inner. *Theorema: International Journal of Philosophy*, 30(3), pp. 15–24.

McDowell, J. (2011c). Some remarks on intention in action. *The Amherst Lecture in Philosophy*, 6, pp. 1–18.

McDowell, J. (2011d). Pragmatism and intention-in-action. In R. M. Calcaterra (Ed.), *New perspectives on pragmatism and analytic philosophy*, pp. 119–28. Amsterdam: Editions Rodopi.

McDowell, J. (2011e). Anscombe on bodily self-knowledge. In A. Ford, J. Hornsby, and F. Stoutland (Eds), *Essays on Anscombe's Intention*, pp. 128–46. Cambridge, MA: Harvard University Press.

McDowell, J. (2012). Concepts in perceptual experience: Putnam and Travis. In M. Baghramian (Ed.), *Reading Putnam*, pp. 341–6. New York: Routledge.

McDowell, J. (2013a). Acting in the light of fact. In D. Bakhurst, M. O. Little, and B. Hooker (Eds), *Thinking about reasons: Themes from the philosophy of Jonathan Dancy*, pp. 13–28. Oxford: Oxford University Press.

McDowell, J. (2013b). Perceptual experience: Both relational and contentful. *European Journal of Philosophy*, 21(1), pp. 144–57.

McDowell, J. (2013c). Tyler Burge on Disjunctivism II. *Philosophical Explorations*, 16(3), pp. 259–79.

McDowell, J. (2014). A note on the significance of the surface inquiry. *International Journal for the Study of Skepticism*, 4(3–4), pp. 317–21.

McDowell, J. (2015). Philosophical method. *Journal of Philosophical Research*, 40, pp. 25–9.

McDowell, J. (2018a). What is the *Phenomenology* about? In A. Abath and F. Sanguinetti (Eds), *McDowell and Hegel*, pp. 29–40, Berlin: Springer Verlag.

McDowell, J. (2018b). Responses. In A. Abath and F. Sanguinetti (Eds), *McDowell and Hegel*, pp. 231–58, Berlin: Springer Verlag.

McDowell, J. (2018c). Perceptual experience and empirical rationality. *Analytic Philosophy*, 59(1), pp. 89–98.

McDowell, J. (2019a). Comments on Brewer, Gupta, and Siegel. *Philosophical Issues*, 29(1), pp. 338–47.

McDowell, J. (2019b). Responses to Brewer, Gupta, and Siegel. *Philosophical Issues*, 29(1), pp. 390–402.

Works by other authors

Alweiss, L. (2005). The myth of the given. In J. Boros (Ed.), *Mind in world: Essays on John McDowell's* Mind and world. Brambauer Pécs, pp. 39–65.

Anjum, R. L., and Mumford, S. (2018). *Causation in science and the methods of scientific discovery*. Oxford: Oxford University Press.

Ayers, M. (2004). Sense experience, concepts, and content – Objections to Davidson and McDowell. In R. Schumacher (Ed.), *Perception and reality: From Descartes to the present*. Paderborn: Mentis, pp. 239–62.

Ayers, M. (2019). *Knowing and seeing: Groundwork for a new empiricism*. Oxford: Oxford University Press.

Baldwin, T. (1988). Phenomenology, solipsism, and egocentric thought. *Aristotelian Society Supplementary Volume*, 62(1), pp. 27–60.

Bartha, P., and Savitt, S. (1998). Second-guessing second nature. *Analysis*, 58, pp. 252–63.
Bayne, T., and Montague, M. (Ed.) (2011). *Cognitive phenomenology*. Oxford: Oxford University Press.
Bennett, J. (1966). *Kant's analytic*. Cambridge: Cambridge University Press.
Bennett, J. (1974). *Kant's dialectic*. Cambridge: Cambridge University Press.
Bermúdez, J. L. (2003). *Thinking without words*. New York, NY: Oxford University Press.
Bird, G. (1996). McDowell's Kant: *Mind and world. Philosophy*, 71, pp. 219–43.
Blackburn, S. (1981). Rule-following and moral realism. In S. Holtzman and C. Leich (Eds), *Wittgenstein: To follow a rule*. London: Routledge and Kegan Paul, pp. 163–87.
Blackburn, S. (1983). *Spreading the word*. Oxford: Clarendon Press.
Blackburn, S. (1984). The individual strikes back. *Synthesis*, 58, pp. 281–301.
Block, N. (1998/2007b). Is experiencing just representing? In his *Consciousness, Function, and Representation* (2007b). Cambridge, MA: MIT Press, pp. 603–10.
Block, N. (2003/2007b). Mental paint. In M. Hahn and B. Ramberg (Eds), *Reflections and replies: Essays on the philosophy of Tyler Burge*. Cambridge, MA: MIT Press. Reprinted in his *Consciousness, Function, and Representation* (2007b). Cambridge, MA: MIT Press, pp. 533–70.
Block, N. (2007a). Consciousness, accessibility, and the mesh between psychology and neuroscience. *Behavioral and Brain Sciences*, 30(5–6), pp. 481–99.
Block, N. (2007b). *Consciousness, function, and representation*. Cambridge, MA: MIT Press.
Block, N. (2007c). Overflow, access, and attention. *Behavioral and Brain Sciences*, 30, pp. 530–48.
Block, N. (2008). Consciousness and cognitive access. *Proceedings of the Aristotelian Society*, 108, pp. 289–317.
Block, N. (2015). The puzzle of perceptual precision. *Open Mind*.
Brandom, R. (1994). *Making It Explicit: Reasoning, representing, and discursive commitment*. Cambridge, MA: Harvard University Press.
Brandom, R. (1996). Perception and rational constraint: McDowell's *Mind and world*. In E. Villanueva (Ed.), *Perception*. Atascadero: Ridgeview Publishing Company, pp. 241–59.
Brandom, R. (2000). *Articulating reasons: An introduction to inferentialism*. Cambridge, MA: Harvard University Press.
Brandom. R. (2002) *Tales of the mighty dead: Historical essays in the metaphysics of intentionality*. Cambridge, MA: Harvard University Press
Brandom, R. (2019). *A spirit of trust: A reading of Hegel's* Phenomenology. Cambridge, MA: Harvard University Press.
Brentano, F. (1889/1973). *Psychology from an empirical standpoint*. (L. L. McAlister trans). Abingdon, UK: Routledge and Kegan Paul.
Brook, A. (1994). *Kant and the mind*. Cambridge: Cambridge University Press.
Brook, A. (2001). Book review: *Self and world. Mind*, 110(437), pp. 190–6.

Burge, T. (2005). Disjunctivism and perceptual psychology. *Philosophical Topics*, 33(1), pp. 1–78.
Burge, T. (2010). *Origins of objectivity*. New York: Oxford University Press.
Burge, T. (2011). Disjunctivism again. *Philosophical Explorations*, 14(1), pp. 43–80.
Byrne, A. (2001). Intentionalism defended. *Philosophical Review*, 110, pp. 199–240.
Byrne, A., and Logue, H. (2008). Either/or. In A. Byrne and H. Logue (Eds) *Disjunctivism: Perception, action, knowledge* (2008b), Oxford: Oxford University Press. pp. 57–94.
Campbell, J. (2002). *Reference and consciousness*. Oxford: Oxford University Press.
Carey, S. (2009). *The origin of concepts*. New York: Oxford University Press.
Cassam, Q. (1997). *Self and world*. Oxford: Oxford University Press.
Cassam, Q. (2002). Representing bodies. *Ratio*, 15(4), pp. 315–34.
Chalmers, D. (1996). *The conscious mind: In search of a fundamental theory*. New York: Oxford University Press.
Chalmers, D. (2004). The representational character of experience. In B. Leiter (Ed.), *The future for philosophy*. Oxford: Clarendon Press, pp. 153–81.
Cheng, T. (2008). Evaluating Williamson's anti-scepticism. *Sorites*, 21, pp. 6–11.
Cheng, T. (2015). Self, action, and passivity. *Philosophical Writings*, 44(1), pp. 1–19.
Cheng, T. (2016). The sceptical paradox and the nature of the self. *Philosophical Investigations*, 39(1), pp. 3–14.
Cheng, T. (2017). Iconic memory and attention in the overflow debate. *Cogent Psychology*, 4(1), pp. 1–11.
Cheng, T. (2018). *Sense, space, and self*. PhD dissertation, UCL.
Cheng, T. (forthcoming, a). Review of: *Perception and reality in Kant, Husserl, and McDowell*. *Phenomenological Review*.
Cheng, T. (Ed.) (forthcoming, b). Self and world, 20 years on. *Analytic Philosophy*.
Cheng, T. (forthcoming, c). Post-perceptual confidence and supervaluative matching profile. *Inquiry: An Interdisciplinary Journal of Philosophy*.
Cheng, T. (in preparation). Supervenience, emergence, and free will.
Cheng, T., Sato, R., and Hohwy, J. (Eds) (forthcoming). *Expected experiences: The predictive mind in an uncertain world*. New York: Routledge.
Chisholm, R. (1957) *Perceiving: A philosophical study*. Ithaca: Cornell University Press.
Christensen, B. C. (2008). *Self and world: From analytic philosophy to phenomenology*. Berlin: Walter de Gruyter.
Chudnoff, E. (2015). *Cognitive phenomenology*. Oxford: Routledge.
Collins, A. (1998). Beastly experience. *Philosophy and Phenomenological Research* 58, pp. 375–80.
Crane, T. (2006). Is there a perceptual relation? In T. S. Gendler and J. Hawthorne (Eds), *Perceptual experience*. Oxford: Clarendon Press, pp. 126–46.
Crane, T. (2009). Intentionalism. In A. Beckermann and B. McLaughlin (Eds), *Oxford Handbook to the Philosophy of Mind*. Oxford: Oxford University Press, pp. 474–93.

Crane, T. (2013). The given. In J. K. Schear (Ed.), *Mind, reason, and being-in-the-world*. The McDowell-Dreyfus debate. New York, Routledge.
Crane, T., and French, C. (2015). The problem of perception (Spring 2017 edition). In E. N. Zalta (Ed.), *Stanford Encyclopedia of Philosophy*, https://plato.stanford.edu/archives/spr2017/entries/perception-problem/
de Gaynesford, M. (2003). Kant and Strawson on the first person. In H-J. Glock (Ed.), *Strawson and Kant*. Oxford: Clarendon Press, pp. 155–67.
de Gaynesford, M. (2004a). *John McDowell*. Cambridge, UK: Polity Press.
de Gaynesford, M. (2004b). On referring to oneself. *Theoria*, 70, pp. 121–61.
de Vignemont, F. (2018). Bodily awareness (Spring 2018 edition). In E. N. Zalta (Ed.), *Stanford Encyclopedia of Philosophy*, https://plato.stanford.edu/archives/spr2018/entries/bodily-awareness/
deVries, W. (2005). *Wilfrid Sellars*. New York: Acumen.
deVries, W. (2017). Hegel's revival in analytic philosophy. In D. Moyar (Ed.), *The Oxford Handbook of Hegel*. Oxford: Oxford University Press, pp. 743–66.
deVries, W. and Triplett, T. (2000). *Knowledge, mind, and the given: Reading Wilfrid Sellars's "Empiricism and the philosophy of mind"*. Indiana: Hackett Publishing Company, Inc.
Dancy, J. (2006). Acting in the light of the appearances. In C. MacDonald and G. MacDonald (Eds), *McDowell and his critics*. Oxford: Blackwell Publishing, pp. 121–34.
Davidson, D. (1970/2001a). Mental events. In L. Foster and J. W. Swanson (Eds), *Experience and theory*. Amherst, MA: University of Massachusetts Press. Reprinted in his *Essays on actions and events* (2001a). Oxford: Clarendon Press, pp. 207–25.
Davidson, D. (1974/2001b). On the very idea of a conceptual scheme. In *Proceedings and addresses of the American philosophical association*, 47; reprinted in his *Inquiries into truth and interpretation* (2001b), Clarendon Press, Oxford, pp. 183–98.
Davidson, D. (1983/2001c). A coherence theory of truth and knowledge. In D. Henrich (Eds), *Kant oder Hegel?* Stuttgart: Klett-Cotta; reprinted in his *Subjective, intersubjective, objective* (2001c), Oxford: Clarendon Press, pp. 137–53.
Davidson, D. (1984/2001b). Communication and convention. *Synthesis*, 59, pp. 3–17; reprinted in his *Inquiries into truth and interpretation* (2001b), pp. 265–80.
Davidson, D. (1986/2005). A nice derangement of epitaphs. In R. E. Grandy and R. Warner (Eds), *Philosophical grounds of rationality: Intentions, categories, ends*, Oxford: Clarendon Press; reprinted in his *Truth, language, and history* (2005), Oxford: Clarendon Press, pp. 89–107.
Davidson, D. (1988/2001c). The myth of the subjective. In M. Benedikt and R. Berger (Eds), *Bewusstein, Sprache und die Kunst*, Edition S. Verlag der Österreichischen Staatsdruckerei; reprinted in his *Subjective, intersubjective, objective* (2001c), pp. 39–52.
Davidson, D. (1991/2001c). Three varieties of knowledge. In A. p. Griffiths (Ed.), *A. J. Ayer memorial essays: Royal institute of philosophy supplement*, 30, Cambridge:

Cambridge University Press; reprinted in his *Subjective, intersubjective, objective* (2001c), pp. 205–20.
Davidson, D. (1992/2001c). The second person. In p. A. French, T. E. Uehling, and H. K. Wettstein (Eds), *Midwest studies in philosophy 17: The Wittgenstein legacy*, Indianapolis: University of Notre Dame Press; reprinted in his *Subjective, intersubjective, objective* (2001c), pp. 107–21.
Davidson, D. (1994/2005). The social aspect of language. In B. F. McGuinness and G. Oliveri (Eds), *The philosophy of Michael Dummett*. Dordrecht: Kluwer Academic Publishers; reprinted in his *Truth, language, and history*, pp. 109–25.
Davidson, D. (1999). Reply to John McDowell. In L. E. Hahn (Ed.), *The philosophy of Donald Davidson*, Chicago, IL: Open Court, pp. 105–8.
Davidson, D. (2001a). *Essays on actions and events*. Oxford: Clarendon Press.
Davidson, D. (2001b). *Inquiries into truth and interpretation*. Oxford: Clarendon Press.
Davidson, D. (2001c). *Subjective, intersubjective, objective*. Oxford: Clarendon Press.
Davidson, D. (2004). *Problems of rationality*. Oxford: Clarendon Press.
Davidson, D. (2005). *Truth, language, and history*. Oxford: Clarendon Press.
Dennett, D. (1987). *The intentional stance*. Cambridge, MA: MIT Press.
Dennett, D. (1988). Quining qualia. In A. Marcel and E. Bisiach (Eds), *Consciousness in contemporary science*. Oxford: Oxford University Press; reprinted in D. Chalmers (Ed.) *Philosophy of mind: Classical and contemporary readings*, Oxford: Oxford University Press, pp. 226–46.
Dennett, D. (1991). *Consciousness explained*. New York, NY: Back Bay Books.
Dingli, S. M. (2005). *On Thinking and the World: John McDowell's Mind and World*. Farnham, UK: Ashgate Publishing.
Dretske, F. (1995). *Naturalizing the mind*. Cambridge, MA: MIT Press.
Dreyfus, H. (2001). Todes's account of nonconceptual perceptual knowledge and its relation to thought. In *Body and world*. Cambridge, MA: MIT Press, pp. xv–xxvii.
Dreyfus, H. (2006). Overcoming the myth of the mental: How philosophers can profit from the phenomenology of everyday expertise. *Topoi*, 25, pp. 43–9.
Dreyfus, H. (2007a). The return of the myth of the mental. *Inquiry*, 50, pp. 352–65
Dreyfus, H. (2007b). Response to McDowell. *Inquiry*, 50, pp. 371–7.
Ducasse, C. J. (1942). Moore's refutation of idealism. In A. Schilpp (Ed.), *The philosophy of G. E. Moore*. Chicago, IL: Northwestern University Press, pp. 225–51.
Dummett, M. (1981). Frege and Wittgenstein. In I. Block (Ed.), *Perspectives on the philosophy of Wittgenstein*. Oxford: Blackwell.
Dummett, M. (1989). Language and communication. In A. George (Ed.), *Reflections on Chomsky*. Oxford: Basil Blackwell, pp. 192–212.
Evans, G. (1982). *The Varieties of Reference*. Oxford: Oxford University Press.
Fodor, J. A. (1989). *Psychosemantics: The problem of meaning in the philosophy of mind*. Cambridge, MA: MIT Press.
Fodor, J. A. (2007). The revenge of the given. In. B. p. McLaughlin and J. D. Cohen (Eds), *Contemporary debates in philosophy of mind*. Oxford: Blackwell.

Frege, G. (1884/1950). *The foundations of arithmetic.* (J. L. Austin, trans.). Oxford: Blackwell.

Frege, G. (1892/1930). On sense and reference. In p. Geach and M. Black (trans) *Translations from the philosophical writings of Gottlob Frege*, 3rd edition. Lanham, ML: Rowman and Littlefield.

Fridland, E. (2015). Automatically minded. *Synthese*, 194(11), pp. 4337–63.

Fridland, E. (2017). Skill and motor control: Intelligence all the way down. *Philosophical Studies*, 174(6), pp. 1539–60.

Fridland, E. (2019). Longer, smaller, faster, stronger: On skills and intelligence. *Philosophical Psychology*, 32(5), pp. 759–83.

Gadamer, H-G. (1960/2004) *Truth and method.* Joel Weinsheimer and Donald Marshall (trans), New York: Continuum.

Gaskin, R. (2006) *Experience and the world's own language: A critique of John McDowell's empiricism.* New York: Oxford University Press.

Geach, p. (1957). *Mental acts: Their content and their objects.* Abingdon, UK: Routledge and Kegan Paul.

Gendler, T. S. and Hawthorne, J. (2006). Introduction: Perceptual experience. In T. S. Gendler and J. Hawthorne (Eds), *Perceptual experience.* Oxford: Oxford University Press, pp. 1–30.

Gettier, E. (1963). Is justified true belief knowledge? *Analysis*, 23(6), pp. 121–3.

Gibson, J. J. (1979) *The ecological approach to visual perception.* Boston, MA: Houghton Mifflin.

Ginsborg, H. (2006). Reasons for belief. *Philosophy and Phenomenological Research* 72, pp. 286–318.

Gomes, A., and Stephenson, A. (Eds) (2017). *Kant and the philosophy of mind: Perception, reason, and the self.* Oxford: Oxford University Press.

Gorner, p. (1971). Husserl and Strawson. *Journal of the British Society for Phenomenology*, 2(1), pp. 2–9.

Grice, H. p. (1961). The causal theory of perception. *Aristotelian Society Supplementary Volume*, 35(1), pp. 121–53.

Gupta, A. (2006). *Empiricism and experience.* Oxford: Oxford University Press.

Gupta, A. (2019). *Conscious experience: A logical inquiry.* Cambridge, MA: Harvard University Press.

Haddock, A., and Macpherson, F. (2008). Introduction: Varieties of disjunctivism. In Haddock, A. and Macpherson, F. (Eds), *Disjunctivism: Perception, action, and knowledge.* Oxford: Oxford University Press, pp. 1–24.

Hanna, R. (2001). *Kant and the foundation of analytic philosophy.* Oxford: Oxford University Press.

Hanna, R. (2006). *Kant, science, and human nature.* Oxford: Oxford University Press.

Hasan, A. (2017). *A critical introduction to the epistemology of perception.* London: Bloomsbury Academic.

Hatfield, G. (1991). *The nature and the normative: Theories of spatial perception from Kant to Helmholtz*. Cambridge, MA: MIT Press.

Hatfield, G. (2009). *Perception and cognition: Essays in the philosophy of psychology*. Oxford: Oxford University Press.

Heidegger, M. (1927/1962). *Being and time*. (J. Macquarrie and E. Robinson, trans). Oxford: Basil Blackwell.

Henry, M. (2000/2015). *Incarnation: A philosophy of flesh*. (K. Hefty, trans.). Evanston, IL: Northwestern University Press.

Hornsby, J. (1980–1). Which physical events are mental events? *Proceedings of the Aristotelian Society* 81, pp. 73–92; reprinted in her *Simple Mindedness: in Defense of Naïve Naturalism in the Philosophy of Mind* (1997). Cambridge, MA: Harvard University Press, pp. 63–97.

Hornsby, J. (1997). *Simple Mindedness: in Defense of Naïve Naturalism in the Philosophy of Mind*. Cambridge, MA: Harvard University Press.

Hohwy, J. (2013). *The predictive mind*. Oxford: Oxford University Press.

Husserl, E. (1913/1982). *Ideas pertaining to a pure phenomenology and to a phenomenological philosophy – first book: general introduction to a pure phenomenology* (F. Kersten, trans.). Dordrecht: Kluwer Academic Publishers.

Husserl, E. (1920–1926/2001) *Analyses Concerning Passive and Active Synthesis: Lectures on Transcendental Logic* (A. J. Steinbock, trans.). Berlin: Springer.

Husserl, E. (1931/2013). *Cartesian meditations* (D. Cairns trans.). Leiden, Netherlands: Martinus Nijhoff.

Husserl, E. (1939/1975) *Experience and judgment* (J. Churchill and K. Ameriks trans). Evanston: Northwestern University Press.

Hyman, J. (2015). *Action, knowledge, and will*. Oxford: Oxford University Press.

Jackson, F. (2004). Mind and illusion. In p. Ludlow, Y. Nagasawa, and D. Stoljar (Eds), *There is something about Mary: Essays on phenomenal consciousness and Frank Jackson's knowledge argument*. Cambridge, MA: MIT Press, pp. 421–2.

Johansson, J. (2007). What is animalism? *Ratio*, 20, pp. 194–205.

Johnston, M. (2004). The obscure object of hallucination. *Philosophical Studies*, 120(1/3), pp. 113–83.

Kalderon, M. E. (2015). *Form without matter: Empedocles and Aristotle on color perception*. Oxford: Oxford University Press.

Kalderon, M. E. (2017). *Sympathy in perception*. Cambridge, UK: Cambridge University Press.

Kant, I. (1787/1998). *Critique of pure reason* (P. Guyer and A. Wood trans). Cambridge: Cambridge University Press.

Kripke, S. (1982). *Wittgenstein on rules and private language*. Cambridge, MA: Harvard University Press.

Kusch, M. (2006). *A sceptical guide to meaning and rules: Defending Kripke's Wittgenstein*. Montreal: McGill-Queen's University Press.

Kvanvig, J. (2003). *The value of knowledge and the pursuit of understanding*. Cambridge: Cambridge University Press.

Landman, R. et. al. (2003). Large capacity storage of integrated objects before change blindness, *Vision Research*, 43(2), pp. 149–64.

Leibniz, G. W. (1714/1991). *Monadology* (N. Rescher trans.). London: Routledge.

Leibniz, G. W. (1765/1999) *New essays on human understanding* (P. Remnant and J. Bennett trans). Cambridge: Cambridge University Press

Lewis, D. (1980). Veridical hallucination and prothetic vision. *Australasian Journal of Philosophy*, 58(3), pp. 239–49.

Lin, C. (2008). Lost world and impalpable environment. *Monthly Review of Philosophy and Culture*, 411, pp. 25–46.

List, C. (2019). *Why free will is real*. Cambridge, MA: Harvard University Press.

Locke, J. (1689/1999). *An essay concerning human understanding*. T. L. Beauchamp (Ed.), New York: Oxford University Press.

McCulloch, G. (2002). Phenomenological externalism. In N. H. Smith (Ed.), *Reading McDowell: on mind and world*. London: Routledge, pp. 123–39.

Maher, C. (2012). *The Pittsburgh school of philosophy: Sellars, McDowell, Brandom*. New York: Routledge.

Mall, R. A. (1973). *Experience and reason: The phenomenology of Husserl and its relation to Hume's philosophy*. Berlin: Springer.

Martin, M. G. F. (2002). The transparency of experience. *Mind and Language*, 17, pp. 376–425.

Martin, M. G. F. (2004). The limits of self-awareness. *Philosophical Studies*, 120, pp. 37–89.

Martin. M. G. F. (2006). On being alienated. In T. S. Gendler and J. Hawthorne (Eds), *Perceptual experience*, pp. 354–410. Oxford: Oxford University Press.

Merleau-Ponty, M. (1945/2013). *Phenomenology of perception*. (D. A. Landes, trans.). London: Routledge.

Merleau-Ponty, M. (1960/1964). *Signs*. (R. C. McCleary, trans.). Evanston, IL: Northwestern University Press.

Merleau-Ponty, M. (1964/1969). *The visible and the invisible*. (A. Lingis, trans.). Evanston: Northwestern University Press.

Miller, A. (2002). Introduction. In A. Miller and C. Wright (Eds), *Rule-following and meaning*, pp. 1–15, New York: Routledge.

Montero, B. (2016). *Thought in action: Expertise and the conscious mind*. Oxford: Oxford University Press.

Montero, B. (2019). Chess and the conscious mind: Why Dreyfus and McDowell got it wrong. *Mind and Language*, 34(3), pp. 376–92.

Murdoch, I. (1970). *The sovereignty of good*. London: Routledge and Kegan Paul.

Nagel, T. (2007). The incompleteness of objective reality. In B. Gertler and L. Shapiro (Eds), *Arguing about the mind*, pp. 36–49. New York: Routledge.

Noonan, H. (2019). *Personal identity*, 3rd edition. New York: Routledge.

Olson, E. (1999). *The human animal: Personal identity without psychology.* New York: Oxford University Press.

Olson, E. (2007). There is no problem of the self. In B. Gertler and L. Shapiro (Eds), *Arguing about the Mind*, pp. 262–77. New York: Routledge.

O'Shea, J. (2007). *Wilfrid Sellars: Naturalism with a normative turn.* Cambridge: Polity Press

Papineau, D. (2003). Is this a dagger? *The Times Literary Supplement*, 5211, p. 12.

Parfit, D. (1984). *Reasons and persons.* Oxford: Clarendon Press.

Parsons, C. (1980). *Non-existent objects.* New Haven, CT: Yale University Press.

Passmore, J. (1961). *Philosophical reasoning.* New York: Charles Scribner's Sons.

Peacocke, C. (1992). *A study of concepts.* Cambridge, MA: MIT Press.

Peacocke, C. (1998). Nonconceptual content defended. *Philosophy and Phenomenological Research*, 58(2), pp. 381–8.

Peacocke, C. (2008). *Truly understood.* Oxford: Oxford University Press.

Pietroski, p. (2000) *Causing Actions.* Oxford: Oxford University Press.

Price, H. (2011). *Naturalism without mirrors.* New York: Oxford University Press.

Prinz, J. (2002). *Furnishing the mind: Concepts and their perceptual basis.* Cambridge, MA: MIT Press.

Pritchard, D. (2005). *Epistemic luck.* Oxford: Oxford University Press.

Pritchard, D. (2012). *Epistemological disjunctivism.* Oxford: Oxford University Press.

Quilty-Dunn, J. (forthcoming). Is iconic memory iconic? *Philosophy and Phenomenological Research.*

Quine, W. V. O. (1951/1961). Two dogmas of empiricism. Philosophical Review, 60, pp. 20–43. Reprinted in his *From a logical point of view*, Cambridge, MA: Harvard University Press.

Quine, W. V. O. (1960) *Word and Object.* Cambridge, MA: MIT Press

Raftopoulos, A. (2019). *Cognitive penetrability and the epistemic role of perception.* London: Palgrave Macmillan.

Redding, p. (2007). *Analytic philosophy and the return of Hegelian thought.* New York: Cambridge University Press.

Redding, p. (2011). The analytic neo-Hegelianism of John McDowell and Robert Brandom. In S. Houlgate and M. Baur (Eds), *The Blackwell Companion to Hegel*, pp. 576–93. New York: Blackwell.

Robinson, H. (1994). *Perception.* London: Routledge.

Rockmore, T. (2012). The Pittsburgh school, the given and knowledge. *Social Epistemology Review and Reply Collective*, 2(1), pp. 29–38.

Romdenh-Romluc, K. (2016). The world and I. In K. Romdenh-Romluc (Ed.), *Wittgenstein and Merleau-Ponty*, pp. 81–99. New York: Routledge.

Rorty, R. (1979). *Philosophy and the mirror of nature.* Princeton, NJ: Princeton University Press.

Rosenberg, J. (2007) *Wilfrid Sellars: Fusing the images.* New York: Oxford University Press.

Rouse, J. (2005). Mind, body, and world: Todes and McDowell on bodies and language. *Inquiry*, 48, pp. 36–61.

Russell, B. (1910–11/1986). Knowledge by acquaintance and knowledge by description. *Proceedings of the Aristotelian Society*, 11, pp. 108–28. Reprinted in his *Mysticism and logic, including a free man's worship* London: Routledge.

Russell, B. (1917). On the notion of cause. In his *Mysticism and logic*, pp. 132–51. London, UK: George Allen and Unwin.

Sachs, C. B. (2017). *Intentionality and the myth of the given*. New York: Routledge.

Sartre, J-P. (1943/2003). *Being and nothingness: an essay on phenomenological ontology*. (H. E. Barnes, trans.). Oxford: Routledge.

Searle, J. (1983) *Intentionality: An essay in the philosophy of mind*. Cambridge, UK: Cambridge University Press.

Searle, J. (1987/2002). Indeterminacy, empiricism, and the first person. *Journal of Philosophy*, 84, pp. 123–46; reprinted in his *Consciousness and language*, pp. 226–50. Cambridge, UK: Cambridge University Press.

Sellars, W. (1956). Empiricism and the philosophy of mind. In H. Feigl and M. Scriven (Eds), *Minnesota Studies in the Philosophy of Science, vol. 1*, pp. 253–329. Minneapolis: University of Minnesota Press.

Sellars, W. (1962). Philosophy and the scientific image of man. In R. Colodny (Ed.), *Frontiers of science and philosophy*, pp. 35–78. Pittsburgh, PA: University of Pittsburgh Press.

Shoemaker, S. (1970). Persons and their past. *American Philosophical Quarterly*, 7, pp. 269–85.

Smith, A. D. (2002). *The Problem of Perception*. Cambridge, MA: Harvard University Press.

Smith, A. D. (2003). *Husserl and the Cartesian meditations*. London: Routledge.

Smith, B. C. (2009). Speech sounds and the direct meeting of minds. In. C. O'Callaghan and M. Nudds (Eds), *Sounds and perception: New philosophical essays*, pp. 183–210. Oxford: Oxford University Press.

Smith, J. (2016). *Experiencing phenomenology*. New York: Routledge.

Smithies, D. (2019). *The epistemic role of consciousness*. New York: Oxford University Press.

Snowdon, p. (1980–1). Perception, vision, and causation. *Proceedings of the Aristotelian Society*, 81, pp. 175–92.

Sokolowski, R. (2000). *Introduction to phenomenology*. Cambridge, UK: Cambridge University Press.

Sperling, G. (1960). The information available in brief visual presentations. *Psychological Monographs: General and Applied*, 74(11), pp. 1–29.

Stanley, J. (2011). *Knowing how*. Oxford: Oxford University Press.

Stazicker, J. (2011). Attention, visual consciousness and indeterminacy. *Mind and Language*, 26(2), pp. 156–84.

Strawson, p. F. (1959). *Individuals: An essay in descriptive metaphysics*. London: Methuen.

Strawson, p. F. (1966). *The bounds of sense*. London: Methuen.
Stroud, B. (1984). *The significance of philosophical scepticism*. Oxford: Clarendon Press.
Thornton, T. (2019). *John McDowell*, 2nd edition. Montreal, Canada: McGill-Queen's University Press.
Todes, S. (2001) *Body and World*. Cambridge, MA: MIT Press.
Travis, C. (2004). The silence of senses. *Mind*, 113, pp. 57–94; reprinted in his *Perception: Essays after Frege*, pp. 23–58. Oxford, UK: Oxford University Press.
Tye, M. (2002). *Consciousness, color, and content*. Cambridge, MA: MIT Press.
Tye, M. (2006). Nonconceptual content, richness, and fineness of grain. In T. S. Gendler and J. Hawthorne (Eds), *Perceptual experience*. Oxford: Oxford University Press.
Tye, M. (2007). Intentionalism and the argument from no common content. In J. Hawthorne (Ed.), *Philosophical perspectives*, 21, pp. 589–613. Northridge: Ridgeview Publishing.
Varela, F., Thompson, E., and Rosch, E. (2017). *The Embodied Mind: Cognitive Science and Human Experience*, revised edition. Cambridge, MA: MIT Press.
Vernazzani, A. (forthcoming). Do we see facts? *Mind and Language*.
Williamson, T. (2000) *Knowledge and Its Limits*. Oxford, UK: Oxford University Press
Wilson, G. (1994/2002). Kripke on Wittgenstein on normativity. In p. A. French and H. Wettstein (Eds), *Midwest Studies in Philosophy*, 19, pp. 366–90; reprinted in *Rule-following and meaning*, pp. 234–59. New York: Routledge.
Wittgenstein (1921/1922). *Tractatus Logico-Philosophicus*. New York: Routledge.
Wittgenstein, L. (1953/2001) *Philosophical investigations* (G. E. M. Anscombe trans.), Oxford: Blackwell Publishing.
Wittgenstein, L. (1956/1978). *Remarks on the foundations of mathematics*. Oxford: Basil Blackwell.
Wittgenstein, L. (1958). *The blue and brown books*. Oxford: Basil Blackwell.
Wittgenstein, L. (1969) *On certainty*. Oxford: Basil Blackwell.
Wittgenstein, L. (1984). *Notebooks, 1914–1916*. (G. E. M. Anscombe trans.), Chicago, IL: University of Chicago Press.
Wright, C. (1989). Wittgenstein's later philosophy of mind: Sensation, privacy, and intention. Presented at an American Philosophical Association symposium on Wittgenstein on December 30, 1989.
Wright, C. (2002). Human nature? In *Reading McDowell: on* Mind and world, pp. 140–59. New York, NY: Routledge.
Wyller, T. (2000). Kant on *I*, apperception, and imagination. In A. Øfsti, p. Ulrich, and T. Wyller (Eds), *Indexicality and idealism: The self in philosophical perspective, vol.2*, pp. 89–99. Mentis Publishing.

Index of Names

Alweiss, L. 181
Anscombe, G. E. M. 183
Aristotle 19–20, 79, 82, 101, 160–1, 172, 181, 187
Austin, J. L. 120
Ayers, M. 50–1, 77–8, 90, 163, 165, 172, 177

Bermúdez, J. L. 2, 4, 134, 159
Bird, G. 184
Blackburn, S. 33, 35, 60, 95, 162, 178
Block, N. 112, 114, 123–4, 145–6, 167, 176, 184, 186
Brandom, R. viii, 3, 12, 14, 26–7, 48–51, 61, 66, 137–9, 160–1, 163, 176–7, 179–80, 189
Brentano, F. 5, 68, 122–3, 186
Burge, T. 53, 158, 187, 189
Byrne, A. 115–17, 122, 125, 167, 185–6

Campbell, J. 2, 4, 159
Carey, S. 175
Cassam, Q. ix, 2, 91, 159, 182, 184
Chalmers, D. 114, 156, 171–2, 174, 183, 185, 189
Chisholm, R. 121
Crane, T. 114–15, 117–26, 143, 167–8, 184–6

de Gaynesford, M. 6, 13, 105–7, 166, 182, 184
de Vignemont, F. 91
deVries, W. 3, 43, 182, 188
Dancy, J. 79
Davidson, D. viii, 13–14, 26–7, 42, 48, 50–3, 68, 71–3, 80, 97–9, 107–9, 111, 127–37, 144, 150, 157, 160–2, 164, 166–8, 171, 173, 175, 177, 179, 183–4, 187
Dennett, D. 174, 179, 185
Descartes, R. 10, 31–2, 95, 102–3, 160, 173–4

Dretske, F. 123
Dreyfus, H. 14, 75, 78–90, 97, 138, 140, 142–3, 159–60, 165, 169, 173, 176, 180–1, 188
Dummett, M. viii, 14, 68–71, 160, 164, 173, 179

Eilan, N. 2, 4, 159
Evans, G. 2, 4, 12, 14, 92, 106, 140, 144, 159, 166, 175–6, 181–3

Fichte, J. G. 153, 188
Fodor, J. viii, 57, 144
Frege, G. 37, 69, 131, 132, 158, 175, 179
Fridland, E. 182

Gadamer, H-G. viii, 24–5, 53, 72–3, 79, 86, 147, 160–1, 169, 180, 184
Gaskin, R. 6, 154, 170, 172
Geach, P. 140
Gendler, T. S. 122, 168, 175
Gettier, E. 33, 38, 41–2, 97, 162
Gibson, J. J. 180
Ginsborg, H. 50–1, 177
Gomes, A. 2, 159, 182
Grice, H. P. 175
Gupta, A. ix, 48–9, 135, 180, 188

Haddock, A. 115
Hawthorne, J. 122, 168, 175
Hegel, G. W. F. 1, 3, 14, 43, 79, 101, 155, 171, 188
Heidegger, M. 12–13, 53, 79, 89, 180
Henry, M. 178
Hinton, J. M. 115, 185
Hornsby, J. 183
Hohwy, J. 188
Hume, D. ix, 98, 108, 111
Husserl, E. 3, 5, 29, 46, 79, 90–1, 171, 176, 180–1
Hyman, J. 180

Jackson, F. 121

Kalderon, M. 186
Kant, I. 1–3, 5, 13–14, 42, 46, 79, 81, 101–7, 109–10, 127–32, 145, 151, 153, 155, 160, 162, 166–8, 171, 176, 182–4, 187
Kripke, S. 2, 14, 52–6, 58, 60–9, 73, 81, 95, 142, 160, 163–5, 177–9, 181, 185
Kusch, M. 64–7, 163–4

Leibniz, G. W. 102, 118–20
Lewis, C. I. 50
Lewis, D. 175
Lin, C-I. viii, 188
List, C. 156
Locke, J. 91–2, 95, 102, 165–6, 182
Logue, H. 116–17, 122, 167, 186
Longuenesse, B. 182

McCarty, D. 177
McCulloch, G. 185
McDowell, J. H. *passim*
McGinn, C. 178
Macpherson, F. 115
Martin, M. G. F. 115, 125, 175, 185–6
Marx, K. 17
Merleau-Ponty, M. 5, 12, 75, 79, 88–91, 160, 165, 178, 182
Miller, A. 177
Montero, B. 182
Murdoch, I. 172

Nagel, T. 172

Olson, E. 11–12, 95

Papineau, D. 4–5, 159
Parfit, D. 14, 92–6, 102–3, 105, 160, 165–6, 183
Parsons, T. 122
Peacocke, C. viii, 132, 135–6, 176, 181, 193
Pietroski, P. 184
Price, H. 35, 171
Prinz, J. 176

Pritchard, D. 175
Putnam, H. 53, 115, 176

Quine, W. V. O. viii, 53, 67–70, 85, 130, 136, 144, 164, 179

Rorty, R. 172
Rouse, J. 181
Russell, B. 30, 172, 186

Sachs, C. B. 182
Schelling, F. W. J. 17
Schopenhauer, A. 29
Searle, J. 53, 62–3, 79, 180, 186
Sellars, W. viii, 1–3, 12, 14, 17–18, 38, 43, 80, 87–8, 130, 135, 138, 142–4, 161, 168–9, 171–2, 177, 182, 188
Shoemaker, S. 166, 183
Smith, A. D. 8–10, 118–19, 160, 171, 176, 185–6
Smith, B. 178
Smith, J. 5, 91
Smithies, D. ix, 174
Snowdon, P. F. ix, 115, 185
Sperling, G. 145–6
Stanley, J. 182
Stazicker, J. 145–6
Strawson, P. F. 1–5, 12, 14, 101, 105–7, 166, 171, 182–4
Stroud, B. 31, 162, 178

Tarski, A. 179
Todes, S. 80, 165, 181
Travis, C. 46, 49, 176
Tye, M. 33, 124–5, 176, 186

Wenzel, C. 174
Williamson, T. 115, 162, 173–5, 182
Wilson, G. 177
Wittgenstein, L. viii, 2, 7, 14–15, 48, 53–64, 66–7, 73–4, 79, 81, 110–11, 136, 142, 148, 155, 163–4, 176, 178–9, 181–2, 184
Wright, C. 22–3, 60–1, 66, 68, 160, 163–4, 172–4, 178

Zahavi, D. ix, 182

Subject Index

a priori 4, 39
absolute idealism 12
act/content distinction 48, 51, 163, 176
action 11, 20, 31, 41, 55, 57–9, 62, 75–9, 81, 83–6, 140, 153, 165, 176, 180–1, 184–5
adverbial theory 120–1, 124–5, 168, 186
affordance 78–9, 87–8, 140, 180, 182
agency 11, 75, 79, 83, 85, 90
agent vii, 11–12, 14, 26–7, 46, 49, 70, 75, 83, 153, 158, 160, 170
animalism 95, 166
anomalous monism 97–8, 144, 166, 183
appearance 31–2, 34–5, 39–41, 117, 122, 125, 128, 150, 184
apperception 102–3, 107, 109, 155, 166, 182, 184
argument from illusion 39, 96, 118–21, 123–5, 167–8, 186
attention ix, 76, 83–6, 92, 102, 124, 142–3, 146, 165, 169, 181, 188

bald naturalism 18–20, 23–6, 44–5, 94, 130, 157, 161, 163
bare presence 136, 139, 140, 142, 188
behaviourism 60, 68, 70, 164, 179
Bildung 20, 23–4, 27, 71, 73, 161, 164
blamelessness 40–1
bodily presence 91, 104, 166
body 5, 30, 80, 86–7, 89–91, 97, 104, 165, 181, 203
broadness 30, 95, 122, 162, 166, 174–5, 182, 185

Cartesian dualism 21, 98, 99, 166, 173
Cartesianism 54, 68, 94–5, 105–6
causality 98, 111, 154–5, 157–8, 161, 166–7, 170, 183
causation 30, 74, 98–9, 122, 153–4, 156–7, 170, 172, 185, 188, 199
Cogito vii, 10, 13, 17, 107, 153, 161, 170
cognitive science 4–5, 13, 132, 159, 169, 171, 176

coherentism 43–5, 48, 88, 110, 130, 135, 162, 176, 184
common kind 117, 119–22, 125–6, 162, 167, 174, 185, 186
concept 5, 11, 24, 26–7, 29, 42, 43, 46–7, 54, 69, 71, 76, 79, 96, 99, 109, 113, 127–9, 131–9, 141, 143, 154, 168, 173, 175–6, 180, 187
conceptual
    capacity 20, 24, 45–6, 74–9, 85, 117, 131–2, 138–9, 141, 144, 155, 165, 176, 180, 181
    content 47, 49, 135, 139, 143, 146, 147, 169, 175
    scheme 108–10, 128, 133–5, 159, 169
conceptualism 46, 75, 77–8, 83, 128–9, 133, 137–40, 164, 180
conceptuality 21, 44, 47, 78, 82, 85, 89, 110, 127, 129, 134–5, 137–9, 142, 147, 151, 165, 167–9, 180, 187–8
consciousness ix, 4–5, 9, 11, 17, 46, 77, 92–6, 101–3, 109, 111–14, 146, 156, 166, 172, 182
    self- ix, 24, 31, 101–2, 109, 165–6, 182
constitution 10, 24, 27, 46, 50, 72–3, 122, 156, 164
constitutive ideal of rationality 97
custom 24, 53, 57–61, 66, 70, 73–4, 81, 163–4

direct realism 8–9
disjunctive conception 35, 47, 116, 184
disjunctivism 114–23, 125–6, 162, 167, 174–5, 185–6
dispositionalism 64–6, 164

emergence 8, 27, 60, 156, 183, 189
embedment 24, 91, 101, 165
embodiment 74–5, 90, 164, 180
empirical content 109, 111
environment viii, 12, 21–2, 24–5, 36, 75, 129, 147–51, 161, 169–70, 173, 180, 182, 188

epiphenomenalism 157, 166
epistemic luck 38-9, 41, 162
ethics 19, 23, 172-3, 178, 189
event dualism 99, 166
evidence 42, 59, 66, 108, 116, 177, 187
evil demon 32, 34, 41
exculpation 41, 136, 162, 175
experience 5, 12, 21, 24, 26, 29, 32-5, 42, 44-51, 76-9, 81, 84, 86, 89, 91, 98, 101, 104, 108, 110-19, 121-2, 124-5, 128-30, 135-9, 141-4, 147-51, 163, 165, 167-9, 171, 176, 181, 184-6, 188
externalism 30, 33, 40, 122, 162, 167, 175, 185

factivism 174
factorization 111, 172
form of life 12, 58-9, 73-4, 81
foundationalism 43, 59, 88, 165, 176
free will 9, 156
full-fledged subjectivity viii, 25

German idealism 110, 155, 170
grounding 156

hallucination 32-3, 96, 115-16, 118-19, 122, 167, 185

idealism 8-9, 47, 110, 163, 176
identification-freedom 92-4, 103, 105, 166, 184
indeterminacy of translation 179
infinite regress of interpretation 56, 64-5, 163-5
information 32, 96, 158, 170
inner space model 31-2, 34-7, 39-42, 48, 53-4, 61-2, 81, 90, 95, 109-11, 116, 162-3, 165, 174-5, 178-9, 183
intellect 19, 78-9, 86, 90, 97, 157, 165, 171, 173, 182
intellectualism 89
intentionalism 33, 113-16, 118-26, 167-8, 174, 184-6
intentionality viii, 1, 14, 45-6, 49-50, 53, 60, 62-3, 82, 86, 88, 95, 109-11, 113, 125, 133, 158, 162-3, 169, 176, 182, 184, 186
internalism 30, 122, 162, 167
introspection 37

intuition 33, 42, 110, 128-9, 131-2, 142, 144, 158, 173, 187
intuitional content 46, 129, 142, 146-7, 169

judgement 22-3, 43-5, 76-7, 113, 128, 131, 142, 168
justification 33-4, 38, 40-3, 50, 55, 58-9, 67, 110, 136-7, 162, 175, 185

KK principle 31, 34-5, 162
knowledge 11, 31-34, 37-42, 45-7, 59-60, 67, 69-70, 75, 85, 92, 96, 101-2, 108, 110, 116, 133-5, 143, 158, 162, 170-1, 173-5, 177-8, 180
 self- 11, 32, 37, 68, 175, 178
Kripkenstein 54-5, 60, 71, 174

language 2, 11, 24, 31, 52-5, 58-60, 62, 64, 68-75, 77, 106, 129, 133, 136-7, 147, 149-51, 161, 164, 167, 169, 173, 179, 181
 games 164
luminosity 174

manifest image 18, 156, 161
memory 96, 166, 183
 quasi- 96-7, 166
mental content 11, 118
mentality 10-12, 14, 43, 95, 113, 156, 159-60
mind-body problem 11, 97-8, 166
mindedness 70, 74-5, 82, 84-6, 89, 142-3, 165, 180, 183
minimal empiricism 48, 108, 130
modesty 69-70
Molyneux's question ix
myth
 of the disembodied intellect 86, 90, 165
 of the given 43-6, 87-9, 110, 128, 130, 133, 135-6, 138, 140-1, 143-6, 162, 169, 175, 180-2, 188
 of the mental 14, 81

narrowness 30
natural science 18-19, 21, 36, 172
naturalism 4-5, 7, 19, 25, 29, 144-5, 147, 157, 159, 161, 170, 183, 188
naturalistic fallacy 18, 130, 144
naturalized platonism 19, 23-4, 29, 161

Subject Index

necessitation 156
non-conceptual content 46, 109, 131–2, 136, 139, 143
normativity 54, 59, 64–5, 67, 177

objectivity 1, 26–7, 46, 67, 101, 104, 111, 150, 158, 166–7, 172, 189
openness 24, 42, 47–9, 51, 161–2, 164
overflow 5, 145, 176
Oxford Kantianism 1–5, 158–9

passive synthesis 5, 46, 181
passivity 26, 43, 45, 78, 87, 143, 165, 180–1
perception 8–9, 11, 22, 31–5, 38, 40–2, 47, 49, 75, 78–80, 85, 92, 102, 112, 114–16, 118–19, 123–5, 128, 147, 150, 160, 162, 165, 168–9, 174–6, 181, 185–6
person 7, 11–12, 14, 27, 37, 46, 58, 61, 66, 71, 75, 87, 90–5, 97–8, 103–4, 108, 139, 153, 155, 158, 160, 164, 170, 183
personhood 90–1, 97, 165–6
phenomenal character 112–13, 115, 117–18, 124–6, 186
phenomenology 3–5, 13, 34, 75, 88, 101, 118, 120, 125, 138, 145–6, 159, 171, 173, 178–9, 185
Phronesis 19, 161, 181
Pittsburgh Hegelianism 1–3, 158–9
primeness 29–30, 41–2, 46–8, 95, 122, 125, 162, 174–5, 185
primitivism 64, 66, 69, 163
private language argument 136, 167
property dualism 183
propositional attitude 11
proto-subjectivity 25, 158
psychologism 68–70, 105, 164, 179

qualia 64, 112–14, 123–6, 167–8, 184–6
quietism 14, 74

rampant platonism 18–20, 22–6, 161
rational animal 18, 20, 38, 40, 76, 78–9, 83, 127, 134, 140–1, 158, 161, 168, 181, 183
rationalism 68, 132
rationality 21, 24, 26, 42, 44, 75–9, 82, 87, 89, 108, 128, 131, 134–5, 138–40, 151, 165, 168–9, 174, 181–2, 187–8

realization 27, 85, 156
realm
  of freedom 14, 43, 153, 156, 170
  of law 18–22, 25, 44–5, 88–9, 98–9, 130, 135, 143–5, 150–1, 154, 156, 158, 161, 165, 170, 172–3
receptivity 29, 45, 47, 132, 188
reduction 24
reductionism 57, 67, 69–70, 92–6, 163–4, 166, 179
reductive physicalism 7, 17, 171
reference 4, 11, 33
relaxed naturalism 26, 98
reliability 40
representational content 37, 135
representationalism 33, 124–6, 167–8, 174, 185–6
residual individualism 14, 26, 49–50, 61, 161, 163
responsiveness to reason 20, 76, 137, 140, 165, 169, 173, 187
rule-following 54, 61, 71–3, 81–2, 164–5, 178–9

sceptical paradox 14, 54–5, 62, 81, 163, 174, 177–8
scepticism 3, 9, 24, 32, 39, 57, 123, 162, 174–5
scheme-content dualism 42, 48, 107, 109–11, 113, 128, 167–8, 184
scientific image 18, 156, 161, 172
second nature 12, 19–23, 27, 29, 130, 137, 144–5, 147–51, 153, 156–7, 161, 170, 173
self x, 11–12, 84–7, 89–92, 104, 127, 160, 177–8, 180, 182, 189
  -determining subjectivity 14, 78, 153, 155–6, 158, 160, 170
  -standing subject 26–7, 161
sense-datum theory 33, 119–21, 186
skillful coping 80, 82, 182
solicitation 78–9, 88–9, 165
space of reasons 14, 17–23, 25–7, 29, 36, 38–46, 50, 70–1, 74, 89, 97, 99, 110, 130–1, 135–6, 139–40, 143–7, 150, 153–8, 161–3, 167, 170, 172–3, 175, 182, 188
spontaneity 18, 21–2, 25–6, 44–5, 48–9, 99, 132, 153, 168

sui generis 18–19, 21–3, 26–7, 44, 69, 89, 99, 130, 135, 143, 147, 154, 163
supervenience 7, 27, 57, 125, 156, 171, 189

transcendental
  anxiety 136
  argument 45–6, 116, 163, 170
  idealism 1
transparency of experience 124, 185
triangulation 26, 161
truth 10, 25, 29, 31–4, 40, 53, 55, 87, 101, 172
two-dimensional semantics 174

wisdom 19–20, 101, 105, 156–8, 170
working memory 176
world viii, 1, 3–4, 7–14, 17, 21, 24–7, 29–32, 34–9, 41–3, 46–51, 53, 57, 61, 74, 78–84, 88–9, 91, 94, 98, 103–5, 107–12, 118, 127, 129–31, 133–40, 142, 147–51, 154–5, 158–62, 165–6, 168–74, 180–4, 187–8
worldly subjectivity 8, 12

Zombie 25

www.ingramcontent.com/pod-product-compliance
Lightning Source LLC
Chambersburg PA
CBHW072233290426
44111CB00012B/2071